PRINCIPLES OF EUROPEAN TRUST LAW

PRINCIPLES OF EUROPEAN TRUST LAW

Edited by

Prof. D.J. Hayton
Prof. S.C.J.J. Kortmann
Prof. H.L.E. Verhagen

Law of Business and Finance
Volume 1

Kluwer Law International - W.E.J. Tjeenk Willink - 1999

Published by:
Kluwer Law International
P.O. Box 85889, 2508 CN The Hague, The Netherlands

W.E.J. Tjeenk Willink
P.O. Box 23, 7400 GA Deventer, The Netherlands

Sold and Distributed in the USA and Canada by:
Kluwer Law International
657 Massachusetts Avenue, Cambridge, MA 02139, USA

Sold and Distributed in The Netherlands by:
Libresso BV, P.O. Box 23, 7400 GA Deventer, The Netherlands
tel. (+31) 570 633 155, fax (+31) 570 621660, e-mail: libresso@kluwer.nl

Sold and Distributed in all other countries by:
Kluwer Law International
Distribution Centre, P.O. Box 322, 3300 AH Dordrecht, The Netherlands

ISBN 90 411 9726 5 Kluwer Law International
ISBN 90 271 5048 6 W.E.J. Tjeenk Willink

Kluwer Law International incorporates the publishing programmes of Graham & Trotman Ltd, Kluwer Law and Taxation Publishers and Martinus Nijhoff Publishers.

W.E.J. Tjeenk Willink is an imprint of Kluwer Juridische Uitgevers, Deventer, The Netherlands

Design: Willy Cremers, Nijmegen, The Netherlands

CONTENTS

Commentary 29

PART II

National Report for Scotland 67

PREFACE

"Like an elephant, a trust is difficult to describe but easy to recognise", wrote Professor David Hayton in his contribution to "Vertrouwd met de Trust (Trust and Trust-like arrangements)", a collection of essays published by the Business and Law Research Centre in 1996. The main objective of the volume was to introduce Dutch lawyers to the common law concept of trust and trust-like arrangements. The enthusiasm and efforts of Professor David Hayton, Visiting Professor Van der Grinten-chair of the Business and Law Research Centre 1995-1996 and 1996-1997, encouraged the Research Centre to continue its research into trust law. In 1996, the International Working Group on European Trust Law was created.

The members of this Working Group are:
- Prof. P.B.H. Birks (All Souls College, University of Oxford, United Kingdom)
- Prof. A. Borrás (University of Barcelona, Spain)
- R.K. Feldthusen (Research Fellow, University of Copenhagen, Denmark)
- Prof. C. González Beilfuss (University of Barcelona, Spain)
- Prof. D.J. Hayton (King's College, University of London, United Kingdom)
- Prof. S.C.J.J. Kortmann (University of Nijmegen, The Netherlands)
- Prof. H. Kötz (Max-Planck Institute, Germany)
- Prof. M. Lupoi (University of Genoa, Italy)
- Prof. A.E. von Overbeck (University of Fribourg (emeritus), Switzerland)
- Prof. K.G.C. Reid (University of Edinburgh, Scotland)
- Prof. Ph. Rémy (University of Poitiers, France)
- Prof. H.L.E. Verhagen (University of Nijmegen, The Netherlands)
- Prof. D.W.M. Waters (University of Victoria, British Columbia (emeritus) and Legal Advisor, Vancouver, Canada)

The secretaries are:
- D.W. Aertsen (University of Nijmegen, The Netherlands)
- Ch.A.M. Domingus (University of Nijmegen, The Netherlands)
- N.E.D. Faber (University of Nijmegen, The Netherlands)

As part of the TMR-Research Network "Common Principles of European Private Law", the Working Group conducted over two years of research into the quagmire of the "European trust". It turned out to be a fascinating experience for all of those involved. The results of the research are presented in this book.

As can be read in the *Introduction* to this book, the purpose of this International Working Group has not been to advocate the adoption by civil law jurisdictions of any trust concept, or to commend the common law trust. Whether the trust in any of its forms, including its Anglo-Saxon form, should find its way into civil law statute or code is for each jurisdiction which thinks fit to consider the matter. The purpose of the International Working Group has rather been to meet the needs of those who have observed the usages to which the trust concept is put, and who see in one or more of those usages a role that a trust might play in the local internal law, but who find themselves puzzling over what exactly are the basic elements of the trust, and in particular of the common law trust.

The Business and Law Research Centre owes a great debt of gratitude to the members of the International Working Group on European Trust Law and to everyone who collaborated to produce the various "National Reports". Thanks to their sustained and generous efforts this book has been completed within a relatively short period of time. Special attention must be drawn to the efforts of Professor David Hayton. The dedication and efficiency with which the secretaries supported the Working Group must also be acknowledged. Finally, Ms Charissa Domingus, who co-ordinated the project, and Ms Gonnie Jakobs, who devised the lay-out, deserve recognition for their outstanding contributions.

The International Working Group would not have been able to complete its work without the generous financial support of both the European Union, through the "TMR-project", and the Nederlandse Vereniging van Banken (The Dutch Bankers Association).

In 1994 the Business and Law Research Centre released its first publication in the series "Onderneming en Recht" ("Business and Law"). We now anticipate the publication of the sixteenth volume in the series. Because the various research projects have an increasingly international dimension, it has been decided to simultaneously release a similar series in English, entitled "Law of Business and Finance". "The Principles of European Trust

Law" will be the first volume in this new series. It is our hope that this volume will inspire future research in this particular area of the law.

Professor Sebastian Kortmann
Chairman of the Board of the Business and Law Research Centre

Nijmegen, December 1998

PART I

Introduction
to the Principles of European Trust Law

A. Trusts in common law and civil law

It will be fairly obvious to the reader that both the Principles of European Trust Law (hereafter: the Principles) and the Commentary are to a considerable extent based on the experience and the terminology of the law of trusts as it was developed in common law jurisdictions. Civil lawyers may therefore be expected to ask a number of penetrating and critical questions: Is the trust not a singularly English institution? Is it not rooted in the duality between law and equity, i.e. in the separation in English legal history of two jurisdictions, namely equity in the Court of Chancery, and law in the common law courts, which finds no parallel in continental legal history? Is the division between legal and equitable ownership on which the trust is based not inconsistent with key elements of the Roman-based civil law systems? What sense does it make to suggest to civil lawyers the adoption of rules based on English trust law if their systems, doubtless for very good reasons, have managed fairly well without it? Would a civilian system not act *contra naturam suam* if it so much as played with the idea of borrowing from the common law experience?

The truth is rather different. The elements of the law of trusts are and always have been present in the Roman-based systems and are to be found in the library of the Roman law itself. The question is only as to the extent to which those foundations are used and built upon. It seems likely, though it is not certain, that even in England it was indeed those foundations in the Roman law library that provided the basis for the development by the Court of Chancery of the protection of "uses" which were the predecessors of trusts.

The experience of two legal systems is especially interesting. Scots law and Roman-Dutch law in South Africa both provide examples of civilian systems which have been exposed to heavy English influence. Neither knew the institutional separation of law and equity. Both have a law of property based on Roman concepts. Both Scots law and South African law have today a vigorous law of trusts, recognizable as such and named as such despite being in some important respects different in detail from the English law. However, though on each case the influence of English case law is undeniable, both Scots law and Roman-Dutch law see their law of trusts not as an artificial implant from an alien system, but as part of a civil law inheritance. In large measure we are witnessing the revivification and revitalization of the familiar Roman institutions of *fiducia* and *fideicommissum*.

In the present volume, the Scottish National Report may prove to be of particular interest to civilians considering the implementation of the trust in their domestic law.

Various forms of trust doctrine are to be found in code or statutory form in many other civil law jurisdictions. In Mexico, Panama, Venezuela and other Central and South American jurisdictions the *fideicomiso* has been known for much of the present century. The proximity of the United States as a trading and financially significant neighbour is generally thought to be responsible for much of this development, as it was in Puerto Rico. The Philippines were in much the same position. In Japan in 1922 the Trusts Law, modelled on U.S. law, was a response, against the background of an adopted German Civil Code, to the felt need to regularize the investment activities of the then trust corporations. And in Ethiopia in 1962 the singular views of the noted French scholar, Pierre Lepaulle, were the inspiration for the introduction into the Code of the *patrimoine d'affectation*, as they had been for Mexico in its Code revision of 1932. British colonial or mandate influences provided the circumstances for the growth of very individualistic trust institutions in each of Ceylon (Sri Lanka), Québec (1879), and Israel, and U.S. common law influenced in 1964 both the adoption and the conceptual structuring of a codified trust in Louisiana. The Quebec *fiducie* was reformulated in 1994 in the new Civil Code.

It is also evident that ends achieved by the trust in the common law have also been achieved by other civil law jurisdictions by way of functionally equivalent, but doctrinally different institutions. The "National Reports" provide many examples of statutory or judge-made rules which seek to deal with situations in which assets have been placed under the control of a fiduciary for the benefit of a beneficiary or for a specified purpose.

Since the trust has become so important on a worldwide scale, this book must be of interest for anyone concerned with, or interested in, the practical uses of the trust. For this reason we will now describe several practical applications of the trust.

B. The trust as an instrument of investment, security and estate planning

The idea of this book sprung from a very particular source. In business and the financing of commerce globalization has given rise to a renewed interest in civil law quarters in common law trust doctrine and the purposes to which that trust form can be put. Security provision and investment, both personal and commercial, are the pre-eminent subject-matters of interest, but the interest extends to the use of the common law trust for property "holding" purposes. It is surprising how often a simple express trust to hold property for the transferor, subject perhaps to a conditional interest in another or others, can be of value in banking and commercial dealings. The professional's "trust account" of his client's moneys is but the most obvious example.

During the last quarter century the variety of uses made of the trust in common law jurisdictions has expanded considerably, and one of the principal causes of this has been, and remains, the globalization of investment and securitization. The volume of usage of the common law trust has also visibly increased, some would say dramatically increased in the areas of corporate pension and disability provision for employees, and of offshore centred personal asset management and disposition. The principal cause is the same.

However, the significant spread of trust ideas has occurred only in very recent years. This is largely as a result of contemporary global investment, but also because of increasing awareness by the public of the advantages of a globally diversified holding and management of family wealth. The trust as an instrument of investment and of family wealth management and disposition has in fact spread like a bushfire throughout the highly competitive offshore financial centres of the world. These - the former "tax havens" - include common law, civil law, and mixed jurisdictions.

The trust institutions in all the above civil law jurisdictions exhibit a range of characteristics, largely the product of history and local circumstances, from those with purely *in personam* fiduciary obligations to those with both *in personam* and *in rem* effects. The *in rem* effects will sometimes constitute a real right against a trustee in possession and sometimes such a right against third parties also.

Each playing a separate role, corporations, limited partnerships, and common law trusts are often used together in connection with the estate planning affairs of higher and middle income individuals, but such combinations are also frequent for business and financial organizational structures, as well as for commercial transactions. The trust was at one time a familiar vehicle on its own as a substitute for incorporation (the so-called "trading trust"), but the trust does not provide trustees with limited liability and for this reason is now in a neutral tax setting less frequently seen. In order to obtain limitation of liability to the assets of the trust, the trust property and its management will be incorporated. The trustees as owners of the issued shares will then appoint themselves or their nominees as directors of the corporation. This too has drawn interest from civilians.

Because it underlies much of the reason for this book, something more should be said of the provision of security by way of trust, investment, and property holding in common law jurisdictions, though it must be recognized that in practice there will be variations of usage, emphasis within uses, and of vocabulary as between continents.

Security provision by way of trusts may be for the protection of investors, such as trusts of corporate assets for debenture holders, and trusts of the real estate for syndicated mortgage lenders. It may also enable holders of receivables and other debt to obtain immediate cash value for those assets. A trust of the receivables or other debt for the benefit of the purchaser ensures immediate beneficial vesting of those assets in the purchaser, while the vendor, though the trust property is not available to his subsequent creditors, will remain obligated to see to the collection. Similarly, prior to the vendor being paid the price, purchasers of goods on credit terms acquire only the beneficial interest in the goods. Pending payment, title to the goods remains in the vendor of the goods on trust, and the unpaid vendor is in this way protected from the purchaser's creditors, even upon the purchaser's resale and his receipt of the proceeds of sale or of a receivable.

In some common law jurisdictions (i.e. where there is no contrary legislation) it is possible for the lender to advance a loan by way of a trust. The borrower's purpose in seeking the loan is to apply the moneys for an object which is to be pursued later. The lender therefore lends the moneys for that purpose, i.e. transfers on trust for that purpose. If the borrower becomes insolvent or bankrupt before the moneys can be applied for that particular purpose, the lender is entitled to priority as a trust beneficiary over the borrower's unsecured creditors. In effect this is another kind of security transaction.

The demand for investment income other than from fixed-interest securities has given rise to unit trusts in all forms of property investment. The most familiar kind of unit investment property is of course securities selected for growth (i.e. "equities") and real estate, and assets of that nature will nowadays be found in unit trusts (or mutual funds) worldwide. Trusts holding "equities" invest on every exchange in the world, and real estate investment trusts will be interested in land to be developed wherever it be. Investment companies in which the investor holds shares are equally useful investment vehicles, but in most jurisdictions tax advantages are greater with unit trusts. In common law jurisdictions lower costs and tax impositions are often the attraction to the investor over the corporate *modus*. Pooled trust funds operated by fiduciary investment companies may be conducted on an invested amount basis rather than through units held, but the effect remains the same, namely, for the medium or small size portfolio diversification of investments for reduced risk and greater return. The sale and assignment of an accounts receivable to a trustee who then makes the fund available to investors by the issue of units - the so-called securitization trusts - are today of increasing significance.

In view of the large sums invested and the swollen trust portfolio sizes, pension fund trusts are probably the most important for modern societies of all forms of trust investment. Such is the influence of their decisions that the investment policies of the managers of these funds have considerable significance for the financial wellbeing of many national economies. Also employees can be encouraged to support seriously their employer's corporate enterprise if trusts of some part of the corporate profit are set up for these employees. Incentive schemes in the form of employee participation trusts often attract tax concessions from the state.

Trusts are frequently drawn whose only function, as we have said, is the "holding" of property as a segregated fund. This may be for the purpose of taking certain assets out of the corporate accounts, or of isolating assets that for tax reasons or because of a dispute can more usefully be administered if set aside. "Hold back" trusts - the so-called mechanics' or builders' lien trusts - ensure that subcontractors and suppliers are protected from the insolvency or failure to pay of the principal real estate site development contractor who has been funded by the site owner or the owner's mortgagee.

Settlement-of-action trusts occur where the defendant agrees to create a fund which with the mediation of a third party will be available to meet the claims of plaintiffs suing as a class. The defendant will take no part in, nor control in any way, how the moneys are divided between those plaintiffs. Trusts to hold insurance proceeds are to be found serving both family and business purposes. Partners may "cris-cross" insure each others' lives, or the lives of the "key" persons of a business may be insured by the corporation, the mode of expenditure of the segregated fund being determined when the insured life determines. The holding by professional bodies of insurance proceeds against client claims for malpractice both spreads the cost of insurance within the profession, and assists in the body's disciplining of those professionals whose fault has directly caused or contributed to the liability. Shares held in an "escrow trust" will ensure that corporate promoters remain investors until the newly-formed corporation is truly established, and so share the previous fate of failure, if it occurs, with the early investors. Stock voting trusts are holding (and voting) arrangements that can be useful in securing the stability of, for example, the family company when the second and third generations are in control. The trust is usually more flexible in this sensitive area than the civil law foundation.

Timesharing ownership of villas and apartments in "the sun belt" is a popular form of trustee holding because it allows each member of an association to assign his or her individual property interest when the family wants a change of geographical location, or to have time-limited interests in two or more holiday resorts.

So much wealth is tied up in the various commercial uses of trusts that one may overlook the original use of the trust in common law jurisdictions and its continuing use, namely, the use of trusts for family purposes, for preserving family capital and looking after the interests of the elderly, the young, the incapacitated and the foolhardy. Instead of family property being divided up by operation of succession law among the members of each successive generation, the property is kept intact by vesting it in trustees to manage it for the benefit of existing and as yet unborn family members for a perpetuity period covering four generations. At the end of such period the capital (or so much of the capital that remains after the expenditure of part for special reasons) can then be appointed to a responsible family member absolutely, who will then re-settle the property upon trustees for a further four generations.

C. The Hague Trust Convention

There are two civil law jurisdictions in which the Hague Trust Convention has entered into effect: Italy and the Netherlands. As a consequence, the legal consequences of a foreign trust must be recognised in these jurisdictions. The introduction of the Hague Trust Convention does not, however, mean that from now on foreign trusts can automatically be used for all kinds of purposes in these jurisdictions. There are several provisions of the Convention which could prevent this. In particular, Article 13 of the Hague Trust Convention gives the court the power to refuse the recognition of a foreign trust if the significant elements of the trust, with the exception of the chosen law and the location of the offices of the trustee, are more closely connected with the law of a country whose substantive laws do not recognise trusts. These "significant elements" are, *inter alia,* the location of the trust assets, the residence or nationality of the persons connected with the trust, the purposes of the trust and the place where these purposes have to be realised. It could be argued that Article 13 of the Hague Trust Convention has the effect that (legal and natural) persons established in a Contracting State, whose substantive law does not recognise trusts, are being discriminated against. For example, a Dutch settlor cannot take advantage of the Convention to create a trust under foreign law over his Dutch real estate in favour of Dutch beneficiaries, particularly not when all of the trust's assets are located in the Netherlands. If he has other trust assets in common law jurisdictions, or one or more of the beneficiaries are resident in a common law jurisdiction, the same real estate can, in principle, be given in trust. In our view this leads to an inequality in law which cannot be justified, but which will continue as long as the substantive laws of the Contracting States do not recognise a real trust-like institution.

In Italy, however, the current situation may be different. Professor Maurizio Lupoi has recently argued[1] that citizens of ratifying countries where trusts are not generally known are entitled to form wholly "domestic" trusts governed by a foreign law. According to Lupoi, this academic argument has been taken up by Italian legal practice and there are now many instances of trusts all the elements of which (with the exception of their governing law) are connected with Italy: Italian assets, Italian trustees, Italian settlors and beneficiaries. One of the major Italian banks has just formed a charitable trust in Milan under English law. In at least two instances "domestic" trusts have been the subject of judicial review which has allowed them to operate in Italy[2]. It goes without saying that should this position gain general acceptance also in other (civil law) countries the need for the Principles should be reassessed. It should be noted, however, that other noted Italian authors (e.g. Broggini) have endorsed a different view. It is suggested by these authors that the Hague Trust Convention assumes an international relationship exists. In purely domestic situations, the choice of a foreign trust law can never set aside the mandatory rules of Italian law. It is possible that where other civil law jurisdictions ratify the Hague Trust Convention, the courts of those jurisdictions will only recognise trusts which have been created in an international setting, and which have genuine common law connections.

It is true that the Hague Trust Convention does not oblige the Contracting States to introduce the trust into domestic law. However, it does constitute a powerful argument for such introduction. To this it may be added that the development of civilian rules for a trust-like institution could also be beneficial to the functioning of the Hague Trust Convention itself. For it would be possible to rely on those rules when a foreign trust is to be recognised in a civil law jurisdiction pursuant to the rules of the Conven-

1 In P. Jackson, D.C. Wilde, The Reform of Property Law, Ashgate, 1997, p. 222.
2 For a reference see the Note by P. Matthews in 11 (1997) Tolley's Trust Law International 20.

tion. Thus, by applying these newly developed rules of domestic trust law, foreign trusts would in many cases be more easy to fit into the system of property law and bankruptcy law of these jurisdictions. Also, this would further reduce the scope of Articles 15, 16 and 18 of the Hague Trust Convention, provisions which otherwise might adversely affect the full recognition of trusts. Finally, the Principles could simply lead to a better understanding of trusts by the courts of the civilian Contracting States.

D. The purpose of this book

The purpose of this book is not to advocate the adoption by civil law jurisdictions of any trust concept, or to commend the common law trust. Whether the trust in any of its forms, including its Anglo-Saxon form, should find its way into civil law statute or code is for each jurisdiction which thinks fit to consider the matter. Our purpose is rather to meet the needs of those who have observed the usages to which the trust concept is put, and who see in one or more of those usages - previously outlined - a role that a trust might play in the local internal law, but who find themselves puzzling over what exactly are the basic elements of the trust, and in particular of the common law trust. If our attention is directed primarily towards the common law trust, it is because general opinion recognizes this as the most developed and universal form of the trust concept. Moreover, it is observable that, when questions are asked as to the basic elements of the trust in the present global scene of investment, security provision and business organization, it is more frequently the common law trust that the speaker has in mind. Finally, even countries that do not plan to implement the trust by legislation might be interested in the Principles for their consequences: the Principles can provide certain default rules that parties may wish to put into their contracts. The Principles could furthermore serve as guidelines to practitioners for interpreting trust-like contracts or institutions.

Our purpose then is to assist those who wish to discover and study the core ideas of the trust. Whether in any jurisdiction those ideas should be adopted is for others to decide. For those jurisdictions which choose to adopt them, it is for them also to decide how those elements or ideas may most usefully be introduced into the local law. By isolating what we consider to be the core ideas, we hope this book will assist in that process.

The "National Reports" are designed to focus attention upon the major issues that exist in respect of the trust, as seen in each of a number of leading jurisdictions.

Principles of European Trust Law

Article I

Main characteristics of the trust

(1) In a trust, a person called the "trustee" owns assets segregated from his private patrimony and must deal with those assets (the "trust fund") for the benefit of another person called the "beneficiary" or for the furtherance of a purpose.

(2) There can be more than one trustee and more than one beneficiary; a trustee may himself be one of the beneficiaries.

(3) The separate existence of the trust fund entails its immunity from claims by the trustee's spouse, heirs and personal creditors.

(4) In respect of the separate trust fund a beneficiary has personal rights and may also have proprietary rights against the trustee and against third parties to whom any part of the fund has been wrongfully transferred.

Article II

Creation of the trust

The general rule is that in order to create a trust a person called the "settlor" in his lifetime or on death must, with the intention of creating a segregated trust fund, transfer assets to the trustee. However, it may also be possible for a settlor to create a trust by making it clear that he is to be trustee of particular assets of his.

Article III

Trust fund

(1) The trust fund consists not only of the original assets and those subsequently added, but also of those assets from time to time representing the original or added assets.

(2) The trust fund is not available to satisfy claims made against the trustee in his personal capacity. Except to the extent that the settlor's creation of the trust contravenes laws protecting his creditors, spouse or heirs, the trust fund is available only for claims made by creditors dealing with the trustee in his capacity as such and, subject thereto, for claims of the beneficiaries or the enforcer, who is an office holder entitled to enforce a trust for purposes.

(3) A trustee of several trusts must keep each trust fund not only segregated from his private patrimony but also from each of the other trust funds, except to the extent that the terms of the trusts otherwise permit.

Article IV

Trusts for beneficiaries or for enforceable purposes

(1) Upon creating a trust, the settlor must designate ascertained or ascertainable persons as beneficiaries to whom the trustee's obligations in respect of the trust fund are owed or will be owed, or must designate purposes in respect of which there is an enforcer.

(2) To the extent that the settlor fails to create rights affecting the whole of the trust fund the trustee will own the assets for the benefit of the settlor or his successors.

(3) Any beneficiary, or any enforcer of a trust for purposes, has a right to information needed to protect his interest and to ensure that the trustee accounts to him.

(4) Subject to the terms of the trust, a beneficiary can make a disposition of his rights.

(5) Any beneficiary, or any enforcer of a trust for purposes, has the right to seek judicial enforcement of the terms of the trust.

Article V

Trustees' duties and powers

(1) The trustee must exercise his rights as owner in accordance with the law and the terms of the trust.

(2) The fundamental duty of a trustee is to adhere to the terms of the trust, to take reasonable care of the trust assets and to act in the best interests of the beneficiaries or, in the case of a trust for purposes, the furtherance of those purposes.

(3) A trustee must keep separate and protect the trust assets, must maintain accurate accounts and must provide the beneficiaries and the enforcer with information requested to protect their interests.

(4) Except to the extent otherwise permitted by the terms of the trust or by law, a trustee must personally perform his functions. He must act honestly and he must avoid all conflicts of interest unless otherwise authorised.

(5) A trustee is accountable for the trust fund, must personally make good any loss occasioned to the trust fund by his breach of trust and must personally augment such fund by the amount of any profits made by him in breach of his duty.

Article VI

Remedies against trustees for breach of trust

Remedies that the court can provide against a trustee for breach of trust include an order restraining particular conduct or removing the trustee from his office and replacing him or decreeing payment of compensation for losses or restitution of profits. The court may also have power to declare that particular assets of the trustee have always been part of the trust fund and never became part of his private patrimony or are to be regarded as security for satisfying his liability.

Article VII

Liabilities of third parties

Where a trustee wrongfully transfers part of the trust fund to a transferee who is not protected as a purchaser in good faith or otherwise, the transferee must make good the loss to the trust fund or may be ordered to hold the assets so transferred (or assets representing them) as part of the trust fund separate from his private patrimony or as security for satisfying his liability. This liability may extend to any subsequent transferee who is not protected as a purchaser in good faith or otherwise.

Article VIII

Termination of a trust

(1) Notwithstanding the terms of the trust, where all the beneficiaries are in existence, have been ascertained, and are of full capacity, then, if all such beneficiaries are in agreement, they can require the trustee to terminate the trust and distribute the trust fund between themselves and their nominees as they direct. However, if some material purpose of the settlor remains to be served then the beneficiaries may not be permitted to terminate the trust.

(2) A trust terminates (a) by virtue of all the trust fund having been distributed to beneficiaries or having been used for trust purposes or (b) by virtue of there being no beneficiaries and no person, whether or not then in existence, who can become a beneficiary in accordance with the terms of the trust, or (c) by virtue of a person exercising a power of termination.

(3) At the close of the permitted period for the duration of the trust (subject to the trustee retaining sufficient assets to make reasonable provision for possible liabilities) the trust fund shall be distributed by the trustee as soon as reasonably practicable in accordance with any terms of the trust setting out how the trust fund should then be distributed. However, if there are no such terms then the trust fund shall be owned by the trustee for the benefit of the settlor or his successors.

(4) In the case of a trust for purposes, where such purposes have been fulfilled so far as possible or cannot now be carried out, then the trust fund shall be owned by the trustee for the benefit of the settlor or his successors, unless the terms of the trust are varied or extended.

Principes de Droit Européen du Trust

Article I

Principales caractéristiques du trust

(1) Dans un trust, une personne appelée "trustee" est propriétaire de biens séparés de son patrimoine personnel; le trustee doit affecter ces biens (le fonds du trust) à l'intérêt d'une autre personne appelée "bénéficiaire" (beneficiary) ou à l'accomplissement d'un but d'intérêt général.

(2) Il peut y avoir plus d'un trustee et plus d'un bénéficiaire; un trustee peut lui-même être un des bénéficiaires.

(3) La séparation du fonds du trust a pour effet de soustraire celui-ci aux prétentions du conjoint du trustee, de ses héritiers et de ses créanciers personnels.

(4) Le bénéficiaire a, sur le fonds du trust, un droit personnel propre contre le trustee et contre des tiers auxquels une partie du fonds aurait été transférée sans droit, il se peut aussi qu'il ait un droit réel à l'encontre du trustee et à l'encontre de ces tiers.

Article II

Création du trust

En règle générale, pour créer un trust, une personne, appelée "constituant" (settlor) doit, de son vivant ou par disposition à cause de mort, transférer des biens au trustee dans l'intention de constituer un fonds de trust séparé. Toutefois, il se peut aussi que le constituant ait la possibilité de créer un trust en statuant qu'il sera le trustee de certains de ses propres biens.

Article III

Le fonds du trust

(1) Le fonds du trust comprend non seulement les biens originaux et ceux ajoutés par la suite, mais également les biens acquis en remploi de ces biens.

(2) Le fonds du trust ne répond pas des dettes personnelles du trustee. A moins que la création du trust ne fût contraire à des lois protégeant les créanciers, le conjoint ou les héritiers du constituant, le fonds du trust ne répond que des prétentions de créanciers à l'encontre du trustee comme tel et, dans la même mesure, des prétentions des bénéficiaires ou du curateur (enforcer), un professionnel (office holder) habilité à assurer l'accomplissement des buts d'un trust d'intérêt général.

(3) Sauf disposition contraire des termes du trust, un trustee de plusieurs trusts doit tenir chaque fonds de trust séparé, non seulement de son patrimoine personnel, mais aussi du fonds de chacun des autres trusts.

Article IV

Trust pour bénéficiaires ou trust d'intérêt général

(1) En créant un trust, le constituant doit désigner des personnes déterminées ou déterminables en qualité de bénéficiaires, envers lesquels le trustee a ou aura des obligations en ce qui concerne le fonds du trust, ou doit désigner un but d'intérêt général pour l'accomplissement duquel un curateur est nommé.

(2) Dans la mesure où le constituant omet de créer des droits sur l'ensemble du fonds du trust, le trustee sera propriétaire des biens dans l'intérêt du constituant et de ses successeurs.

(3) Tout bénéficiaire, et tout curateur d'un trust ayant un but d'intérêt général, a droit aux informations nécessaires pour sauvegarder ses intérêts et s'assurer que le trustee lui rende des comptes.

(4) Un bénéficiaire peut disposer de ses droits dans les limites des termes du trust.

(5) Tout bénéficiaire, et tout curateur d'un trust ayant un but d'intérêt général, peut poursuivre en justice l'exécution des termes du trust.

Article V

Les devoirs et les pouvoirs du trustee

(1) Le trustee doit exercer ses droits conformément au droit et aux termes du trust.

(2) Le devoir fondamental d'un trustee est de se conformer aux termes du trust, de gérer raisonnablement les biens du trust et d'agir dans l'intérêt bien compris des bénéficiaires ou, en cas de trust ayant un but d'intérêt général, de promouvoir l'intérêt en question.

(3) Un trustee doit garder les biens du trust séparés et les protéger, tenir des comptes précis et fournir aux bénéficiaires ou au curateur les informations nécessaires à la sauvegarde de leurs intérêts.

(4) Sauf autorisation contraire découlant des termes du trust ou de la loi, un trustee doit remplir ses fonctions personnellement. Il doit agir honnêtement et, sauf autorisation contraire, éviter tout conflit d'intérêts.

(5) Un trustee est comptable du fonds du trust, il doit personnellement réparer toute perte causée au fonds du trust par une violation du trust (breach of trust). Il doit personnellement ajouter à ce fonds tout profit que lui aurait procuré la violation de ses devoirs.

Article VI

Remèdes juridiques contre le trustee en cas de violation du trust

En cas de violation du trust, le juge peut notamment interdire certains actes au trustee, le destituer et le remplacer, ou ordonner la réparation de pertes ou la restitution de profits. Il se peut aussi que le juge ait le pouvoir de déclarer que certains biens du trustee ont toujours fait partie du fonds du trust et ne sont jamais entrés dans son patrimoine personnel ou doivent être affectés en garantie de sa responsabilité.

Article VII

Responsabilité de tiers

Lorsqu'un trustee transfère sans droit une partie du fonds du trust à un acquéreur, qui n'est pas protégé en qualité d'acheteur de bonne foi ou autrement, cet acquéreur doit réparer la perte subie par le fonds du trust, il se peut qu'il soit enjoint de tenir les biens ainsi transférés (ou des biens les représentant), séparés de son patrimoine personnel en tant que partie du fonds du trust ou en tant que garantie de sa responsabilité. Il se peut que cette responsabilité s'étende à tout tiers acquéreur subséquent qui n'est pas protégé en tant qu'acheteur de bonne foi ou autrement.

Article VIII

Fin du trust

(1) Nonobstant les termes du trust, si les bénéficiaires sont tous en vie, ont été déterminés et ont pleine capacité, ils peuvent, d'un commun accord, exiger du trustee de mettre fin au trust et de distribuer le fonds du trust entre eux ou les personnes qu'ils désignent. Toutefois, si quelque but du constituant restait à atteindre, il se peut que les bénéficiaires ne soient pas autorisés de mettre fin au trust.

(2) Un trust prend fin (a) lorsque le fonds du trust a été tout entier distribué à des bénéficiaires ou a été utilisé pour servir les buts du trust, ou (b) lorsque il n'y a pas de bénéficiaires ni de personne, existante ou non, qui puisse le devenir selon les termes du trust, ou (c) lorsqu'une personne exerce un pouvoir de mettre fin au trust.

(3) A l'expiration de la durée permise du trust (le trustee devant toutefois conserver suffisamment de biens pour faire face à des engagements prévisibles) le fonds du trust sera distribué par le trustee aussi rapidement que possible, conformément aux termes du trust indiquant comment en pareil cas le fonds du trust devrait être distribué. Toutefois, si ces termes sont muets à cet égard, le fonds du trust sera la propriété du trustee dans l'intérêt du constituant ou de ses successeurs.

(4) Lorsque les buts d'un trust d'intérêt général auront été atteints dans toute la mesure du possible, ou ne peuvent plus être accomplis, le fonds du trust sera la propriété du trustee dans l'intérêt du constituant ou de ses successeurs, à moins que les termes du trust ne soient modifiés ou prorogés.

Commentary

A. General introduction to the wide-ranging trust concept[1]

Reaction to hearing the word "trust" may well be one of caution and fear because it is natural to be fearful of what one does not really understand. The word is versatile and chameleon-like, taking its meaning from its context, which has to be closely examined to reveal the full ramifications of the concept. The concept also has much historical baggage that makes it taken for granted in common law jurisdictions but makes it difficult to comprehend in other jurisdictions.

Indeed, in common law jurisdictions the trust is regarded as a very worthy and respectable institution, a vast amount of wealth being held by trustees, while some other jurisdictions may consider the trust to be somewhat dubious, a device, perhaps, for avoiding claims of creditors, heirs and the tax authority. In reality, in all jurisdictions there are laws preventing transfers of assets from having the effect of defeating claims of the transferor's creditors, spouses and heirs, and also laws that prevent tax evasion and unacceptable types of tax avoidance.

Years ago, common law authors were too keen to assert the uniqueness of the common law trust, particularly by emphasising the contrast between the trustees having legal ownership of the trust assets and the beneficiaries having equitable ownership; they also pointed out that the beneficiaries not only have personal rights to sue for losses and profits arising from a breach of trust but also have equitable proprietary interests in the trust assets that can bind third parties who acquire legal ownership of the assets. Today, in

---

1 For treatises see Scott on Trusts, 4th edn (USA); Waters, Law of Trusts in Canada, 2nd edn; Underhill & Hayton, Law of Trusts & Trustees, 15th edn (England & Wales); Wilson & Duncan, Trusts, Trustees & Executors, 2nd edn (Scotland); Delany, Equity and the Law of Trusts in Ireland (1996); Jacobs, Law of Trusts in Australia, 5th edn; Honoré, South African Law of Trusts, 4th edn. For digests and legislation worldwide see Glasson, International Trust Laws. For an English student textbook and casebook see Hayton & Marshall, Commentary & Cases on Law of Trusts and Equitable Remedies, 10th edn (1996). For an English introductory book for laymen and foreign lawyers see Hayton, Law of Trusts, 3rd edn (1998).

the light of vigorous trust laws in South Africa, Scotland, India, Japan, and Sri Lanka and pockets of law dealing with segregated funds (on lines somewhat analogous to common law trust funds) in civil law jurisdictions discussed after this commentary, we can see that the common law trust is at one extreme end of the spectrum of the trust concept. Such concept does not require any division of legal ownership and equitable ownership but can leave the trustee as full owner, although subject to special obligations to beneficiaries in respect of particular assets that he must keep separate from his own private property, so as to be free from claims of his spouse and heirs and his private creditors. Hence, a segregated trust fund owned by trustees for the benefit of beneficiaries or the furtherance of purposes is at the core of the trust concept in these Principles.

Not every concept that is called "a trust" in English or translated into English as "a trust" is "a trust" within the meaning of Article I. To include all so-called "trusts" within Article I would make any definition of a trust virtually meaningless. Deliberately excluded are cases where assets are not owned by the trustees but either form an ownerless fund dedicated to the benefit of beneficiaries or for the furtherance of a purpose (e.g. Quebec "trusts") or are owned by the "beneficiaries" and managed by the "trustees" (e.g. the Dutch *bewind* or one type of South African "trust"). Moreover, cases where "beneficiaries" of a trust have no enforceable rights are excluded from being trusts for the "beneficiaries": the trustees have a segregated trust fund, but a lack of "beneficiaries" means that the fund is held for the settlor (the person who created the trust), although the trustees have power to benefit the "beneficiaries", who really should be characterised as "objects" of a power (as explained further in the commentary to Article IV(3)).

A trust has no legal personality, so that a company or a foundation that is a legal person cannot qualify as a trust. It should also be apparent that the relationship of agency or mandate cannot be a trust where ownership of the assets is not vested in the "trustee"-agent but remains with the principal. Furthermore, if a person sets aside particular property of his as security to satisfy debts due to a creditor this is not the creation of a trust, even if he uses the word "trust", but the creation of a charge which may well need to be registered if it is to be effective against other creditors of the chargor. Moreover, if property worth x pounds is charged or assigned by A to B to secure a debt of x pounds, but on sale of the property on A's default some years later x + y pounds are received, B can only claim x pounds. If the property instead had been settled by A on trust for B then B would be entitled to x and y pounds.

It is vital to appreciate that if a settlor, S, transfers property to a trustee, T, on trust for W, X, Y and Z and their (as yet) unborn children, this is very different from a contract between A and B for the benefit of W, X, Y and Z and their unborn children. Apart from the obvious requirement for property to be vested in T if there is to be a trust, the death or mental illness of S or T or a breach of trust by T does not affect the validity of the trust, although the death or mental illness of A and B or a breach of contract by B can terminate the contract or afford grounds for the termination of the contract. The obligations of a trustee (a person holding the office of trustee) are different from the obligations of a party to a contract, just as the obligations of such a party are different from the obligations of a person liable for a tort or delict.

Once T owns assets as trustee (whether as a result of a contract or a donation) the trust is a free-standing institution with a life of its own: the settlor, S, cannot revoke or terminate the trust wholly or partially unless he reserved such a power to himself when he created the trust. One can liken the trust to a rocket which is launched by a contract or a donation: only if the settlor inserted a special button in the rocket which he can activate from the ground can he bring the rocket down to earth.

In common law jurisdictions, in the absence of such power of revocation or termination, the settlor and the trustees cannot agree to treat the trust as revoked or terminated once it has been created, even if the beneficiaries have not accepted their interests in the trust fund or have not yet been informed of their interests e.g. because minors or not yet born. The beneficiaries, once born, have vested (unconditional) or contingent (conditional) interests from the outset unless they disclaim their interests as soon as possible (so that such interests either revert to the settlor or accelerate the interest of a subsequent beneficiary, such as a remainderman after a life interest has been disclaimed). However, in other jurisdictions it is compatible with the concept of a trust to allow the settlor scope to prevent a trust obligation arising in favour of an intended beneficiary before such beneficiary has accepted his rights, so that until such acceptance the trustee holds the trust fund on trust for the settlor or for those beneficiaries who have accepted their rights.

In such other jurisdictions, accustomed to contracts for the benefit of third parties which are enforceable by the third party as well as the contracting parties, it may well be that the settlor is permitted a right in his lifetime to enforce the trust in addition to the rights of the beneficiaries to enforce the trust. This is also compatible with the existence of a trust for beneficiaries. However, if the beneficiaries do not have any rights to enforce the trust, then no trust for beneficiaries exists: there will only be a trust for the settlor, although the trustees may have a power to benefit the "beneficiaries" characterised as merely "objects" of a power, as discussed in the commentary to Article IV(3).

In respect of the trust fund it is fundamental that the trustee owes duties to the beneficiaries who have correlative rights against the trustee. To be able to enforce their rights it is crucial that the beneficiaries have a right to make the trustee account for his management of the trust property. In the case of charitable purpose trusts the right of enforcement is vested in a representative of the State, while in the few jurisdictions with statutes that allow non-charitable purpose trusts to be validly created this is only the case if the settlor appoints a specific person to be "enforcer".

In common law jurisdictions the settlor in his capacity as settlor has no right to enforce his trust: like the maker of a gratuitous disposition he drops out of the picture once he has made the disposition. The courts are then only concerned to regulate the internal trustee - beneficiary relationship according to trust law and the external relations between the trustees and third parties according to the relevant law governing such relations e.g. contract, tort (or delict). Exceptionally, however, the settlor may be a beneficiary, in which case he can exercise the rights of a beneficiary, or as settlor he may reserve to himself some powers (e.g. a power of revocation, or a power of removal and appointment of trustees, or a power of appointment of capital to beneficiaries, or a power to add or delete beneficiaries) or the functions of enforcer of a statutory purpose trust. Where such powers or functions are reserved the settlor is entitled to have enforced by the court the directions he makes in the exercise of his powers or functions if the trustees refuse to obey such directions.

Except for the special case of a bare trust where S transfers property to T to hold to the order of S as absolutely entitled beneficiary (or of X, Y and Z as absolutely entitled beneficiaries of full capacity), a trustee must decide for himself what to do with the trust property within the parameters laid down by the trust instrument. He must always act honestly and, except to the extent that he is authorised to act to the contrary, he must loyally use his position exclusively to further the interests of the beneficiaries or the trust purposes in unprejudiced fashion. Thus, *subject to a contrary authorisation,* he is subject to the "no profit" rule and the "no conflict" rule.

By the "no profit" rule a trustee cannot use his position (including any knowledge or opportunity derived from his position) to obtain a profit for himself or for a third party. By the "no conflict" rule a trustee cannot place himself in a position where his duty to his beneficiaries conflicts with his self interest or with his duty to another set of beneficiaries. If any conflict does arise between his self interest and his duty to his beneficiaries he must prefer his duty to his beneficiaries, while if a conflict arises between his duties to two sets of beneficiaries he may have to resign both trusteeships.

In most cases, however, the trustee will be authorised to charge for his services and to place business with an associated firm or company without the trustee or such firm or company being liable to account to the beneficiaries for any commission made. The trustee can never be allowed to act other than in good faith but may be exempted from liability by the trust instrument for negligent behaviour if the settlor approves such exemption when he creates his trust, and if legislation does not prevent the trustee being exempt from liability for negligence or, at least, gross negligence.

Having a life of its own, a trust is not allowed to fail for lack of a trustee, so it will not cease to exist if the trustee ceases to exist by dying or, if a company, by being dissolved. Whoever then comes to own the trust fund becomes obliged to own it as a separate fund dedicated to benefiting the beneficiaries or furthering the purposes of the trust until a new trustee is appointed by an appropriate procedure e.g. by the new owner of the trust fund or by the settlor or by the court. If there is more than one trustee, then in common law countries the trustees will hold the trust fund as joint tenants, so that if there are three trustees T1, T2 and T3, then on T1's death the fund vests automatically in T2 and T3, while on T2's death the fund vests solely in T3 who should appoint new trustees. If T3 dies without having appointed new trustees, then the person upon whom T3's estate devolves must keep the trust fund separate from his private patrimony and hold it as trustee until he exercises his power to appoint new trustees.

Over the course of time it is up to each jurisdiction in its own legal, cultural and historical context to determine the extent to which a segregated trust fund should be protected by the provision of a personal right (as in Scotland or South Africa) with different degrees of protection against third parties (other than purchasers in good faith) to whom some part of the trust fund has been wrongfully transferred or a proprietary right against such third parties (as in England and other common law jurisdictions). It is a matter for each jurisdiction whether it distinguishes between solvent and insolvent third parties or between knowledgeable and innocent third parties. Each jurisdiction also needs to determine precisely where it draws the line between the interests of general creditors of an insolvent third party, who has acquired wrongfully transferred trust property, and the interests of the beneficiaries who make the opposing claim that they are entitled to such property. Development by case law is generally a gradual process, while legislation can take greater strides where a justifiable need is perceived.

B. Implementation of these Principles

These Principles are not intended to provide a comprehensive code. They are intended to facilitate dealings within or across European borders by generating an understanding of the trust and by enabling most European countries to appreciate that within their own domestic legal systems they may have the trust as described in Article I, even if they do not have the elaborate type of trust that common law countries like England and Ireland have. The Principles are intended to enable civil law countries to recognise the potential for development of their domestic legal relationships and to provide guidance as to various ways in which this development may occur within differing cultural, legal and socio-economic heritages.

It is up to each country to develop its own type of trust law in its own fashion, recognising the defining common core elements prescribed in Article I. Thus, within the United Kingdom, Scotland, with its civil law background, has developed its own type of trust concept which creates extensive personal obligations, while Jersey and Guernsey have developed their own legislative trust concept. In the United States of America, Louisiana with its French law background has developed a trust concept to facilitate inter-State dealings, as has Quebec in Canada, albeit in unusual fashion. Moreover, in federal countries like the USA and Canada, each State or Province has its own law of trusts differing subtlely from the law of each other State or Province, although there is an extensive common core element that textbooks and professors of law concentrate upon for the purpose of generating an understanding of trust law. Similarly, in the off-shore common law trust world, each Island has developed its trust law beyond English trust law, so as to make its laws more flexible and facilitative, but in different ways for each Island.

The purpose of these Principles is to increase possibilities and thereby facilitate a wide range of commercial or family activities involving wealth generation, whether within or across borders, as indicated in the last part of the Commentary's General Introduction. Implementation of The Hague Convention on Recognition of Trusts can usefully provide the excuse for developing the core trust concept described in Article I of the Principles, whether by way of a self-sufficient statute or by amending provisions of the Civil Code.

At the core of the trust concept is the ownership by the trustee of a separate fund of assets segregated from his private patrimony and in respect of which the trustee is accountable to the beneficiaries or the enforcer of the trust. However, of course, the separate fund cannot be protected from the overriding domestic laws that protect creditors, spouses and heirs of the settlor. The consequences of recognition of the separate fund need to be made clear: namely, that the existence of the separate fund should survive the death, divorce or insolvency of the trustee. It is also necessary to make clear what exactly the fund is: namely, not just the original transferred assets but also the assets from time to time replacing assets within the fund, including assets intended by the trustee to be trust assets when he purchased them with trust money or obtained them by virtue of being trustee, and, perhaps, including such purchased or obtained assets even where the trustee wrongfully intended them to become part of his patrimony. The latter situation creates problems in civil law jurisdictions (see e.g. the Roman-Dutch South African trust law) where the local legal and commercial context requires assets apparently owned by a person as part of his private patrimony to be available for that person's creditors. In England, for centuries creditors have been well aware that a debtor may be a trustee or a beneficiary with a limited interest (e.g. a life interest until remarriage), so if worried about creditworthiness they take security over the debtor's private property or a secured or unsecured guarantee from a third party: otherwise they take a risk.

In introducing local trusts it may be deemed advisable to proceed slowly e.g. only allowing licensed companies of good financial standing to be trustees or, at least, trustees of certain types of commercial trust; by requiring a notarial deed for the creation of a trust; by requiring ownership of trust assets to be made apparent on any registers of ownership of particular types of asset. It may even be that settlors, at first, may not be permitted to become sole trustee of assets distinguished from the rest of their property. However, if they are permitted to add their own assets to segregated assets of which they are already trustee for others, it is difficult to understand why they should not be allowed to create a trust consisting exclusively of their own assets which they have segregated from their other assets.

Provision needs also to be made for appointment to, and retirement and removal from, the office of trustee[2]. Here, one has to face up to the special advantages flowing from the common law concept of co-ownership as joint tenants. If A and B are joint tenants of property, then each is regarded as owning the whole property and on the death of A, by virtue of the right of survivorship (like a tontine arrangement), B becomes sole owner, A having nothing that he can pass to his heirs under his will or intestacy. Joint tenancy, while useful for spouses, is crucial to trusteeship.

If there are two trustees, T1 and T2, and T1 dies, then no trust property passes under T1's will or intestacy. The trust property is solely owned by T2, who in common law jurisdictions has power to appoint more trustees (commonly up to a limit of four trustees in total). If T2 dies without having appointed more trustees, then in common law jurisdictions the trust property passes to the executor of T2's will (or his administrator if he died

2 E.g. English Trustee Act 1925 ss 36-39 (and 41) as amended by Trusts of Land and Appointment of Trustees Act 1996.

intestate) to own it as a separate fund until exercising his power to appoint new trustees[3].

It is possible that the courts in non-common law jurisdictions could develop rules that, although on a co-trustee's death his proportionate share of the trust fund passes to his heir, the heir is subject to an obligation to own the fund as a separate fund under a duty to transfer it to the surviving co-trustee(s); and that if a sole trustee dies, then his heir must hold the trust fund as a separate fund until appointing new trustees and transferring the fund to them, with the court having a reserve power to appoint new trustees if necessary.

It would, however, seem better if legislation provided that on the death of one of the co-trustees nothing is to pass to the heir of the deceased trustee, the trust fund accruing to the surviving trustees. Provision can also be made for the insolvency of a trustee, whether to make his trusteeship automatically determine or to make the insolvency an event enabling his co-trustees to appoint a new trustee in his place. Having a sole corporate trustee can avoid many of the above problems but not those arising upon the insolvency or dissolution of the corporate trustee, except that its liquidator may have power to appoint new trustees.

Legislation will also be needed if, as in traditional trust jurisdictions[4], a formal appointment of new trustees is automatically to transfer ownership of the trust assets to the new trustees (together with any continuing trustees) except for assets like land and company shares, where ownership only passes by entry of the new owner on the land or share register.

In the area of appointment and removal of trustees the court needs to have reserve powers where it is inexpedient, difficult or impracticable to do without the assistance of the court[5]. Indeed, since more doubts are likely to arise upon the introduction of a developing trust concept than arise upon the operation of the trust in a well established traditional trust jurisdiction, and since the latter type of jurisdiction has found it very useful indeed for the trustees to have the right to obtain the advice of the court

---

3 E.g. English Trustee Act 1925 s 18.
4 E.g. English Trustee Act 1925 s 40.
5 E.g. English Trustee Act 1925 s 41.

upon any matter where doubts arise, it will be very helpful if legislation enables there to be a specialist judge to whom the trustees can have recourse for advice in doubtful matters. Trustees will then be fully protected if they act upon such advice.

As a last resort, in a case where a trustee is, or may be, liable for a breach of trust, but has acted honestly and reasonably and ought fairly to be excused for the breach of trust and for omitting to seek the advice of the court (where such advice is available), it is also very helpful if the court has power to relieve the trustee wholly or partly from liability[6].

Developing a flexible concept through the courts and the legislature is never an easy task and always a lengthy task. It is hoped that this project clearly reveals how worthwhile is the extra wealth-generating and wealth-preserving facility provided by the trust concept in the commercial as well as the family context, so that the task of developing such concept within diverse European jurisdictions will be taken up. It is further hoped that the guidance provided by the Principles and the Commentary will facilitate the success of this task.

In reading the Principles it is vital to appreciate that the word "may" is deliberately used to introduce optional possibilities that may represent the law in some jurisdictions (e.g. common law jurisdictions) but need not represent the law in other jurisdictions.

C. Commentary on the Principles article by article

Article I. Main characteristics of the trust

Paragraphs (1) and (2)

Fundamental to a trust is the requirement that the trustee owns particular assets as a segregated fund for the benefit of beneficiaries or the furtherance of purposes[7]. The trustee does not manage trust assets owned by some other person(s); the trust assets are owned by the trustee. Hence, no

6 E.g. English Trustee Act 1925 s 61.

7 Underhill & Hayton, Law of Trusts & Trustees, 15th edn (henceforth "U&H"), Articles 8 and 9.

use was made of the ambiguous definition of a trust in Article 2 of The Hague Trusts Convention:

> "The term 'trust' refers to the legal relationship created by a person, the settlor, when assets have been placed under the control of a trustee for the benefit of a beneficiary or for a specified purpose. A trust has the following characteristics - (a) the assets constitute a separate fund and are not part of the trustee's own estate; (b) title to the trust assets stands in the name of the trustee or in the name of another person on behalf of the trustee".

This unsatisfactory definition arose to deal with the common practice of having shares owned by custodians to facilitate speedy and inexpensive dealings in shares. A purchaser of, say, 5,000 X plc shares does not normally become registered shareholder of such shares. Instead, he will be recorded (electronically in a computer, nowadays) as interested in 5,000 of 1 million shares in X plc owned by a nominee custodian company. The layman will consider the purchaser's assets to include 5,000 X plc shares owned by the nominee but under the control of the purchaser, and if the purchaser were a trustee, T, the layman would similarly consider the 5,000 shares as trust assets.

However, a trust lawyer will consider that T is the owner of a half per cent share of the nominee's 1 million shareholding: this is the trust asset and T has title to it. Thus, Article 2 need only be concerned with the case where title to the trust assets stands in the name of the trustee and where assets have been placed in the ownership of the trustee.

Unfortunately, because the majority of delegates at The Hague Conference considered the trust lawyer's technical view a little complex for understanding by non-trust lawyers Article 2 was expanded so as to cover "assets placed under the control of a trustee for the benefit of a beneficiary or for a specified purpose", so that it appears, at first sight, that trust assets can be owned by someone other than the trustee, e.g. by the settlor.

If this be possible then, surprisingly, there can be an Article 2 "trust" where O, the owner of an asset, remains owner and merely gives control of it to A, under an agency or mandate arrangement, for the benefit of O or others, P and Q. However, Article 2(a) requires that "the assets constitute a separate fund and are not a part of the trustee's own estate" as one of "the characteristics which an institution must show in order to fall under the

Convention's coverage" (as emphasised in paragraph 36 of the Von Overbeck Official Report on the Convention). Thus, it would appear that if the asset owned by O is not a separate fund excluded from being part of O's own estate then there can be no trust of such asset.

Be that as it may, such problems are avoided in the Principles, which clearly do not extend to agency or mandate arrangements, by requiring the settlor to confer ownership of the trust assets upon the trustee (as apparent in Articles I(1) and V(1)).

It is crucial that the settlor does not intend the assets to be part of the trustee's private patrimony, but to form a trust fund set aside for benefiting the beneficiaries or the purposes of the trust, so that it is not available to satisfy claims made against the trustee in his private capacity (e.g. by his spouse, heirs or creditors) as opposed to his capacity as manager of the trust fund.

Also fundamental to a trust (as developed in Article IV) is the obligation owed by the trustee to the beneficiaries to account for how he has dealt with the trust fund. In the case of trusts for purposes the right to make the trustee account for his trusteeship is vested in a representative of the State if the purposes are charitable[8]. Non-charitable purpose trusts cannot be created in most jurisdictions. However, in those jurisdictions with legislation permitting such trusts[9], such trusts can only be created if the settlor appoints a specific person to be enforcer of the trust.

Just as a person cannot contract with himself, so a person cannot be sole trustee for himself as sole beneficiary. However, most jurisdictions permit a trustee to be one of the beneficiaries under the trust of which he is one of the trustees or even the sole trustee, enforceability by the other beneficiaries underpinning the existence of the trust in the latter eventuality.

8 E.g. the Attorney General (representing the Crown as *parens patriae*) or a statutory body like the English Charity Commissioners.

9 E.g. Bermuda, Jersey, Guernsey, Isle of Man, Cayman Islands.

Paragraph (3)

It is crucial that the trust fund is immune from claims by the trustee's spouse, heirs and creditors dealing with the trustee otherwise than in his capacity as trustee. The trust fund is liable only to claims by creditors dealing with the trustee in his capacity as trustee[10] (subject to any prior overriding claim by the settlor's creditors, heirs or spouse claiming that the settlor's transfer of the property to the trustee contravened laws protecting such claimants[11]) and, then, to the rights of the beneficiaries[12].

Any rights that a beneficiary has in respect of the trust fund (e.g. as life tenant, entitled to income, or as remainderman, entitled to capital on the death of the life tenant) are, of course, available to satisfy any claims that his spouse, his heirs or his creditors may have against him (or his estate on his death, assuming that he was not simply a life tenant). If the beneficiary has only an interest in a discretionary trust then he has no rights that can be seized and sold for the benefit of his creditors, although if he receives anything pursuant to the exercise of the trustee's discretion his creditors are entitled to it. Some common law jurisdictions[13] as a matter of policy have made it possible for persons to create special trusts, providing a measure of protection against creditors, for spendthrift relatives or dependants who need protection against their own improvident, foolhardy habits.

Paragraph (4)

So that the separate trust fund is immune from claims by the trustee's spouse, heirs or creditors dealing with the trustee not as a trustee but in his private capacity, the beneficiaries *must* have a personal claim against the trustee, so that the trust fund itself can be recovered from the trustee in priority to the claims of such persons. Indeed it *may* be that, as in common law jurisdictions, the beneficiaries have a proprietary *in rem* claim to the trust fund. It is crucial to appreciate that the word "may" is used simply to indicate optional possibilities that may represent the state of the law in some jurisdictions but not in others.

---

10 U&H, Article 86.

11 U&H, Articles 16, 17, 18 and 19.

12 U&H, Articles 2, 33, 45, 95 and 104.

13 E.g. English protective trusts under s 33 Trustee Act 1925 (U&H Article 11 (1)(c)) and American spendthrift trusts on which see Scott on Trusts, paras 151-152.

When part of the trust fund is wrongly transferred by the trustee to a third party, who is a donee or who is not an acquirer for value in good faith, then the dedication of such property for the benefit of particular beneficiaries or for furthering particular purposes may be recognised by the transferee being ordered in some jurisdictions to pay compensation for the value received. However, a common law jurisdiction[14] will go further and compel such a transferee to hold the property or any property representing such property for the benefit of the particular beneficiaries or purposes: it regards such transferee as always having owned such property as a trust fund that was never part of his private patrimony.

In common law trust jurisdictions the trust concept straddles the law of property and the law of obligations because of the historical development of a Court of Equity (orginating in a royal prerogative jurisdiction delegated to the Lord Chancellor) separate from the Common Law Courts to deal with cases where no remedy or no adequate remedy was available in those Courts. The Court of Equity looked on as done that which ought to be done and treated defendants as good men: thus a defendant trustee could not claim that the trust property belonged to him beneficially and that he was liable only to pay compensation to the plaintiff beneficiary for the loss of the trust property. In feudal society it was crucial that a plaintiff knight, who had conveyed his land to the defendant to hold for the plaintiff until he returned from the Crusades, could recover that specific land from the defendant, who would also be personally accountable for what he had done with the land. The rule developed that if Equity considered that there was an enforceable obligation owed to the plaintiff by a defendant in respect of particular property, then the plaintiff was treated as having an equitable interest in the property, which bound the legal owner of the property, unless he happened to be a bona fide purchaser without notice of the equitable interest. Alongside equitable obligations there thus developed *equitable* property interests, binding all persons other than bona fide purchasers without notice, as opposed to *legal* property interests that were rights that bound everybody. However, trusts can flourish without the need for any such divided ownership of property as apparent in Scotland, India and South Africa.

14 U&H, Article 104.

Article II. Creation of the trust

A trust cannot exist without a fund owned by a trustee obliged to deal with it as a segregated fund according to the terms of the trust prescribed by the settlor at the time he creates the trust[15]. The settlor must therefore ensure that ownership (see Articles I(1) and V(1)) of the intended trust assets is transferred to the trustee, whether by will or in his lifetime pursuant to a contract for value or gratuitously. The trustee will retain ownership of the trust assets, which may include anything which is capable of being transferred to another person (including the benefit of enforceable promises or contractual rights) or he may transfer the trust assets into the name of a nominee. In the latter case the trustee has the right to call for the assets (e.g. shares in quoted companies) to be transferred to himself or to such person (e.g. a purchaser) as he directs, although, technically, his rights against the nominee can be regarded as trust assets vested in him.

In some special circumstances[16] the *lex situs* may be prepared to treat a transfer by a transferor-settlor as effective from the time when the transferor had done everything obligatory upon him to do to effect the transfer, although title had not actually passed (e.g. because title does not pass until the transfer of shares or land has been formally registered by a company registrar or the Land Registry). It is worth noting that a settlor in jurisdictions like England or Scotland can enter into an enforceable promise to transfer a sum of money or a particular asset to a trustee with the intention that the benefit of such promise will be owned by the trustee for the benefit of beneficiaries or the furtherance of purposes: a trust then arises of the right to enforce such promise[17].

If a trustee of a trust created, for example, by his brother for his brother's descendants can add his own assets to the segregated trust assets, so distinguishing such settled assets from the rest of his assets, there seems little reason why he should not be able simply to create his own exclusive trust by distinguishing from his assets particular assets that he makes clear he will be holding as trustee on trust for specified persons or purposes. Of course, it will need to be clear to which assets the intention to create a trust

15 U&H, Article 9.
16 U&H, pp. 133-134.
17 U&H, pp. 147-160.

relates, and clear proof of such intention will be required[18]. Such trust may also be vitiated by the usual mandatory rules if created in order to defeat the claims of creditors or heirs or a spouse.

Once a person can own a trust fund separate from his private patrimony it is difficult to justify distinguishing between the case where that situation is brought about by the act of another person and the case where it is brought about by himself. The matter ceases to be one of principle and becomes one of evidence. Common law countries and hybrid countries like Scotland thus permit a settlor to be sole trustee of his own trust for the benefit of persons or purposes. However, as use of the word "may" indicates, it is up to each jurisdiction to decide whether or not it will permit creation of a trust by a settlor making himself trustee of particular assets of his distinguished from his other assets, and what evidence will suffice to establish such a trust.

Article III. Trust fund

Paragraph (1)

As may be the case for identifying what property from time to time represents property subject to a partnership or a particular matrimonial property regime or mutual (agreed to be irrevocable) wills of spouses or persons in other close relationships, the terms of the trust apply not just to the original trust assets (often a nominal sum of money paid to the trustee) and subsequently added assets, but also to assets from time to time representing such assets[19] e.g. where the trustee sells ICI plc shares and uses the proceeds to purchase Whizzo Ltd shares, or the trustee uses trust income to purchase Sainsbury plc shares, or the trustee receives compensation from the wrongful damager of trust property or the insurer of a trust painting destroyed by fire, or the trustee receives bonus shares in respect of a trust shareholding, or uses trust money to build a house on trust land. Indeed, it is common for the trust instrument expressly to define the "Trust Property" or the "Trust Fund" as "the Initial Property specified in the Schedule hereto and any property subsequently transferred to the Trustee as

18 U&H, pp. 61, 125-128: Scotland also allows this: *Allan's Trustees v IRC* 1971 SLT 62, *Clark Taylor & Co Ltd v Quality Site Development* 1981 SLT 730; so long as the trust is created in writing: Requirements for Writing (Scotland) Act 1995 s 1(2)(a)(iii).

19 U&H, Articles 33, 95 and 104.

additions to the Trust Fund and any property from time to time representing the Initial Property or the subsequently transferred property or the fruits thereof". Civil lawyers will recognise in this the concept of real subrogation.

Whether or not there is such an express definition of Trust Fund, the beneficiaries are regarded as being interested in a trust "fund" comprising whatever assets from time to time represent the original and subsequently added assets. The trustee cannot claim that he was a bad man and wrongfully used trust income to purchase Sainsbury plc shares for himself, so that he is only under a personal obligation to pay compensation to the beneficiaries, where he is authorised as trustee to purchase such shares. Even where he used trust money wrongfully to buy for himself shares that he was not authorised by the trust instrument to buy for the trust e.g. Whizzo Ltd shares, he is not allowed to deny the beneficiaries' claim that he acted as a good man in committing an advantageous breach of trust (that they are prepared to forgive) by purchasing the Whizzo shares for the trust fund. He cannot plead his own dishonesty to the advantage of himself at the expense of the beneficiaries: his trustee in bankruptcy and his general creditors stand in his shoes so that they, too, cannot take advantage of his dishonesty to prefer themselves at the expense of the beneficiaries. In civil law terminology the principles of real subrogation operate whether the trustee acts rightfully or wrongfully[20]. The trustee is presumed to have acted properly: *omnia praesumuntur rite esse acta* in the words of the Latin maxim.

Where the trustee sells trust assets and dishonestly pays the proceeds into his own bank account (instead of the trust fund) and so mixes trust money with his own money before purchasing some asset for himself, each jurisdiction needs to develop special identification rules to identify an asset that can be claimed as part of the trust fund (or perhaps as security for a claim for compensation where the asset has depreciated in value). Common law jurisdictions have developed rules that work against the trustee (and thus against his trustee in bankruptcy and general creditors) and favour the beneficiaries: the wrongful mixing of the trust moneys with his own moneys prevents the trustee from disproving whatever the

20 *Attorney General for Hong Kong v Reid* [1994] 1 AC 324.

beneficiaries claim as the asset that represents what they claim to be their trust moneys: see commentary to Article VI.

Paragraph (2)

As emphasised by Article 11 of The Hague Convention on Recognition of Trusts and paragraph 108 of the Von Overbeck Report thereon, it is, of course, the key to the trust that the trust fund is immune from claims of the trustee's private creditors, his spouse and his heirs (although if the trustee is also a beneficiary then, of course, his rights as a beneficiary are available to satisfy such claims). The trust fund is subject first to the overriding possibility that the settlor's transfer of property that created the trust fund may be attacked for breaking laws protecting creditors, heirs or spouses of the settlor[21]. The fund is subject secondly to the claims of the trustee for reimbursement of expenses and the claims of creditors dealing with the trustee as owner and manager of the trust fund[22]. Finally, the net fund after payment of such claims is available for the beneficiaries (and of creditors of the beneficiaries) or for relevant purposes.

For purpose trusts to be enforceable there must be a person whose function is to act as enforcer. In the case of charitable (public benefit) trusts such person is a state official[23]; otherwise, the settlor should initially appoint the enforcer in the trust instrument and make arrangements therein for succession to the office of enforcer, with legislation or the inherent jurisdiction of the court otherwise providing for who is to hold office as enforcer[24].

This core notion of a protected separate fund is already present in many civil law systems as appears in the commentaries on such systems that follow this Commentary.

Paragraph (3)

While the normal duty of a trustee of several trusts is to keep each trust fund distinct, a settlor can by the terms of his trust authorise a trustee to pool specific types of fungible (i.e. interchangeable) trust assets with the

21 U&H, Articles 16, 17, 18 and 19.
22 U&H, Article 86.
23 See note 8.
24 See note 9.

same types of assets of other trusts of which the trustee is also the trustee, so that the pooled assets are held by the trustee for the benefit of each trust in proportions reflecting the contributions of each trust[25]. Indeed, a settlor can authorise the trustee to pool trust assets with the trustee's private assets (which otherwise would have to be segregated from trust assets): then, ownership of the pooled assets is held by the trustee for the benefit of the trust fund and the private patrimony of the trustee in the proportions contributed by each. Thus if, pursuant to an authorisation in the trust instrument, T pooled £10,000 of his own money with £20,000 from Trust B and £30,000 from Trust C to purchase 600 Mega plc shares in his name, then on T's insolvency only 100 shares would be available for T's private creditors, 200 and 300 shares respectively being regarded as part of the trust funds of Trust B and Trust C. In common law countries having an equitable jurisdiction, T would have legal title to the 600 shares but the beneficiaries of Trust B and Trust C would, respectively, have the equitable title to 200 and 300 shares. In civil law countries, it should be that T's right to the 600 shares, a chose in action, is regarded as part of his private patrimony as to one sixth but as part of the trust fund of Trust B as to one third and as part of the trust fund of Trust C as to one half: cp the interest of an investor pooled with interests of all other investors in fungible securities accounts with Euroclear (of Belgium) and Cedel (of Luxembourg).

In an exceptional case the terms of the settlor's trust may even authorise the trustee to lend trust money to itself so that the money moves from the trust fund to the private patrimony of the trustee, who is then only personally liable as a debtor in respect of the amount of the loan[26]. Indeed, it is possible, for example, that if T is a company that is a market-maker in shares of particular companies (e.g. Global plc), then it will be authorised in the trust instrument to sell to the trust at the proper market price any Global shares that it owns and to retain the proceeds and any profits as part of its private patrimony, or to purchase from the trust Global shares for itself or its holding company and retain any commission it receives as part of its private patrimony.

---

25 *R v Barlow Clowes* (No 2) [1994] 2 All ER 316, *Re Goldcorp Exchange Ltd* [1995] 1 AC 74.

26 *Space Investments Ltd v Canadian Imperial Bank of Commerce Trust Co Ltd* [1986] 1 WLR 1072.

Article IV. Trusts for beneficiaries or for enforceable purposes

Paragraph (1)

No trust can exist unless the trustee is, or will be, under an obligation to another in respect of the trust fund[27]. Thus, there must be a beneficiary with a right to enforce the terms of the trust against the trustee or an office-holder with a right to enforce the purposes of the trust. To the extent that the settlor does not effectively place the trustee under obligations to another person, the trustee will hold the trust fund on a resulting trust for the settlor. Thus, if the settlor transferred property to the trustee to be held for such worthy purposes as the trustee may see fit, there will be a resulting trust for the settlor (or, if he is dead, his heirs) because such trust purposes, not being exclusively charitable, are void for uncertainty[28].

For a trust for purposes to be valid, the trust must either be a charitable trust (viz trusts for purposes beneficial to the community) so that some representative of the State can enforce it in the public interest, or it must be a non-charitable purpose trust made valid by legislation that provides some special procedure for enforcement of the purpose (if expressed in sufficiently clear enforceable terms) against the trustee e.g. an enforcer named as such in the trust document and, usually, having to be a lawyer qualified to practise in the State that validates such non-charitable purpose trusts.

For a trust for persons to be valid, the settlor must designate ascertained or ascertainable persons as the actual or potential beneficiaries[29]. It is possible that a civil law jurisdiction may require beneficiaries to be in existence when the trust is created if there is to be a valid trust for them, even if this drastically reduces the flexibility of the trust concept. Common law jurisdictions, however, permit a trust to be valid so long as ascertainable beneficiaries qualify to take an interest before the end of a period known as the perpetuity period, which may be a fixed period, like 100 years, or an

---

27 *Armitage v Nurse* [1998] Ch 241, 253 where Millett LJ states "There is an irreducible core of obligations owed by the trustees to the beneficiaries and enforceable by them which is fundamental to the concept of a trust. If the beneficiaries have no rights enforceable against the trustees there are no trusts".

28 *Re Gillingham Bus Disaster Fund* [1959] Ch 62.

29 U&H, Article 8.

uncertain period expiring 21 years from the death of a specified person alive at the date of the creation of the trust.

In such jurisdictions the fact that on or before the expiry of the perpetuity period there will be some beneficiary with a right to enforce the trust by seeing the trust documents and accounts and then, if necessary, by making the trustee account for losses occasioned by breaches of trust or profits made for the trustee personally in breach of trust, is sufficient to establish the requisite trustee-beneficiary duty-right relationship. A valid trust thus exists where the trustee has power to accumulate income (viz add income to capital) for 100 years and then must distribute the capital between such of the settlor's then living descendants born in the preceding eighteen years as it sees fit (or in default of any such descendants to such charitable corporations then in existence as the trustee may select) but with the trustee to have power at any time within the 100 year period to appoint income or capital as it sees fit to any of the settlor's descendants or their spouses (such descendants and their spouses not being beneficiaries under a discretionary trust but simply being objects of a discretionary power as explained below under paragraph (3)).

Paragraph (2)

To the extent that a settlor in his lifetime (or a testator by his will), after transferring ownership of his property to the trustee, fails effectively to place the trustee under fully comprehensive obligations to beneficiaries or enforcers of purposes, the trustee will hold the trust property on trust for the settlor or his heirs. This will occur where a settlor transfers property to T upon trust for A for life, without stating what happens after A's death, so there is then a resulting trust in the settlor's favour. This is also the case where, after a period, obligations intended to arise outside such a period are either void for uncertainty (e.g. for "worthy causes" after the death of A) or for infringing a rule that makes obligations void if arising too far in the future (e.g. where a discretionary trust for the descendants of A is followed by a discretionary trust for the descendants of B after there are no longer any descendants of A). Exceptionally, if the purposes of a charitable trust can no longer be carried out effectively, then the trust fund will be authorised by the court to be applied to a closely similar purpose, as explained below in the commentary to Article VIII(3). Indeed, in a jurisdiction permitting non-charitable purpose trusts, it may be that a similar cy-près jurisdiction is available.

Paragraph (3)

No beneficiary or office holder can be in a position to enforce a trust unless he knows of the trust. Thus, the trustee should ensure that a beneficiary of full capacity knows that he has a conditional or unconditional fixed interest (e.g. a life interest or an interest in remainder, which may, or may not, be subject to some condition such as attaining a specified age or surviving a specified person). So far as practicable, the trustees should even inform beneficiaries interested only under a discretionary trust[30] (e.g. the trustee holds income and capital upon trust for distribution in his absolute discretion in favour of such of the settlor's descendants as he sees fit over the next 80 years). Similarly, a trustee must inform an office holder of a valid purpose trust.

A beneficiary or office holder then has a right to obtain from the trustee all information needed to protect his interest, but must pay for copies of any relevant documentation unless the terms of the trust require otherwise[31]. However, there is no right to confidential information[32] e.g. where the settlor provided the trustee with a confidential letter of wishes (which is not a legally binding document, unlike the trust instrument) or where a beneficiary disclosed intimate health or financial details to the trustee in order to obtain money from the trustee. Neither is there any right to see documents or parts of documents that may reveal the reasons for the trustee exercising discretions conferred on him as trustee (unless the terms of the trust require otherwise)[33]. However, if a beneficiary can establish a sufficient basis for a breach of trust action against the trustee, then, under rules of court governing discovery in the course of litigation, the trustee will be forced to disclose documents that may possibly advance the beneficiary's case or adversely affect the trustee's case[34].

While even a discretionary beneficiary has the right to be informed he is a beneficiary and a right to see the trust documents and accounts, a person who is simply the object of a power vested in the trustees need have no

30 U&H, pp. 610-611, *Re Murphy's settlements* [1998] 3 All ER 1.
31 U&H, Article 62.
32 U&H, pp. 45, 660.
33 U&H, pp. 659-660.
34 U&H, pp. 45, 660.

such rights[35]: the trustee-beneficiary duty-right tension is the necessary prerequisite for the existence of a trust. To illustrate the distinction between beneficiaries under a discretionary trust and objects of a power, take the case where a trustee holds the trust fund for the perpetuity period on discretionary trust to use the income at his absolute discretion to benefit such of the descendants of A as he chooses, but has power, instead, in his absolute discretion to use the income to benefit such of the descendants of B as he chooses, while at the end of the perpetuity period he must distribute the capital equally between the descendants of A in stirpital shares, although he has power to appoint capital instead to such of B's descendants as he may choose.

Here, A's descendants are the primary objects of the settlor's bounty, B's descendants being secondary objects who will only be benefited if the trustee positively decides to exercise his optional powers in their favour. If the trustee's power to appoint income to such of B's descendants as he sees fit is not exercised within a reasonable time of receipt of the income by the trustee, then the trustee must distribute the income between such of A's descendants as he chooses[36]: a new trustee will be appointed by the court to carry out this duty if the trustee does not perform his duty[37]. If at the end of the perpetuity period the trustee decides not to appoint capital to any of B's descendants or only to appoint one quarter of it amongst some of B's descendants, then the trustee must divide all or three quarters (as the case may be) of the capital amongst the descendants of A per stirpes and the court will so divide the capital if the trustee does not. Thus, in essence, a power is simply a permission granted to the trustee to do something he otherwise could not do; while a trust obligation compels a trustee to act in particular ways unless he has power to do something different and chooses to exercise such power. To underpin such trust obligations, the beneficiaries must have a right to all information needed to make the trustee account for his conduct as trustee; objects of a power may have such a right if the settlor intended this, but not if he did not so intend.

35 U&H, p. 611, Trends in Contemporary Trust Law, AJ Oakley (ed), pp. 49-52.
36 U&H, p. 23.
37 U&H, p. 68.

In exceptional circumstances it may be possible for a beneficiary to be excluded from having rights of information[38] e.g. while he is Government Finance Minister or Chief of the Anti-Corporate Fraud Office or while his rights are contingent or while he is director of a company which is a competitor of a company owned and controlled by the trustees.

Paragraph (4)

Like the owner of any asset, a beneficiary can dispose of his rights as beneficiary under a trust. The transferee will then have the same rights that the transferor-beneficiary owned. However, some jurisdictions for public policy reasons (e.g. designed to protect spendthrifts or pension fund beneficiaries against their foolhardiness) may permit or impose certain restrictions on the alienability of beneficiaries' rights.

Paragraph (5)

Irrespective of whether a jurisdiction allows a settlor to have power to enforce the terms of his trust, it is crucial that judicial remedies are available to a beneficiary (or office holder), on which see Article VI and commentary thereon.

Article V. Trustees' duties and powers

Paragraph (1)

The trustee as owner of the assets comprising the trust fund has all the powers of an owner unless restricted by the terms of the trust or by legislation. In common law jurisdictions, legislation often limits the management powers of trustees, so that they can only invest in safe types of investment unless the settlor expressly confers wider powers on trustees in the trust document setting out the terms of the trust. However, the developing trend is to have new legislation permitting trustees to exercise the full powers of owners, so long as they exercise the standard of care of a prudent investor. Just as two or more owners must exercise their powers jointly so must two or more trustees.

38 U&H, pp. 662-663.

Paragraphs (2) and (3)

A trustee must first ascertain who are the beneficiaries, what are their rights in respect of income or capital, and what powers he has to further their interests[39]. The trust document provides him with most of this information but legislation may automatically confer various common powers upon trustees[40] or enable the court[41] to provide the trustee with extra powers, while he may have to make inquiries as to the whereabouts of beneficiaries and of documentation relating to the trust assets and to any assignments of interests of beneficiaries. Almost invariably there will be a trust document, but a trust may be created orally in simple situations.

Where a new trustee takes over from another trustee he must ensure that all the trust fund is transferred to him, e.g. where he takes over from a retiring trustee or a deceased trustee. He must earmark the trust fund so that it is clearly segregated from his personal patrimony and other trust funds vested in him[42]. If, as explained in the commentary to Article III(3), he has a right to pool fungible trust assets with similar assets of other trust funds or even of himself, he must take particular care to keep accurate records and to allocate promptly to particular funds particular sold or replaced assets.

The trustee must ensure that beneficiaries know that they are beneficiaries and inform office holders of the terms of trusts for valid purposes. He must keep accurate up-to-date accounts so that relevant beneficiaries or an office holder can obtain all the information they need to protect their interests as discussed in the commentary to Article IV(3).

The trustee must comply strictly with the terms of the trust in benefiting beneficiaries or furthering trust purposes and must take reasonable care[43] in investing the trust fund and in exercising his other managerial and administrative powers.

---

39 U&H, Article 48.
40 E.g. English Trustee Act 1925 ss 15, 23, 31 and 32.
41 E.g. English Trustee Act 1925 s 57.
42 U&H, pp. 58-59 and 855.
43 U&H, Article 54 and pp. 597-600.

Because the duties of trustees are onerous and because they may get caught in the cross-fire between two sets of beneficiaries with competing interests, common law jurisdictions afford trustees the opportunity to apply to the court (at the expense of the trust fund) for advice or for approval in relation to matters where the trustees are uncertain as to their position[44]. The trustees can then safely proceed in accordance with such advice or approval (so long as they put the court fully in the picture and did not mislead it).

Paragraph (4)

The trustee must act personally and not delegate any of his functions (particularly his property-owning function, any discretionary powers as to distribution of income and capital and his discretionary management function) unless so authorised by the terms of the trust or by specific legislation[45]. He must act in unprejudiced fashion and keep a fair balance between the competing interests of those interested in a high income and those interested in high capital growth (unless the terms of the trust otherwise permit e.g. to prefer the interest of the life tenant who is the testator's widow to that of the remainderman who is a distant relative or a charity)[46]. He must always act honestly[47].

The trustee must not profit from the trust nor breach the "no conflict" rule unless otherwise authorised by the settlor when creating the trust[48], as mentioned in the General Introduction to the Commentary. He must consciously and independently consider from time to time the exercise of his powers to benefit beneficiaries or objects of discretionary powers and he must not exercise these powers arbitrarily, capriciously or for a purpose perverse to any sensible expectation of the settlor[49] (viz he must loyally act in good faith).

---

44 U&H, Article 90.
45 U&H, Article 57.
46 U&H, Article 50 and pp. 599-600.
47 *Armitage v Nurse* [1998] 8 Ch 241, 253.
48 U&H, Articles 60 and 61.
49 U&H, pp. 77-78 and Article 63.

Paragraph (5)
Accountability of the trustees to the beneficiaries or to the enforcer is at the core of a trust for beneficiaries or for purposes. When the beneficiaries or the enforcer examine the trustee's accounts they can seek to show the accounts to be erroneous, whether by falsifying the accounts or surcharging the accounts[50]. The accounts are falsified where an item entered in the accounts is false because it represents a wrongful application of part of the trust fund so that the item is disallowed. Thus, if T wrongfully sells an authorised investment to purchase an unauthorised investment the sale and purchase will be disallowed: T will be treated as if he had acted properly and had retained the authorised investment which he will have to replace at its current market value. However, if the unauthorised investment is worth more than the authorised investment the beneficiaries will elect not to exercise their right to falsify the account.

The accounts are surcharged where the trustees should be liable for a higher amount to the beneficiaries or the enforcer because such higher amount should feature in the accounts as representing what the trustees ought to have received but for their failure to comply with their obligations to the beneficiaries or as representing profits actually made by the trustees for themselves in breach of trust (even though such breach was an innocent or honest breach which caused no loss to the trust fund or even enabled the trust fund to make a profit as well as the trustees)[51].

Further on the extent of the liabilities of the trustee see the commentary to Article VI.

Article VI. Remedies against trustees for breach of trust

If, in his investment or managerial role or in appointing or supervising an authorised agent the trustee neglects to exercise the standard of care expected of him he will be liable to make good any consequent losses[52]. Where there are two or more trustees each must actively involve himself in decision making in trust affairs: if the passivity of a trustee allows[53] his

50 U&H, p. 828, *Lord Justice Millett* (1998) 114 LQR 214, 225-227.
51 U&H, Article 33, *Boardman v Phipps* [1967] 2 AC 46.
52 U&H, Articles 54, 55, 57 and 92.
53 U&H, Article 58.

co-trustee to commit a breach of trust he will himself be liable for the loss occasioned by such breach. Each trustee is normally liable for the whole loss when caused by the joint default of all the trustees[54].

Arising from his status as trustee, a trustee must account for what he has done with the trust fund. Thus, if the trustee distributes any part of the trust fund to persons who are not beneficiaries, or spends it on non-trust purposes, or without authority delegates discretionary management of the trust fund to another, or without a requisite consent appoints capital to a beneficiary, the trustee commits a breach of trust and must reinstate the trust fund to its previous value[55] (although credit will be given for anything recovered from any recipient of the wrongfully transferred trust fund). A breach of trust also renders the trustee liable to be removed by the court, whether or not any loss results from the breach e.g. where without a requisite consent the trustee sells particular trust assets to a purchaser for the full purchase price, or where the trustee in breach of the "no profit" or "no conflict" rules makes a profit for himself, even if he also makes a profit for the trust.

Indeed, where in breach of trust a trustee makes a profit for himself he is subject to a strict rule of deterrence that makes him liable to augment the trust fund by the amount of his profit (even if he occasioned no loss to the trust fund or even if the trust fund also profited from his behaviour) and in some jurisdictions he will be treated as holding the profit as part of the trust fund from the moment he received it: "profits" can extend to bribes and secret commissions and property representing such bribes or commissions[56].

Some jurisdictions have developed sophisticated rules as to a tracing process available to protect vulnerable beneficiaries against a trustee taking advantage of them[57]. Thus, if a trustee, T, takes a bribe of £5,000 or £5,000 proceeds of sale of a trust asset and pays such £5,000 into his private bank account already containing £5,000 and then purchases a painting for

54 U&H, Articles 93 and 101.
55 U&H, Articles 56 and 92, *Attorney General for Hong Kong v Reid* [1994] 1 AC 324, *Boardman v Phipps* [1967] 2 AC 46, *Target Holdings v Redferns* [1996] AC 421, 440.
56 U&H, Article 33.
57 U&H, Articles 95 and 104.

£10,000, the painting can be traced to enable him to be treated as owning the picture as to one half for himself and one half as part of the trust fund. Thus, the beneficiaries will be in an advantageous position if the painting appreciates in value or if T becomes bankrupt. If the painting depreciates in value then the beneficiaries are treated as secured creditors having a charge over the painting to secure repayment of £5,000 plus interest. The tracing process is thus a vital preliminary to the assertion of a claim to whole or partial ownership of a particular traced asset or to a charge over such traced asset.

If it so happens that out of the mixed £10,000 T spent £5,000 on a painting that appreciates in value to £7,500, while the remaining £5,000 in the account is dissipated, then T is not allowed to claim that the painting is part of his private patrimony. His mixing of the trust £5,000 with his own £5,000 prevents him from disproving the beneficiaries' claim that it was their £5,000 that was used to purchase the painting.

If it so happened that out of the mixed £10,000 he dissipated £5,000 leaving £5,000 in his account he is not allowed to deny that he acted as a good trustee in spending his own money first so as to leave the £5,000 as part of the trust fund.

The position of those deriving title under T is the same as T, so that his trustee in bankruptcy, spouse or heirs cannot be in a better position than T, and so that the position of vulnerable beneficiaries cannot be worsened by the bankruptcy, divorce or death of T.

In civil law jurisdictions there may already be some sophisticated rules so that property from time to time representing property subject to a partnership or a matrimonial property regime or mutual (agreed not to be revocable) wills may be traced so as to establish ownership thereof. Any such rules could thereof be applied by analogy to trace property from time to time representing part of the trust fund.

It is possible that, initially, a jurisdiction may only allow the proceeds of sale of an asset that was part of the trust fund to be traced so as to establish ownership of a new asset purchased with such proceeds (so that such new asset from the time of its purchase is regarded as part of the trust fund) where such proceeds have not been mixed (other than *de minimis*) with the trustee's private money. If this be the case then, where there has been mixing, for example, of £5,000 trust money with £5,000 of the trustee's private money to purchase for £10,000 Whizzo shares for the trustee's private patrimony, a jurisdiction may, perhaps, permit the beneficiaries to be regarded as secured creditors, having a security interest in the Whizzo shares for the purpose of satisfying their claim for £5,000 and interest, or if the shares have doubled in value, perhaps for the purpose of satisfying a claim for £10,000 and interest so as to prevent the unjust enrichment of the trustee (and his creditors if he is insolvent).

Because a trust can endure for 100 years or so, while the office of trustee is an onerous one and one where the interests of some beneficiaries may conflict with other beneficiaries, it is normally possible for the trustee to seek guidance from the court in respect of any matters where he is uncertain as to what is the scope of a particular duty or power of his before he commits himself to taking any action[58]. In some circumstances where there is an acceptable reason for the trustee not to have sought and obtained the court's guidance, the court may have a discretion to excuse the trustee wholly or partly from liability for breach of trust[59] e.g. where paying trust money to a person who appeared to be a genuine beneficiary by virtue of forged documents that would have fooled anybody but an exceptionally skilled expert.

Indeed, it is very common for the settlor in his trust instrument to excuse the trustee from liability for breach of trust unless the trustee was negligent or even to excuse the trustee from liability unless he acted recklessly or in bad faith, so that he cannot then be made liable for grossly negligent breaches of trust[60]. Experience, however, has shown that legislation[61] may have to intervene to protect beneficiaries in certain types of trust such as unit trusts, debenture trusts and pension trusts by outlawing clauses that purport to prevent the trustee from being liable for negligent conduct, or legislation (as in Jersey) may generally outlaw clauses purporting to exempt trustees from liability for gross negligence.

---

58 U&H, Article 90.

59 U&H, Article 98.

60 *Armitage v Nurse* [1998] Ch 241.

61 E.g. English Companies Act 1985 s 192, Financial Services Act 1986 s 84, Pensions Act 1995 s 34.

Article VII. Liabilities of third parties

Where T in breach of trust transfers part of the trust fund to X, then T is personally liable to augment the trust fund by the amount of loss suffered by reason of the transfer[62]. Thus, if T made a wrongful gift of a trust painting to X when the painting was worth £x, and when the breach of trust is discovered the painting is worth £2x, T will have to pay £2x compensation. After all, there should appear in the trust account an item consisting of a painting worth £2x.

If T is insolvent, or is dead and his estate distributed by the time the breach is discovered, the question arises whether X can be made personally liable for £x or £2x (with or without the painting being security for such sum) or can be placed under a liability to return the painting itself as always having been part of the trust fund[63]. If X no longer has the painting because he sold it to a bona fide purchaser for £1½x and used this money to purchase a new painting now worth £3x, the further question arises as to whether X can be made personally liable for £1½x or £3x (with or without the painting being security for such sum) or can be placed under a liability to hand over the new painting as always having been part of the trust fund since he acquired it[64].

In some jurisdictions the answer to the question may depend upon X having knowledge that T had acted wrongfully or having suspicion that T had probably acted wrongfully and, then, upon X deliberately or recklessly (and so dishonestly) refusing to make further inquiry for fear of what he would probably learn. In common law jurisdictions the simple fact that X was a donee and would be unjustly enriched at the beneficiaries' expense will render X liable to pay compensation or to hand over the painting[65].

In this area there is much scope for jurisdictions to develop their own rules and, perhaps, have rules that depend on whether the defendant is or is not insolvent, as well as rules that depend upon whether the defendant knew

62 U&H, Article 92.
63 U&H, Article 95.
64 U&H, Article 104.
65 *Ibid.*

or had reason to know that the transfer to him was wrongful or probably wrongful.

If T holds property on trust for B alone, but in breach of trust gives it to X, who has knowledge of B's interest, why should X not be bound to deliver the property to B? Why should the position be any different if X has no knowledge of B's interest but would still be unjustly enriched as a donee if allowed to retain the property for himself? Why should the existence of the trust fund not be recognised by compelling X to deliver the property up to B, or to the replacement trustee for the wrongdoing T where T held the property on trust for X, Y and Z or for such of X, Y and Z and their spouses and descendants as the trustee shall select during the next 80 years? Should the bankruptcy of X make any difference? This may depend upon the extent to which in modern society creditors really deal with a person only after checking out that he appears to be a person of wealth, so that they are misled to act to their detriment if it transpires that some of his wealth is not part of his private patrimony. Many common law jurisdictions[66] have abandoned insolvency rules which provide that property reputedly owned by an insolvent passes to his trustee in bankruptcy. It should be noted, however, that such rules have never applied to trust funds: indeed, such funds have never been part of the trustee's estate capable of passing on bankruptcy to his trustee in bankruptcy. However, many civil law jurisdictions still place much emphasis on publicity of ownership.

The above questions can also be raised in respect of the situation where X is not a donee but an acquirer for value ("a purchaser") although not in good faith. Clearly, there can be no question of X being liable if he is a purchaser in good faith of the trust asset whereupon T holds X's money or other exchanged property as part of the trust fund. Similarly, there can be no question of X being liable where he is protected by legislation designed to enhance the marketability of particular types of property, e.g. land. In common law jurisdictions it is common to find that if X pays his purchase money for land (or money he is lending on the security of land) to two trustees or to a sole trust corporation, then X takes a perfect title to the land (or the mortgage), detached from the interests of any beneficiaries which

66 E.g. English Insolvency Act 1986 s 283 definition of bankruptcy estate not extending to property of which the bankrupt appears to be the owner.

are "overreached" by being attached to the purchase money or the mortgage money[67]. Only if the terms of the trust expressly required the consent of specified beneficiaries to any disposition of the house would X have to obtain their consents (although if more than two consents are requisite legislation, designed to simplify conveyancing, usually permits overreaching to occur if two consents are obtained).

Where X is not protected as a purchaser in good faith or by overreaching legislation, then once he knows that T transferred the property to him in breach of trust, so that he has been unjustly enriched, but subsequently sells the property and dissipates the proceeds of sale (e.g. by living the high life) so that no order can be made to deliver up particular property, he will be personally liable for the value of the property[68].

Article VIII. Termination of a trust

Paragraph (1)
Just as B can terminate a trust of property held by T for B absolutely, so can B, C, D and E terminate a trust of property held by T for B, C, D and E absolutely, or F, G and H terminate a trust of property held by T on trust for F for life, remainder to G for life, remainder to H absolutely, or on trust to distribute income and capital among such of F, G and H as T may decide in his absolute discretion[69]. However, if some material purpose of the settlor remains to be accomplished the beneficiaries may not be permitted in some jurisdictions to terminate the trust[70].

Take the case of a testator who, in his lifetime, transferred a 25 per cent shareholding in his company to his second child, B, and by will left a 51 per cent shareholding to B on trust for B's siblings, A, C and D equally. B

67 E.g. English Trustee Act 1925 s 14 and Law of Property Act 1925 s 27.

68 U&H, pp. 412-413. From *Westdeutsche Landesbank Girozentrale v Islington B C* [1996] AC 669 it appears that X cannot be personally liable to account as constructive trustee until acting wrongfully after knowing that the transfer to him was wrongful. However, if X innocently used trust money to pay off his existing unsecured or secured creditors, the beneficiaries by way of subrogation will stand in the shoes of such creditors, so as to be able to claim repayment of their moneys paid to such creditors: *Banque Financiere de la Cité v Parc Battersea Ltd* [1998] 1 All ER 737.

69 U&H, Article 72.

70 Scott on Trusts, para 337.

is managing director of the family company and the testator's intention was to ensure that B controlled the company and kept it as a family company so long as B continued as managing director. However, A, C and D want their 17 per cent shareholdings so that together they can sell a majority shareholding to X.

Under English law persons having interests in property have freedom to do what they please with their property so that A, C and D, as absolutely entitled to the shares, are entitled to have their property and deal with it as they please. Under many USA jurisdictions greater emphasis is placed on the settlor's wishes so that A, C and D are not so entitled until B ceases (by death or resignation) to be managing director. To achieve this in English law, the interests of each of A, C and D should be conditional upon each of them being alive when B ceased to be managing director or, if predeceasing such cesser of B's managing directorship, upon each having left children surviving such cesser, in which case such children would take the share their parent would have taken if alive at the date of such cesser.

In order to protect a beneficiary from his own profligacy a settlor can settle property on B for life or until he does or attempts to do anything (e.g. becomes bankrupt or tries to sell his interest) whereby if the income were payable to him for his life he would be deprived of the right to receive all or any part of the income, in which event the income will be held on discretionary trusts for B, his spouse, C, and any children born to them in such shares as the trustee shall in its absolute discretion determine during B's lifetime, with capital to pass to X on B's death[71]. If B tries to arrange with X for B and X to divide the capital between them, so that B will cease to become entitled to all of the income from all of the capital, then B will forfeit his life interest and become simply one of the discretionary beneficiaries comprising B, C and, say, their two children D and E, who are adults of sound mind. If C is past the age of child-bearing so that there cannot be any future-born children then B, C, D, E and X can agree to divide the trust property between themselves as they unanimously agree, although this would not be possible if future-born children were capable of coming into existence.

71 E.g. English Trustee Act 1925 s 33.

Paragraphs (2) and (3)

The settlor will normally intend the trustees for beneficiaries or for permitted purposes to distribute the income and the capital of the trust fund before the end of a specified period or at the end of such a period to the extent not already distributed to beneficiaries or for trust purposes. Usually the law governing the trust will prevent a trust, other than a trust for exclusively charitable purposes, from lasting for longer than a perpetuity period e.g. a certain period of 80, 100 or 120 years or an uncertain period of the expiry of 21 years from the death of a specified person alive at the date of the creation of the trust[72]. This is to prevent the dead from ruling the living for too long, especially if the settlor can require persons if they are to benefit as beneficiaries not to marry persons of a particular religion or profession or colour or ethnic origin and themselves to adopt the family name of the settlor, if this is not already their family name, and to be members of a particular religion or profession. However, increasingly, jurisdictions are enacting legislation to make such discriminatory requirements void even for private trusts as opposed to charitable purpose trusts.

A person may have a power to terminate the trust under the terms of the trust document. The settlor may expressly reserve a power of revocation which, if exercised, will lead to the settlor recovering what then remains in the trust fund. The trustees may have conferred upon them a power to terminate the trust prematurely e.g. by advancing the "Closing Date" specified in the trust document, whereupon the trust fund will be distributed as set out in the trust document.

If the settlor's trust document does not make provision for what is to happen at the end of the trust or if the class of beneficiaries dies out, for example, because there are no longer any descendants of the settlor, then the settlor has not fully disposed of his interest in the trust fund. Thus, the trustee holds the fund on a resulting trust for the settlor or, if he is dead, on a resulting trust for his estate, so that it forms part of his estate at his death passing to those then entitled to such estate[73]. Thus, property may pass as part of the settlor's estate to the settlor's heir's estate and, such heir being

72 U&H, Article 11.
73 U&H, Articles 29 and 32.

dead, to the heir of such heir's estate. However, the trustee may retain sufficient trust assets to cover any liabilities, and once those liabilities are satisfied pay over the balance to the relevant person entitled to the balance of the trust fund.

As emphasised in this Commentary's General Introduction, it is vital to appreciate that, once created, a trust has a life of its own and continues despite the death or mental incapacity of the settlor or the trustee[74] or the temporary absence of ascertained beneficiaries (where such beneficiaries are capable of coming into existence before expiry of the trust period) or the commission of a breach of trust by the trustee, who then has to restore to the trust fund whatever value he has deprived it of.

Paragraph (4)

Exceptionally, in the case of property owned by trustees for charitable trusts, so that it is devoted to charity to the exclusion of any interest of the settlor or his heirs, but the original purposes can no longer be carried out properly, such property will be owned for purposes as similar as possible to the original purposes, as determined by the court or some statutory body having power in this connection[75]. It is up to the trustee, or in default, to some public officer with responsibility for charitable trusts to make the necessary application to the court or relevant statutory body.

In some of the jurisdictions which permit the validity of non-charitable purpose trusts there is available a statutory procedure, analogous to the charitable procedure, if the original purposes can no longer be carried out properly[76].

---

74 Trusts do not fail for lack of a trustee: U&H, p. 60.

75 E.g. English Charities Act 1993 ss 13 and 16. This is also the case where the charitable trusts fail at the outset but the settlor had a paramount charitable intention: if such intention is absent then there is a resulting trust to the settlor or his estate.

76 E.g. Cayman Islands, Special Trusts Alternative Regime Law 1997 s 11; Jersey Trusts (Amendment No. 3) Law 1996 Article 7.

PART II

National Report for Scotland

K.G.C. Reid*

A. Introduction[1]

There is in Scotland a fusion of the two great legal traditions of Europe, of the civil law and the common law, and Scots law is in this sense a mixed (or hybrid) system. But the property law of Scotland is entirely civilian in character. The distinction between real rights and personal rights is strictly observed. There is a *numerus clausus* of real rights. The real right of ownership is indivisible[2]. And there is no place for the distinction of English law between law and equity, and between legal ownership and equitable ownership. But despite this resolutely civilian background, Scotland has the trust. Why?

One might equally ask, why not? It is possible to have the trust and yet still remain virtuous. To adopt the trust is not, or not necessarily, to sink into the arms of equity. A civilian system cannot readily have the *English* trust, it is true. Probably it would be ill-advised to make the attempt. But there are other models on offer.

In Scotland trusts in the modern sense date from the seventeenth century, although notarial protocol books reveal examples from earlier periods of

---

* Prof. K.G.C. Reid is professor of property law, University of Edinburgh and Law Commissioner for Scotland.

1 The standard modern work is W.A. Wilson and A.G.M. Duncan, Trusts, Trustees and Executors (2nd edn, 1995). For a summary account in German, see D. Krantz, *Trusts im schottischen Recht* (1997). G.L. Gretton, Trust and Patrimony in: H.L. MacQueen (ed), Scots Law into the 21st Century: Essays in Honour of W.A. Wilson (1996) is an important contribution to the theory of trust, drawing on the work of Lepaulle. For the wider background see K.G.C. Reid, The Law of Property in Scotland (1996).

2 In theory Scotland still retains a feudal system of land tenure, under which *dominium* is divided (into *dominium utile* and *dominium directum*). But feudalism is moribund in practice and is shortly to be abolished.

property being transferred from A to B for the "utility and profit" of C[3]. An important source seems to have been the *fideicommissum* of Roman law[4]. English law gave the Scottish trust its name (i.e. "trust"), but in other respects exercised surprisingly little influence until the nineteenth century, by which time the essentials of the Scottish trust were already well established. Hence throughout its long history the Scottish trust has remained an institution of the civil law rather than of the common law.

B. Existing law

1. *Patrimony and personality*

In a Scottish trust there is separation of patrimony without separation of personality; and from this fundamental idea many of the consequences of trust flow.

In a trust, assets are held by a trustee for the benefit of a beneficiary. By "held" is meant owned: the only real right encountered in trusts is the real right of ownership which is vested in the trustee. A trustee therefore has assets of two distinct types. On the one hand there are his private assets, the assets to which he is beneficially entitled; and on the other hand there are the assets which are held in trust. Two sets of assets means two separate patrimonies (or "estates", to use the word more commonly found in the legal literature of Scotland). But both patrimonies are held by the same person, and from the point of view of property law the ownership of the trust assets is no different from the ownership of the private assets.

Each patrimony forms a separate and exclusive fund. A creditor of one patrimony has no claim against assets which form part of the other patrimony. If an asset is sold or exchanged, the proceeds of the sale or exchange are allocated to the patrimony from which the asset was taken. There is in other words real subrogation, or "tracing" in common law parlance. A trust patrimony can become bankrupt in the same way as a private patrimony,

3 The leading modern study of the history of trust in Scotland is by G.L. Gretton, in: R. Helmholz and R. Zimmermann (edd), Itinera Fiduciae: Trust and Treuhand (1998).

4 See further D.E.L. Johnston, The Roman Law of Trusts (1988).

although this is rare in practice, and it is possible for one patrimony to be solvent while the other is insolvent. If a trustee dies, his private patrimony passes to his heirs and is broken up, while the trust patrimony lives on, in the hands of a new trustee.

There can, of course, be difficulties in practice. When a trust is first set up, the assets which are to be placed in trust must be clearly demarcated. But over time a trustee may fail to keep his patrimonies distinct. He may use assets from one to service the other. He may pay funds from both into the same bank account. Cases may arise in which an accurate attribution of patrimony becomes impossible. It is then necessary to have special rules for dealing with mixed assets[5]. Difficulties of this kind would be more easily avoided, although not avoided completely, if the trust were itself a separate juristic person. Each patrimony would then have its own personality. But in any event such difficulties arise only rarely in practice. Most trusts are carefully managed. Usually there is more than one trustee, and the trust patrimony is managed professionally, on behalf of all trustees, by a solicitor or accountant. As a general proposition, trustees may be trusted.

Occasionally the separation of patrimonies is disregarded. A person who contracts with a trustee has a right of recourse against the trustee's whole property, including his private assets. Trust law does not usually restrict liability to particular assets of the trustee, and in the case of trust debts the private patrimony is liable along with the trust patrimony[6]. However, if a contract is entered into on the basis that the trust patrimony alone is to be liable, the private patrimony is then exempt. The rules just described apply only to creditors *of the trust*. Where the person holding the office of trustee contracts in a *private* capacity, the segregation of patrimonies holds firm and the private creditor has no claim against the trust patrimony.

2. *The beneficiary*

In a common law trust, the right of the beneficiary is often characterised as a right *in rem*. In the civil law trust used in Scotland the right of a beneficiary is characterised as a personal right only.

5 These rules are necessarily quite complex. The general commentary to Article VI gives an impression of how these rules work in common law jurisdictions.

6 Thus a person seeking limited liability must form a corporation and not a trust.

At first the Scottish approach may seem surprising. It is a familiar feature of trusts that the claim of a beneficiary is preferred to the claims of the personal creditors of the trustee. This means that if the trustee becomes insolvent, the beneficiary can obtain the relevant trust asset free from the claims of the personal creditors. A right which prevails against other creditors has the appearance of a real right. But here appearances mislead. The beneficiary's preference is based, not on real right, but on separation of patrimony. The personal creditors have a claim against the private patrimony of the trustee. The beneficiary has a claim against the trust patrimony. Neither claim is affected by the other. If the private patrimony is insolvent, the personal creditors must go without. They cannot claim from the trust patrimony. But the same is true, in reverse, if the trust patrimony becomes insolvent. The beneficiary is not protected against the creditors *of the trust*. Quite the contrary. If the trust patrimony has been administered unwisely and has incurred indebtedness, the claim of the beneficiary is postponed to the claims of the other unsecured creditors. For a beneficiary's right is residual in character[7]. He receives what is left of the trust patrimony once all other trust creditors have been paid. If there is nothing left, a beneficiary receives nothing.

Of course, in practice insolvency is much more likely to affect the private patrimony than the trust patrimony. For this reason the rule is often expressed, incompletely, as being that the trust beneficiary prevails against the personal creditors of the trustee. And this approach has at least the merit of giving prominence to one of the most attractive features of trusts, namely that if A gives assets to B to be handed over in 20 years' time to C, neither A nor C need concern themselves with the possibility that B might become (personally) insolvent.

There are technical reasons why the right of a beneficiary is only a personal right. A real right is a right in a thing; and in many trusts there is no stable "thing" to which the beneficiary's real right could attach. The trust patrimony is often an ever-changing fund. Of course this is not always so. A trust might provide that a particular house, or a particular painting, is to be transferred to the beneficiary. In that case the real right (if one was to be

7 In this respect it resembles the (personal) right of a member of a corporation. In company law creditors come before shareholders.

recognised) could attach to the house or painting. But much more often the entitlement of the beneficiary is merely to money, and the trust patrimony will consist of shares and other investments which change over time[8].

There is also a second difficulty with real rights. Because a real right has the potential to affect everybody, there is usually a requirement of publicity. Typically this is achieved either by registration or by possession. But there is no publicity for the trust. Indeed secrecy is often seen as its greatest advantage.

It follows from what has been said that, in Scotland at least, the law of trusts belongs more to the law of obligations than to the law of property. Trusts concern property, of course, as many obligations do, while the separation of patrimony is clearly an aspect of property law. But the central relationship in a trust - the relationship between beneficiary and trustee - is obligational in character. In an earlier period attempts were made to explain that central relationship in terms of the law of contract. On this view a trust was a contract *in favorem tertii*, combining elements of mandate and deposit. The modern approach is to accept trust as a distinct and separate branch of the law of obligations.

Of course the personal right of the beneficiary could, like any personal right, be fortified by a real right in security. There is no reason why, in creating the trust, the settlor[9] could not arrange for the beneficiary's right to be secured on one or more of the trust assets. But such a security would require to be properly constituted under the general law. In practice such arrangements are never made.

Not much need be said about the content of the beneficiary's right. The right is held against the trustee, and may be enforced against his private patrimony as well as his trust patrimony. The beneficiary is entitled to see the trust properly administered, both under the general law of trusts and

8 If a real right was to be admitted, it would probably have to be modelled on the floating charge. A floating charge is a right over a patrimony with shifting contents. The right is personal only until the charge attaches on the occurrence of a particular event (such as the appointment of a receiver). On attachment the charge then becomes a real right in security, affecting the assets which formed part of the fund at that time.

9 In Scotland "truster" is used instead of "settlor".

under the particular rules laid down by the settlor for this particular trust. And the beneficiary is entitled, when the time comes, to receive the particular benefit which the trust exists to provide. The right of a beneficiary is excluded from negative (extinctive) prescription.

3. *The trustee*

The trustee owns the trust property, but he cannot use it for his own benefit. Rather he must do with the property as he is directed by the terms of the particular trust. Usually these terms are set out in a formal deed of trust drawn up by the settlor. In most trusts, the property is to be held for a period of time before it can be distributed to beneficiaries. During this period the trustee must administer the property to a high standard. He must take appropriate professional advice. If the assets consist of money, he must invest the money prudently and, where appropriate, make changes to his investment strategy. The assets cannot be used for the trustee's personal benefit. In short, the relationship between trustee and beneficiary is fiduciary in character, and the usual rules of fiduciary relationships apply[10].

The trustee may often be involved in buying and selling assets, if only as a matter of business prudence, and in general such sales and purchases are unobjectionable. Very occasionally a sale may be in breach of trust. This occurs where the sale is contrary to the terms of the trust, whether expressly or by implication. For example, a trustee who is directed by the deed of trust to hold family jewelry until the intended beneficiary reaches the age of 25 is in breach of trust if he sells the jewelry or, worse still, if he gives it away. What happens then? Can the intended beneficiary recover from the buyer or donee? The answer depends on the circumstances. A transfer made in breach of trust is perfectly effective as a matter of property law. The trustee really does own the property. The restriction imposed by the trust is obligational only. Hence the trustee is able to transfer ownership to the buyer or donee[11], and in return any proceeds of sale form part

10 See further the discussion of the "no profit" and "no conflict" rules in the general introduction to the Commentary.

11 This was settled as early as the seventeenth century. Stair wrote (Institutions of the Law of Scotland (1681) 1.13.7) that "the property of the thing intrusted, be it land or moveables, is in the person of the intrusted, else it is not a proper trust: so

of the trust patrimony. The question which then arises is whether the beneficiary is able to insist that the transfer be undone.

Donations of trust property can always be undone, but the position for sales is more complex and, until 1961, depended on the state of knowledge of the buyer. Up until 1961 a buyer who was in good faith was unaffected by the trust, but if he knew of the breach of trust his title could be set aside. This rule was inconvenient in practice[12]. In Scotland there are very many trusts, and hence very many sales by trustees. Buyers, particularly of land, began to worry about whether such sales were, or were not, in breach of trust. Sometimes the answer depended on the interpretation of the deed of trust, and was contested. In such cases the buyer, being naturally cautious, would refuse to proceed with the sale. The position was altered by legislation[13]. Since 1961 a buyer of trust property is always protected, even if he is in bad faith. However, in cases of fraud there is liability in delict.

The fact that assets can be alienated free from the trust is fully consistent with the idea of the trust right as a personal right. A trust cannot, and probably should not, do the work of a real right. In practice the limited scope of a trust right has not caused problems in Scotland. For while a trustee may become bankrupt, he does not routinely alienate in breach of trust.

4. *Complexities*

Up until now we have been considering a trust in which there is only one trustee and one beneficiary. It need hardly be said that life is not usually so simple. Except in the case of trusts used in a commercial context, it is normal to have several trustees and several beneficiaries.

Usually there are at least two trustees. For charitable trusts, statute now requires a minimum of three. In long-standing public trusts there might be ten trustees, or more. A trust with several trustees begins to look like a

if it be transmitted to singular successors, acquiring *bona fide*, they are secure, and the trustee is only liable personally upon the trust".

12 There is an obvious parallel here with the move to protect third parties dealing with companies against the effects of the *ultra vires* doctrine.

13 Trusts (Scotland) 1961 s. 2. The provision probably does not apply to money.

corporation, in which the trustees are the directors and the beneficiaries the shareholders. In practice trustees may change in much the same way as directors, and the day-to-day business of the trust is often conducted by a managing trustee or by a professional manager appointed from outside. The trust itself may last for many years. Some public trusts last for a hundred years or more. In cases like this there is no opportunity for confusion of patrimony. Indeed the relationship between individual trustee and trust patrimony is little more than notional. From time to time the trustee is asked to sign something. Otherwise he has no direct dealings with the trust property. When he resigns, or dies, his notional share in the property passes automatically to the remaining trustees. The "ownership" by the trustees seems no more than a technical device to accommodate the absence of legal personality. For the trust property has to be owned by someone. But for many practical purposes the trust operates as a separate juristic person.

Sometimes there are no trustees. This happens when a trust is first set up. The deed of trust will nominate trustees, but a person cannot be a trustee until he has accepted that nomination. It also happens if all the trustees die. That a trust can exist without trustees is a further indication of its status as a quasi-person. But there are theoretical difficulties. What owns the trust property if there are no trustees? And who is the debtor in the personal right held by the beneficiaries? These questions can be answered, although perhaps not very convincingly, but the problem is in any event reduced by a statutory rule which prevents a person who is sole trustee from resigning without first having appointed a new trustee in his place.

The number of beneficiaries may also vary. Sometimes there is one beneficiary, or five, or a hundred. In the course of the life of a trust there may be periods when there are no beneficiaries at all. For example a trust may be set up for the benefit of children who are not yet born. In public trusts (i.e. trusts for the benefit of the public, or a section of the public) the trustees often have a broad discretion as to the nomination of beneficiaries, and until a particular nomination is made a person is not a beneficiary. This prompts the question of enforcement of public trusts. The principal enforcing agent in Scotland is the Lord Advocate, who is the senior law officer, and charitable trusts in particular are subject to close supervision.

Roles can be combined. The settlor can be one of the trustees as well as one of the beneficiaries. In 1971 the House of Lords[14] decided that the settlor can be the *sole* trustee, a result which has important consequences for the use of trusts in a commercial context[15]. However, the same person cannot be at the same time settlor, sole trustee and sole beneficiary. Such a trust would fail by the doctrine of confusion.

5. *Creation*

A trust can be created more easily even than a contract, for while a contract requires an act of will by two different people, a trust requires an act of will by only one, by the settlor, who is creating the trust. The juridical act required to create a trust is a declaration of the trust by the settlor. The procedure is exceptionally informal. Usually there is no need to use writing, far less the services of a notary public. I can declare a trust merely by speaking the words. However, writing is required in the case of *mortis causa* trusts (i.e. trusts created by testament), and also in trusts where the settlor is to be the sole trustee. In practice writing is used in other cases also.

The cause of the declaration varies. There may be a prior contract to create a trust, as sometimes happens in a commercial context, but more usually the cause is donation. Since Scotland accepts the abstraction principle, the validity of a trust would not be directly affected by an invalidity in the underlying cause.

The declaration of trust must nominate the assets which are to be put in trust and the purposes for which those assets are to be held. Usually it will also nominate the trustees. If the declaration is in writing, it does not take effect until the writing is delivered to one of the trustees or, in cases where the settlor is also the sole trustee, until the existence of the trust is notified to one of the beneficiaries.

The trust is born with the declaration. From that moment the settlor is under an enforceable obligation to transfer the nominated assets to the

14 As in the rest of the United Kingdom, the House of Lords is the final appellate court for Scotland in civil matters.

15 *Allan's Trs v Lord Advocate* 1971 SC(HL) 45.

trustees, and the beneficiaries hold rights under the trust[16]. But until they are transferred to the trustees, the trust assets are vulnerable to the personal creditors of the settlor. The normal rules of property law govern the transfer. In a case where the settlor is also sole trustee, no transfer takes place because the trustee is already owner, and separation of patrimony is achieved by the declaration of trust alone.

6. *Secrecy*

The creation of a trust is not only a private act, it may be a secret one. Only the settlor and the trustee need know. There are obvious advantages in this secrecy, at least for the people most immediately concerned. But there are also disadvantages. Trust brings about a separation of patrimonies. If that separation is not visible to the outside world, then outsiders may be misled, to their disadvantage. The problem is most serious for assets where the title is recorded in a public register. Indeed for a long period in its history, Scots law took the view that a trust could not affect land unless its existence was noted on the land register. However, this approach was overturned by a decision of the House of Lords in 1892[17]. Under the modern law the register need do no more than indicate the ownership of land, without specifying whether that ownership is absolute or in trust.

The problem should not, however, be exaggerated. In most cases the existence of a trust is highly visible. And in the case of charitable trusts there are now statutory rules of disclosure. The real difficulty lies with trusts used as security rights, a subject which is taken up again below.

7. *Termination*

Normally a trust comes to an end only when the trust assets have been distributed in accordance with the trust purposes. If there is no trust property left, and no prospect of further property being received, the trust is at an end. Occasionally a trust may be terminated for some other reason.

---

16 One way of analysing this is to say that the enforceable obligation (i.e. promise) created by the declaration constitutes the initial asset of the trust. Hence, as soon as there is a declaration there is also a trust asset. See on this point the general commentary on Article II.

17 *Heritable Reversionary Co Ltd v Millar* (1892) 19 R(HL) 43.

The declaration of trust might provide for early termination. The settlor may have reserved a right of revocation. All the beneficiaries, if of full age, may agree that the trust property is to be distributed and the trust brought to an end. Finally, a trust is brought to an end if the trust purposes can no longer be fulfilled, for example because there are no extant beneficiaries and no possibility of beneficiaries in the future. In that case the assets are returned to the settlor or, if the settlor is dead, to his heirs.

8. *Uses of the trust*

What are trusts used for? One might almost as well ask what are contracts used for. The strength of the trust lies in its flexibility. Like the contract, the trust can be put to innumerable, and diverse, uses. It is not possible here to do more than indicate some of the more characteristic examples.

In the lawyer's mind the paradigm trust is the private trust, typically used in a family context. A person wants to make a gift to members of his family. He wants to make the gift now, but he wants the family to receive the gift later. There may be cogent reasons why he wants to make the gift now. Reducing his assets may bring tax advantages. It will also protect the assets that are given away from his creditors. Equally, there may be cogent reasons why he does not want the members of the family to receive the gift until later. They may be too young. In some cases they may not yet be born. The gift may be subject to conditions which, by their very nature, cannot be met immediately. And so on. For situations like this the trust forms an ideal mechanism. The donor can make an immediate transfer of the assets to trustees. When the time comes the trustees can pay out. And for as long as the trust continues the assets are protected, by the doctrine of separate patrimony, against the insolvency, both of the trustees and of the settlor.

The example just given was of an *inter vivos* trust. But family trusts are also very frequently created in testaments.

The widespread use of the family trust has tended to lead, in Scotland, to the neglect of the real right of *usufruct* (or "liferent" as it is normally called). Where a donor wishes to confer a right of use for life, this is most conveniently done through a trust. An obvious advantage of this approach is that the trustee can adjudicate in any disputes between the usufructuary and the person who is ultimately entitled to unqualified ownership. The right of a trust usufructuary is of course personal and not real.

A second paradigm is the charitable trust. This plays a similar role to that of the foundation or *Stiftung* which is encountered in many other European countries. A charitable trust is a "public" trust in the sense that its beneficiaries are members of the public at large. Charitable trusts may run for many years, and have numerous trustees. In Scotland charities are sometimes organised as corporations, as elsewhere in Europe, but the distinctive advantage of the trust lies in its simplicity, informality and, therefore, in its cheapness.

Trusts are used for many other purposes. Some of the commercial uses were mentioned in the general introduction to this volume. They include unit trusts, pension fund trusts, and trusts for the operation of time shares of immovable property. In addition, there is a trust every time someone dies. The executor who administers the assets of a deceased person is a type of trustee. The executor acquires ownership of the deceased's assets by virtue of a court decree (in practice a simple administrative process, not requiring an appearance before a judge). Usually such trusts are brief in duration. The executor collects together all the assets, pays any outstanding debts, and then distributes the remaining property in accordance with the deceased's testament or with the rules of intestate succession[18].

Personal bankruptcy operates in much the same way as death. The bankrupt's assets are collected together and administered by a trustee in sequestration, who is appointed by the court and who receives ownership under a court decree. The rule for corporate insolvency is different: a liquidator does not, in the ordinary course of events, become owner of the assets of the insolvent company.

18 In Scotland executors act also in cases of intestacy.

C. Further developments of trusts

1. *Trusts as security devices*

In the last 30 years attempts have been made to use trusts as pseudo rights in security. These attempts are controversial, and although the issue has been considered by courts on a number of occasions it is too early to say whether such trusts have a future in Scotland[19].

The fundamental idea is well-known, but perhaps bears repeating here. Suppose that A owes B money. B may be content that A should not pay immediately, but at the same time B would like some form of security. In theory it would be open to B to seek a real right in security over one or more of A's assets, but in practice that may be impossible, or at least undesirable. There may be a wish to avoid publicity. The credit given by B may be too shortlived to make a security a worthwhile exercise. In Scotland a common problem is that all of A's assets may be subject to a floating charge, and that the charge contains a "negative pledge" clause (i.e. a clause prohibiting the creation of any right in security having priority over or equality with the floating charge). Some of the effects of a security can be obtained by using a trust. What happens is this. A signs a declaration that particular assets are now held in trust by him for B. A is thus both the settlor and the sole trustee, and B is the sole beneficiary. The trust is a so-called "bare" trust, that is to say, a trust the only purpose of which is that A must hold to the order of B. If B demands the assets, A must transfer them. In practice B will not demand the assets, unless A becomes insolvent without having paid the debt. In that case B will enforce the trust. Since the trust creates a separate patrimony, B can in principle require that the assets be transferred to him without regard to the claims of the personal creditors of A.

Of course security trusts do not usually arise in so pure a form. No bank would advance a loan on the strength of a security trust. Typically, security trusts are used as a means of securing temporary grants of credit made in the course of some quite different transaction.

---

19 See generally chapter 4 of Wilson & Duncan. There has been similar controversy in England: see D.J. Hayton's contribution to D.J. Hayton *et al.* (edd), *Vertrouwd met de Trust* (1996), pp. 44-45.

Often the transaction is sale. In the sale of goods, trusts can be used as a second line of defence once an initial clause of retention of title has ceased to work. Suppose that X sells goods to Y and retains ownership pending payment of the price. Y may be unable to pay X until he has resold to Z; but if Y resells to Z, and Z is in good faith, Z will become owner[20] and X will lose the protection provided by the initial retention of title. Thus it is common for a contract of sale to provide that any proceeds received by Y from the subsale to Z are to be held in trust by Y for X. If the trust is effective, and if the proceeds can be identified, X is then protected in the event of Y's insolvency[21].

A number of objections can be, and have been, made to the use of trusts in this way.

First, there is no proper trust. Trusts are about fiduciary administration. Here there is none. The "trustee" makes no distinction in practice between his private assets and his "trust" assets. Both are used for his own benefit and without regard to the interests of the "beneficiary". The trustee's balance sheet is quite likely to be silent. In short, the separation of patrimonies is nothing more than a sham. So is the trust.

Secondly, there is no proper publicity. The "beneficiary" is obtaining some of the benefits of a right in security without having taken the trouble, or incurred the publicity, which is normally required of a real right. In most cases the "trustee" is a company, and under company law rights in security (with some exceptions) must be registered with the registrar of companies[22]. A trust evades the registration requirement. Further, since the "settlor" and "trustee" are one and the same person, the separation of patrimony will not have been marked by any transfer of the affected asset.

20 Sale of Goods Act 1979 s 25. This is an exception to the usual rule, which is *nemo plus juris ad alienum transferre potest, quam ipse haberet*.

21 In the only Scottish case on this subject, *Clark Taylor & Co v Quality Site Development (Edinburgh) Ltd* 1981 SC 111, the trust was held not to be effective. In *Tay Valley Joinery Ltd v C F Financial Services Ltd* 1987 SLT 207 a trust was upheld to secure assets (receiveables) which had been paid for but not yet transferred to the buyer. This seems a more appropriate use of trust, although it is not clear that the decision can be reconciled with *Clark Taylor*. In a later case involving similar facts (*Macioca v Alma Holdings Ltd* 1993 SLT 730) the court was able to avoid giving a concluded view.

22 Companies Act 1985 s. 410.

Arguably this lack of publicity is objectionable in principle. But in any event it may serve to mislead other creditors. A person who has given credit without taking security will be dismayed to find, on insolvency, that the apparently unsecured assets of his debtor were actually subject to a trust.

Thirdly, the widespread use of security trusts would have a marked impact on the law of insolvency and on the general principle of *paritas creditorum*. Some unsecured creditors would be more equal than others[23]. Whether this is a welcome or an unwelcome development is a matter to be determined by insolvency lawyers rather than by trust lawyers. The important point for present purposes is that the effect of security trusts is not neutral. If creditor A gains through use of a trust, then creditors B, C and D (being unsecured) suffer a corresponding loss. In an insolvency the cake always remains the same size. All that can be altered is the way in which it is divided up.

In Scotland security trusts are popular with certain sectors of the business world. That is hardly surprising. A creditor is always likely to be enthusiastic about a cheap, and covert, way of securing a loan. Whether such trusts are in the interests of commerce, viewed more generally, is a much more difficult question to which the courts or legislature have, so far, offered no definitive answer[24].

One practical answer is that security trusts may come to be seen as less useful than they once seemed. A security trust is not a real right, and is far

23 This point has been judicially noticed in the *Clark Taylor* case (at p. 116) where the Lord President of the Court of Session warned, disapprovingly, that "if a condition (...) designed only to freeze assets of a debtor and to keep them out of other creditors' hands until a particular creditor's debt is paid in full, were to be regarded as constituting a proper trust in accordance with the law of Scotland, and were to be adopted widely by sellers of goods, the damage which would be done to the objectives of the law of bankruptcy and of liquidation would be incalculable."

24 In general the approach of the courts has been to refuse recognition to commercial trusts on the ground that the rules of constitution have not been properly complied with. The most recent decisions are *Balfour Beatty Ltd v Britannia Life Ltd* 1997 SLT 10, *Mercedes-Benz Finance Ltd v Clydesdale Bank plc* 1997 SLT 905, and *Style Financial Services Ltd v Bank of Scotland* 1997 SCLR 633. Perhaps understandably, the courts have been reluctant to grapple with the larger issue of the desirability of using of trusts in a commercial context.

less effective than a real right in security. In particular, the "beneficiary" in such a trust is extremely vulnerable both to the sale of the trust asset, and to its burdening by a (genuine) real right in security.

2. *Constructive trusts*

A constructive trust is a trust which arises by operation of law, without express constitution. In certain situations the court finds that a trust exists even though the parties have taken no steps to create one. Since the main effect of such a finding is to create a preference in bankruptcy, an expansive approach by the courts would in time have a major impact on the law of insolvency. For this reason Scots law has been cautious about recognising such trusts and, so far at least, has restricted constructive trusts to a small number of well-known situations[25]. In a case decided in 1997 a judge of the Court of Session confessed to having "an almost instinctive abhorrence of the notion of constructive trusts in the law of Scotland"[26]. By contrast, in England and in other common law jurisdictions constructive trusts are widely recognised.

Constructive trusts are not touched on by the Principles, and nothing further will be said here.

D. Commentary on the Principles article by article

Except where indicated below, the Principles may be taken as an accurate statement of the law of trusts in Scotland.

Article I. Main characteristics of the trust

Paragraph (4)
The beneficiary has a personal right (and hence a personal remedy) against the trustee. In general the law of trusts in Scotland gives no right against

---

25 A pioneering analysis is G.L. Gretton, Constructive Trusts (1997) 1 Edinburgh Law Review 281 & 408.

26 *The Mortgage Corporation v Mitchells Roberton* 1997 SLT 1305 at p. 1310A. The judge was Lord Johnston.

a third party, although some qualifications to this rule are mentioned in the commentary to Article VII.

Article II. Creation of the trust

Both methods of creation are permissible under Scots law. The intention to create a trust is usually expressed by a written declaration of trust.

In relation to the first method of creation (where trustee and settlor are different people), the normal practice is for the transfer of assets and declaration of trust to take place at the same time. However, if the declaration takes place first, the trust comes into existence immediately. This is because the enforceable rights conferred on the trustee by the declaration are viewed as an initial asset of the trust.

Article III. Trust fund

This is an accurate statement of the law of Scotland.

Article IV. Trusts for beneficiaries or for enforceable purposes

Paragraph (1)
A public trust may be enforced either by the Lord Advocate (the senior law officer) or by any person falling into the class of potential beneficiaries.

Paragraph (4)
Similarly, the rights of a beneficiary can be attached by his creditors.

Article V. Trustees' duties and powers

Paragraph (5)
The liability of the trustee is personal. Hence the claim of the beneficiary is, for once, against the private patrimony of the trustee.

Article VI. Remedies against trustees for breach of trust

Profits made by a trustee acting in breach of trust might be treated as held in a constructive trust for the beneficiaries of the trust property. However, a court has no power to declare a "security" *stricto sensu*.

Article VII. Liabilities of third parties

Even a *mala fide* buyer receives an unchallengeable title, but his conduct may attract liability in delict.

The title of a donee could be set aside by an action of reduction, with the result that the property wrongfully given away would return to the trust patrimony. A subsequent donee would be in the same position. But probably there would no constructive trust in the period prior to the reduction, and there would certainly be no security.

Article VIII. Termination of a trust

Paragraph (3)
In Scots law there is no perpetuity period restricting the duration of a trust. But while no "permitted period" is laid down by law, the settlor can prescribe a period of his own. (There are, however, restrictions on the accumulation of income comparable to those existing under English law.) Thus Article VIII(3) has no application in Scotland.

National Report for Germany

H. Kötz*

A. Introduction

Nowhere in German law can one find any single institution which by itself performs all those functions for which the common lawyer deploys the trust. The idea of having two persons occupying owner-like positions with regard to the same thing in such a way that one of them, as "legal owner", has powers of disposition "at law", and the other, as "equitable owner", has certain rights recognised "in equity" is a concept that seemed to Maitland "almost essential to civilization"[1]. Yet there is nothing quite like it in German law. On the other hand, it goes without saying that German legal practitioners and the German courts must deal with situations in which assets have been placed under the control of a fiduciary for the benefit of a beneficiary or for a specified purpose. This paper will deal with the rules which German lawyers will invoke in such cases and which may therefore be called the functional counterparts in German law of the rules governing trust relationships in common law jurisdictions.

I will first deal with a few situations arising under German law which fit the general description of a trust relationship - i.e. assets placed by a settlor under the control of a trustee for the benefit of a beneficiary or for a specified purpose - but which, for various reasons, will not be discussed in any detail in this paper (3-5). I will then discuss the general structure of the *fiduziarische Treuhand* (6) and a few major applications of this concept in commercial or business contexts (7). A number of practical problems that have occupied the courts will then be addressed (8-9). A concluding section will speculate on why the trust has not been developed as a general concept in German law, why there is a relative dearth of case law and technical refinement in the field of trust law in Germany, and what need,

---

* Prof. H. Kötz is Director at the Max Planck Institute for foreign and International private law in Hamburg.

1 Maitland, Equity; A Course of Lectures, 2nd edn by Brunyate, 1936, p. 23.

if any, there is in Germany for introducing an institution equivalent to the common law trust (10).

B. Existing law

1. *Testamentary trusts*

The most important function performed by the trust in a personal or family context is that of permitting the testator to tie up his property. A typical case is where a testator leaves his property to a trustee on the terms that the trustee is to administer the estate in favour of the surviving spouse until remarriage or death, and thereafter for the children of the marriage, with the provision that as soon as the youngest child reaches majority the estate is to be divided in determined proportions among the surviving children and their offspring. A German testator may reach practically the same result by combining certain institutions of the law of succession, namely the *Nacherbfolge* (§§ 2100-2146 Civil Code), the *gemeinschaftliches Testament* (§§ 2265-2273 Civil Code) and the *Testamentsvollstreckung* (§§ 2197-2228 Civil Code)[2].

According to § 2100 Civil Code, a testator may provide in his will that his estate shall pass to A as "first heir" (*Vorerbe*) and then, upon A's death (or upon any other event to be specified in the will) to B as "second heir" (*Nacherbe*). Similarly, a husband and his wife may make a "joint will" (*gemeinschaftliches Testament*) in which they provide that the estate of the pre-deceasing spouse shall pass to the surviving spouse and that the surviving spouse's estate shall pass to the surviving children and their offspring. Testamentary dispositions both of the "first heir" and the surviving spouse are in principle null and void to the extent to which they are in conflict with the disposition made in favour of the "second heir" (in the case of *Nacherbfolge*) or the surviving children (in the case of a *gemeinschaftliches Testament*). The "first heir" does have a (limited) right to dispose *inter vivos* of the assets belonging to the estate, and the surviving spouse's

2 The following observations are based on Fratcher, Int.Enc.Comp.L. Vol. VI (Property and Trust), Chapter 11 (Trust), s. 127-128 (1973). See also Kötz, *Trust und Treuhand, Eine rechtsvergleichende Darstellung des anglo-amerikanischen trust und funktionsverwandter Institute des deutschen Rechts*, (1963), p. 97 *et seq.*

dispositions *inter vivos* will equally be valid, at least in principle. However, the testator may exclude the first heir's or surviving spouse's power to make dispositions *inter vivos* by appointing a testamentary executor (*Testamentsvollstrecker*) who has the sole power to dispose of the estate according to the testator's instructions. While the ownership in the assets of the estate is in the "first heir" or the surviving spouse, for whose benefit the testamentary executor must manage the property, the power to dispose of these assets *inter vivos* is vested solely in the testamentary executor.

It follows that if a testator combines *Nacherbfolge* or *gemeinschaftliches Testament* and the appointment of a *Testamentsvollstrecker,* which is frequently done, the practical results will be very similar to those achieved in the common law by a testamentary trust. The situation is well summarised by Professor Fratcher as follows:

> "On the one hand, the estate will be tied up so as to pass from the 'first heir' (or heirs) to the 'second heir' (or heirs) or from the surviving spouse to the children of both spouses. On the other hand, the 'first heir' and the 'second heir' as well as the surviving spouse and the children will not be able to either manage or dispose of the estate but will be limited to receiving the income of the estate from the Testamentsvollstrecker according to the testator's instructions. Thus, the 'first heir' and the surviving spouse are in a position similar to that of the holder of a life estate in the common law whereas the position of the 'second heir' or of the children under a 'joint will' may be likened to that of a remainderman."[3]

No further details on arrangements of this type will be given here since the focus of national reports is to be on applications of the trust in a commercial or business context.

3 Fratcher (preceding note) s. 128. It may be added that the German Civil Code has long and elaborate provisions governing the guardianship of the property of minors, mental incompetents and spendthrifts. Such guardianship is vested in tutors, curators and other so-called "legal representatives" whose powers are very similar to that of a *Testamentsvollstrecker*. Similar powers are held by a *Konkursverwalter* (trustee in bankruptcy) and a liquidator who are appointed by the court to manage and dispose of the property of insolvent debtors.

2. *Charitable trusts*

In the common law there is a charitable trust where assets are transferred to a trustee not for the benefit of named beneficiaries but for a specified charitable purpose such as the relief of poverty, the advancement of education, the advancement of religion or some other purpose sufficiently beneficial to the community to justify an exemption from various taxes and the inapplicability of the Rule against perpetuities. German law provides for various substitutes. The settlor may establish a charitable foundation (*Stiftung*) which is an independent juristic entity capable of owning property and of suing and being sued (§§ 80-88 Civil Code). The creation of a foundation usually requires approval by some governmental agency which will normally be withheld unless the assets of the foundation are to be devoted to a purpose deemed to be charitable. The government exercises a fairly strict supervisory control over the management of the assets of a foundation. The settlor may, by will or by a disposition *inter vivos*, transfer assets to a foundation he himself has created, or he may transfer such assets to an existing foundation established by somebody else. According to § 87 Civil Code the competent government authority may modify the charitable purpose of the foundation if the purpose originally specified by the settlor can no longer be achieved because of a change of circumstances. This rule is clearly equivalent to the doctrine of cy-près.

Since the establishment of a charitable foundation is a fairly expensive and complex affair, a settlor may simply transfer assets to another on the understanding that the assets shall constitute a separate fund, shall not form part of the transferee's own estate and that the transferee shall have the power and the duty to manage the assets for the charitable purpose specified by the transferor. In this alternative, the legal relationship between the parties will be analyzed by a German lawyer as a *fiduziarische Treuhand* which will be discussed in greater detail further below.

3. *Trusts as a security device*

German law has no separate legal regime for the creation of security interests in movable property and accounts receivable. While the Civil Code does have detailed provisions on the creation of a pledge in such assets, these rules are largely impracticable because they require, in the case of movable property, a transfer of possession to the pledgee (§ 1205 Civil Code) and, in the case of accounts receivable, a disclosure to the debtor of the creation of the pledge (§ 1280 Civil Code). The German courts have stepped into the breach by recognizing what is called, in the case of movable property, *Sicherungsübereignung* and, in the case of accounts receivable, *Sicherungszession*. Thus, in order to provide security for a debt, a debtor may transfer the ownership in a movable thing to his creditor. This does not require a transfer of possession. Likewise, the debtor may assign a contractual right to his creditor without giving notice to the third party. In both cases, the creditor acquires full title to the movable or the right. However, this is based on the parties' understanding that the transferee is to acquire only a security interest in the subject matter and shall exercise his power to dispose of the asset only in accordance with the terms laid down in the security agreement, i.e. only where the debtor becomes insolvent. Technically, the transferee may be viewed as a trustee. However, as the applicable rules form part of a special field of law whose functional counterpart is to be found in Article 9 Uniform Commercial Code and similar rules, rather than in the general rules of trust law, no further details will be discussed here.

4. *The fiduziarische Treuhand as a trust-like device*

In most other situations in which assets are to be entrusted to others to be managed, administered or kept safe for the benefit of certain beneficiaries the legal technique devised by German law to back up such arrangements is the *fiduziarische Treuhand*. It is created by a transfer of assets to the *Treuhänder* coupled with a contractual agreement made between him and the transferor under which he assumes, normally in consideration of a fee, a contractual duty to manage the assets in a particular way for the benefit of the beneficiaries. Usually, the parties intend to confer on the beneficiaries a right to enforce the agreement by way of a direct claim against the *Treuhänder*. In this case such right will arise as a *ius quaesitum tertio* under a stipulation for the benefit of a third party. Note, however, that beneficiaries under a *fiduziarische Treuhand* have, subject to a qualification to be made later, only the ordinary rights *in personam* of parties to a contract, and that their interest in the *Treuhand* assets is not a *ius in re aliena*[4].

The *Treuhänder's* duties are called fiduciary duties. It does not matter whether they are laid down explicitly in the *Treuhand* agreement or are supplied by the court by way of filling gaps in the agreement or by implying default rules such as the rule that the *Treuhänder* must avoid conflicts of duty and interest, must keep the *Treuhand* assets separate from his own estate, must keep clear and accurate accounts of his administration of the assets, must permit the settlor and/or the beneficiary to examine the accounts, must not enter into a transaction or continue a situation in which his personal interest is adverse to that of the beneficiary, must not mix *Treuhand* money in a bank account with his personal money, must account for any profit made in the course of administration, must not turn his office to his own advantage, must not exploit business opportunities which became available to him in the course of exercising his fiduciary obligations and must comply with a general duty of loyalty, which is the form that the principle of good faith takes in a fiduciary relationship of this kind.

If the *Treuhänder* fails to carry out the *Treuhand* agreement according to its terms or is found in breach of any fiduciary duty, the beneficiary's primary remedy is a personal action for damages. Despite the general principle of separation of assets, in such an action for damages the *Treuhänder's* personal assets are available to satisfy any liability that is found to exist. True, the beneficiary's action is not one for the breach of an "equitable" duty as in the common law, nor is it based on delictual fault. It is an action for breach of contract. But this does not seem to be very important. One might, indeed, say that the difference between the common law and German law is not significant if the *Treuhänder* is solvent and financially

4 It is also possible, even if rare, to construe the position of a *Treuhänder* on the analogy of that of a *Testamentsvollstrecker*, executor, tutor, guardian, curator or of other "legal representatives" (see preceding note). In that event, the settlor does not divest himself of title or ownership in the assets, but merely grants the *Treuhänder* a power to manage and to dispose of them in accordance with the settlor's instructions. Thus, where somebody sells goods on credit he may reserve title and grant the buyer a power to dispose of the goods in the ordinary course of business. However, apart from the case just described, arrangements of this nature are fairly rare in practice even though it is in the end a matter of convenience in whom the title to the *Treuhand* assets is located.

able to satisfy the beneficiary's claim for damages[5]. It is arguable, though, that the common law, with its characteristically sharpened perception of the dangers arising from conflicts of interests, imposes stricter standards of behaviour on trustees than German law.

Another difference between the common law trust and the *fiduziarische Treuhand* is that there is no general competence of the German court to exercise the supervisory and administrative functions needed to make the trust an efficient device for the management of property. A *Treuhand* intended to function over a long time may operate reasonably well where the instrument creating it makes elaborate provision dealing with all problems and emergencies. However, if no such precautions have been taken difficulties might result from the failure of German law to vest in the court a general jurisdiction to remove and appoint a *Treuhänder*, to advise a *Treuhänder* on his rights and duties in an unexpected situation, or to permit him to deviate from the terms of the *Treuhand* agreement when changed conditions make deviation essential to achievement of its primary purposes. It is only fair to say, though, that the failure of German law to establish such judicial procedures has not yet been regarded as a serious gap in the system so that no proposals have been made to remedy the situation[6].

5. *Applications of the fiduziarische Treuhand*

It might be instructive to describe a few situations in which use is made in Germany of the *fiduziarische Treuhand*.

(a) Brief mention must be made of investment companies (*Kapitalanlage-gesellschaften*) whose business it is to collect money from their clients and invest it on their behalf in land, mortgages on land, bonds, debentures, shares in corporations etc. Investment companies are regulated in great detail by a special Statute (*Gesetz über Kapitalanlagegesellschaften* of 14 January 1970). The statute provides that the assets acquired by the company constitute a separate fund to be managed with the care and skill a reasonable businessman would use in his own affairs. The assets stand in

5 See below no. 8 and 9 on the differences arising where a *Treuhänder* is insolvent or has improperly alienated *Treuhand* assets.

6 Such procedures do exist for the management of property by a *Testamentsvoll-strecker*, guardian, curator, tutor or other "legal representative".

the name of the company or in the name of another person on behalf of the company and the rights flowing from the ownership of the assets are to be exercised by the company in its own name and in accordance with the terms of the agreement and the duties imposed by the statute. The assets are not liable to be taken in execution by the company's private creditors nor do they fall into the company's own insolvent estate.

(b) A *Treuhand* for the benefit of creditors is sometimes used as a substitute for bankruptcy because bankruptcy would involve greater expense or delay or would be too radical a measure. It arises from a transfer by a debtor in financial difficulties of all or part of his assets to a *Treuhänder* whose duty it is either to continue the debtor's business or to liquidate the assets, to pay the creditors so far as possible and, if there is a surplus, to return it to the debtor.

(c) A *Treuhandkonto* is an account opened by somebody with a bank on the understanding that all moneys paid into the account either by himself or by third parties will be held by him as *Treuhänder* for one or more beneficiaries. Thus it is standard procedure to provide in a contract for the sale of land (which is valid only if created in a document drawn up and attested by a notary) that the buyer is to pay the purchase money not to the seller directly but into a *Treuhandkonto* (also known as *Anderkonto*) opened by the notary with a bank. The notary, as *Treuhänder* of the money paid into the account, is under a fiduciary duty to deal with it in accordance with the parties' instructions and must not make any payment to the seller unless the conditions specified in the contract have been complied with. The money in the *Treuhandkonto* does not fall into the notary's private insolvent estate. It does not form part of his estate on death nor is it part of his or his spouse's matrimonial property. Nor are the notary's own creditors able to reach the money in satisfaction of their claims. The banking industry has developed special standard terms of business for the opening by notaries, attorneys and accountants of *Treuhandkonten* or *Anderkonten* in which the banks waive their right to withhold payment or operate a set-off on the basis of their own claims against the notary or other account holder.

(d) Bonds, debentures and the like issued to a large number of investors are sometimes secured by a mortgage or other security interest in the issuer's land. Since it would be impracticable to convey to each bond or debenture holder a fraction of the security interest it is quite common to transfer title to the security interest to a bank or other financial institution which, as *Treuhänder,* is under a duty to administer the security interest for the benefit of all bond or debenture holders.

(e) For a variety of reasons a need may arise to separate control of a corporation from the beneficial ownership of its shares. A similar need may arise where, as is quite common in Germany, an enterprise is established in the form of a limited partnership (*Kommanditgesellschaft*) with one general partner - often a limited liability company - and a great number of individuals as limited partners. In many cases it is impracticable to invite all limited partners to general meetings of the company and to let them exercise rights of control, of receiving annual balance sheets, of checking their accuracy on the basis of the partnership's books, and of requiring information on all matters affecting the partnership. In this situation arrangements will often be made for the transfer of the limited partners' interests to a *Treuhänder* who must use the voting rights attaching thereto for the benefit of, and account for dividends arising therefrom to the limited partners as beneficiaries of the *Treuhand.* Such arrangements will also be used to secure continuity of corporate policy despite changing beneficial ownership of the stock. A prospective lender may require the creation of such a *Treuhand,* with a *Treuhänder* satisfactory to him, as a condition of lending money to the corporation.

6. *The protection of Treuhand assets*

A *fiduziarische Treuhand* is created by a transfer *inter vivos* of assets to the *Treuhänder* coupled with an agreement by which the *Treuhänder* assumes a contractual duty vis-à-vis the settlor and the beneficiaries (as third party beneficiaries) to manage the assets for the benefit of the beneficiaries (of which the settlor may be one) in accordance with the settlor's instructions. The *Treuhänder* acquires a full and unrestricted title to the *Treuhand* assets, whereas the beneficiaries' interests are, at least in theory, merely the ordinary rights *in personam* of parties to a contract. However, German courts have made a significant inroad into this principle. There is clear authority for the rule that if A transfers property to B on the understanding that it shall be managed by B as *Treuhänder* on behalf of certain beneficiaries, B's creditors are not entitled to seize that property unless the debt has been incurred by B while properly administering the *Treuhand*. It has also been held that the beneficiaries are entitled in B's bankruptcy to demand a release of that property from the bankrupt's estate[7]. Obviously, this rule does not sit well, and is really incompatible with the theory that the beneficiaries' interest in the *Treuhand res* is a mere right *in personam*. The courts have rationalized their position by arguing that the *Treuhänder* owns the property "in form only", not "in substance" and that the assets were transferred to him "in a formal and legal sense, but not from a substantive and economic viewpoint".

It might seem that the position of German law is very similar to that of the common law. Closer scrutiny reveals, however, that the rule is given a more restrictive scope in German law. It does apply to assets which have been directly transferred to the *Treuhänder* by the settlor and still exist in his hands in their original form. But the courts have taken a different position where the assets were transferred to the *Treuhänder* by a third party. Many writers have argued that it should make no difference whether it was by the settlor himself or by a third party (perhaps acting on the settlor's instructions) that the asset was transferred to the *Treuhänder*: In both cases the beneficiaries should be given priority over the *Treuhänder's* private creditors[8]. So far, this view has been accepted by the courts only in cases in which the third party paid money into a *Treuhandkonto* or *Anderkonto*[9].

There is a related aspect of trust law with which, it may be argued, German law cannot cope. It involves what is called the doctrine of "real subrogation". If a trustee disposes of assets and acquires other assets with the proceeds, the new assets are trust assets regardless of whether or not the trustee's disposition was in breach of trust. The new assets are therefore protected from the trustee's private creditors and form part of the fund available to satisfy claims of the trust beneficiaries and trust creditors. Thus, the beneficiary is allowed to "trace" the original trust assets into the newly acquired property. German law reaches the same result where the

---

7 *Reichsgericht* 23 December 1899, RGZ 45, 80; *Reichsgericht* 10 October 1917, RGZ 91, 12; *Reichsgericht* 9 June 1931, RGZ 133, 84; *Bundesgerichtshof* 7 April 1959, Neue Juristische Wochenschrift 1959, 1223.

8 See Coing, *Die Treuhand kraft privaten Rechtsgeschäfts*, (1973), p. 178 *et seq.*; Kötz (*supra* n. 2), p. 129 *et seq.*; Gernhuber, *Die fiduziarische Treuhand*, Juristische Schulung 1988, 350, p. 360/361.

9 See Bundesgerichtshof 7 April 1959 (*supra* n. 7); *Bundesgerichtshof* 16 December 1970, Neue Juristische Wochenschrift 1971, 559.

"old" and "new" assets form part of a deceased's estate (§§ 2041, 2111 Civil Code). However, there is no clear authority yet for the rule that the doctrine of "real subrogation" also applies to assets forming part of a *fiduziarische Treuhand*. Thus, if a *Treuhänder* purchases property with money supplied by the settlor or with the proceeds of sales of the original property, or obtains property in exchange for the original property, it is not clear whether the beneficiaries will be awarded a proprietary right in the substitute property and on this basis take priority over the *Treuhänder's* private creditors. There is nothing in the structure of German law that would preclude this conclusion. But it does raise the policy question whether real subrogation should be stretched that far becauce reasonable men may differ as to how a fair balance ought to be struck between the claims of beneficiaries and the *Treuhänder's* private creditors.

Another problem concerns mixing. In the common law, if a trustee mixes trust money in a bank account with his own money, not only is the beneficiary's claim for part of the resulting mass good against the trustee's creditors in bankruptcy, but the common law has also developed a number of presumptions to determine the size of the beneficiary's part, such as the presumption that a trustee with a mixed account honestly spends his own money first, unless the beneficiaries prefer to claim as their own the asset purchased with such money because it has increased in value and the trustee's wrongful mixing makes it impossible for him to disprove such claim. Under German law it would be difficult, if not unacceptable on both policy and doctrinal grounds, to grant different persons rights *in rem* over parts of a fluctuating bank account whose size would depend on whether, and at what dates, "private money" or "trust money" was paid into, or withdrawn from, the account, and whether or not money was spent wisely or unwisely.

7. *Alienation of Treuhand assets*

What is the beneficiary's position if the *Treuhänder*, in breach of the settlor's instructions, alienates an asset forming part of the *Treuhand* estate? In the common law, if the transfer is a breach of trust and the third party is a donee or a purchaser with actual or constructive notice of the breach, he takes "subject to the trust". Consequently, the beneficiary may compel him to reconvey the asset to the trustee or his successor, and this claim will be given priority over the claims of the third party's own creditors. German law would find it very difficult to reach this result since the *Treuhänder* has full and unrestricted ownership of the *Treuhand* assets and there is therefore no reason to apply the rules on the *bona fide* acquisition of title from a *non-dominus* (§§ 932 *et seq*. Civil Code). True, if the *Treuhänder* and the third party conspired to defraud the beneficiary or if the third party knew of the breach and took an active part in it, it is possible to regard the transfer of ownership as null and void as contrary to the *boni mores* (§ 138 Civil Code). In other cases, however, e.g. where the third party has merely constructive notice of the breach or is a donee, while German law would order him to make restitution, this claim will lie in tort or unjust enrichment and will therefore be *in personam* only[10].

8. *Reception of the trust in Germany?*

According to traditional wisdom, the special style of legal thought in the civil law is characterized by a tendency to deduce the decision for the case in hand from overriding principles and basic general concepts, whereas the common law, with its pragmatic and dimensional way of seeing things, instead of committing itself to supposed universals, seeks to develop piecemeal solutions in response to distinct types of disputes and problems. In the field discussed in this article, however, the reverse seems to be the case. In his contribution to the International Encyclopedia of Comparative Law Professor Fratcher lists no less than 26 different purposes for which the unitary concept of a trust may be used[11], and the trust, doubtless, deserves its description by Professor Scott as "one of the most flexible instruments in the armoury of our jurisprudence"[12]. In German law, however, the transfer by a testator of assets to another for the benefit of successive beneficiaries would be seen as a problem of the law of inheritance. If somebody wishes to transfer property to another on the understanding that the other is to administer it for the achievement of a charitable purpose, a German lawyer will turn to the law relating to foundations and the rules on the *fiduziarische Treuhand*, and it will not be

10 The courts have denied the beneficiary a right *in rem* if the transferee had merely constructive notice of the breach. See *Bundesgerichtshof* 4 April 1968, Neue Juristische Wochenschrift 1968, 1471; *Bundesgerichtshof* 4 November 1976, Wertpapiermitteilungen 1977, 525, p. 527. *Contra:* Coing (*supra* n. 8), p. 166 *et seq.*; Kötz (*supra* n. 2) 138 *et seq.*

11 Fratcher (*supra* n. 2) s. 1.

12 Scott, Fifty Years of Trusts, Harv.L.Rev. 50 (1936) 60, p. 76.

at all self-evident to him that the legal rules governing these diverse cases are to be cut from the same cloth.

It has been shown (*supra* n. 3) that the practical results of German law are rather similar to those reached by the common law rules on testamentary trusts. Not only are the *Testamentsvollstrecker's* own creditors unable to take in execution the assets of the estate, but also the doctrine of "real subrogation" applies to deceased's estates (§ 2111 Civil Code) so that the "tracing" of assets is accepted to a limited extent. There is even a functional counterpart of the Rule against perpetuities since § 2109 Civil Code provides, in essence, that the appointment of a "second heir" becomes invalid if it turns out that his interest vests more than thirty years after the testator's death. Nonetheless, a common lawyer will be appalled by the dearth of case law and the lack of technical refinement of the rules governing the fiduciary duties of testamentary trustees. There is, indeed, a less pressing need in Germany for the development and refinement of legal institutions serving the purposes which in common law countries have always been satisfied by testamentary and charitable trusts. The reason seems to be, first, that under German law the part of a person's property freely disposable by testament is much smaller than in common law countries and, second, that for reasons based on the political and religious history of Germany and, indeed, continental Europe, the state is viewed as the main provider of public benefits and there is therefore nothing similar to the deeply ingrained habit of well-to-do Anglo-American testators to set aside a part of their estate for the achievement of a charitable purpose[13].

The only remaining question is whether there exists a plausible case for the adoption of a statute by which the rules of German law on the *fiduziarische Treuhand* would be clarified and improved and, perhaps, rendered more similar to those of the common law trust. In my submission, an overwhelming case for introducing such a statute cannot be made out. True, a common lawyer would have no difficulties in identifying a number of "weaknesses" of German law. Most of these "weaknesses" could be remedied by the courts themselves, and academic writers have made proposals to this effect which have sometimes been based on a comparison

13 See Kötz (*supra* n. 2), p. 163 *et seq.*, Fratcher (*supra* n. 2) s. 110.

of German law and the common law, and might well be based in the future on the Principles of European Trust Law. It has been argued, for example, that the beneficiaries should in the event of the *Treuhänder's* bankruptcy take priority over his own creditors regardless of whether the trust assets have been transferred to him by the settlor or by a third party, and a strong argument has also been made out for the application, by analogy, of the principle of "real subrogation" to property transferred to the *Treuhänder inter vivos* (see *supra* n. 8). In the case of an improper alienation of a trust asset the common law gives the beneficiary a claim to the asset against anyone who acquired it except a purchaser in good faith and for value. In order to reach the same result in Germany there is no need to give the beneficiary an "equitable property interest" in the asset. All that would be needed would be the recognition by the court of a rule that an improper alienation of an asset by a *Treuhänder* is to be treated on the same footing as an improper alienation of an asset by a *Testamentsvollstrecker*. In the latter case, the courts have held that a third party acquired no good title to the asset if he has constructive notice of the *Testamentsvollstrecker's* breach[14]; why not apply this rule, by analogy, to a disposition made by a *Treuhänder*?

There is, however, a serious problem in cases in which land forms part of the *Treuhand* assets. Under the law as it stands the *Treuhänder* would be entered in the land register as the unrestricted owner, and there is no possibility of qualifying his title by adding a note in the register that he owns the land merely "as *Treuhänder*". If such a possibility were created by statute, this would mean imposing a serious cost on third parties contemplating acquiring the land. They would be bound to inquire whether the *Treuhänder* has power to act or is properly exercising his power. This would, I believe, be unacceptable to German lawyers. Of course, the statute might say that the existence of trust powers and their proper exercise may be assumed by the third party without inquiry. In that event, however, it might be asked whether such a change in the law is needed in the first place.

---

14 *Reichsgericht* 15 February 1911, RGZ 75, 299; *Reichsgericht* 10 December 1913, RGZ 83, 348; *Reichsgericht* 20 October 1930, RGZ 130, p. 131.

In general, the technical and doctrinal obstacles to giving effect to some trust law principles in German law do not seem to be insuperable. In some cases, however, the adoption of such principles raises serious issues of policy, and what a common lawyer would describe as a "weakness" of German law might well turn out to be a strength. For example, it is an open question whether the common law always strikes the right balance between the claims of trust beneficiaries and those of the trustee's own creditors. Take the case of tracing the beneficiary's interests to private and trust moneys mixed in a bank account: Should German law stretch the doctrine of "real subrogation" as far as the common law has done? I do not think so, and while I admire the refinement of the rules developed by English judges in this field I am not at all sure whether the common law is not too tender to the beneficiary at the expense of the trustee's own creditors and whether the advantage to the beneficiary, if advantage it is, is not outstripped by the unavoidable cost of such refinement, i.e. legal uncertainty.

C. Commentary on the Principles article by article

Article I. Main characteristics of the trust
and
Article II. Creation of the trust

A situation very similar to that described in Article I exists in German law where assets have been transferred by A (settlor) to B (trustee, in German: *Treuhänder*) on the basis of a contractual agreement ("trust agreement", *Treuhandvertrag*) under which B assumes a duty to segregate the assets from his other property and to manage them in a particular way for the benefit of one or more beneficiaries. The contractual duty to deal with the assets as specified in the "trust agreement" will normally be owed by B to A, but if A and B intend to confer a right to enforce the agreement on one or more third parties (the beneficiaries) such intention will take effect by way of a "contract for the benefit of a third party" fully recognized in German law according to §§ 328 BGB.

Note that German law makes a sharp distinction between the agreement needed (among other things) to transfer title to property ("transfer agreement"), and the "trust agreement" which is the source of the trustee's contractual duties to deal with the assets in a certain way. The "transfer agreement" must comply with any applicable statutory rules, particularly the formal requirements provided by such rules. Thus, if real estate is to be transferred the conditions laid down in §§ 873 *ff.* BGB must be satisfied. The transfer of title to movable things is dealt with by §§ 929 *ff.* BGB, the transfer of receivables (choses in action) by §§ 398 *ff.* BGB, the transfer of shares in a limited liability company by § 15 para. 3 GmbHG, and so on. Both the "transfer agreement" and the "trust agreement" are viewed as contracts governed by the general rules of contract law. Both agreements may therefore be set aside on the ground of deceit, misrepresentation or duress, and they may be void as against public policy if they were made in an attempt to defraud creditors or if they lead to the result that the settlor divested himself of so much of his property as to virtually deprive himself of all ability to make independent decisions. In some cases formal requirements must be complied with to give effect to a "trust agreement". If, for example, a "trust agreement" imposes a duty on the trustee to hold real estate for a beneficiary and eventually to transfer title to him the agreement must be notarized under § 313 BGB, and the same formal requirement applies under § 15 para. 4 GmbHG if the trustee must eventually transfer to the beneficiary shares in a limited liability company. Both the "transfer agreement" and the "trust agreement" are treated as distinct "legal transactions", and it is therefore possible, at least in theory, that the transfer of the assets to the trustee is valid, while the "trust agreement" is not, and *vice versa*.

There would be no objection in principle against allowing a person to set himself up, as to some of his assets, as a trustee for the benefit of a beneficiary. There would be no transfer of assets in this case. What would be needed, however, is a contract between the trustee and the beneficiary under which the trustee assumes a duty vis-à-vis the beneficiary to manage the assets for his benefit in a certain way. It goes without saying that clear proof of such intention will be required, and that it must also be clear to which assets such intention relates. As to the question whether the assets will be immune from claims by the trustee's private creditors see below commentary to Article III.

Article III. Trust fund

Article III identifies the assets constituting the trust fund (paragraph 1) and provides that the trust fund shall not be available to satisfy claims made by the trustee's private creditors (paragraph 2). German law recognizes the rule laid down in paragraph 2 but would not nearly go as far as paragraph 1 in identifying the assets to be protected from the trustee's private creditors.

There is authority for the rule that the settlor or a beneficiary is entitled under § 771 ZPO to set aside acts of sequestration, seizure or garnishment brought by the trustee's private creditors against clearly definable assets held by the trustee under a "trust agreement". Likewise, in the trustee's bankruptcy, a settlor or beneficiary may demand from the trustee in bankruptcy (*Konkursverwalter*) a release of such assets under § 43 *Konkursordnung* (see *supra* n. 8 and the cases cited in footnote 7).

However, it is not clear to which assets these rules apply. The general rule is that they are applicable only where assets have been directly transferred to the trustee by the settlor and still exist in the trustee's hands in their original form. It is doubtful, however, whether a similar protection against the trustee's general creditors will be extended to assets transferred to the trustee by a third party. This is the case where the trustee sells shares held on trust to a buyer and the buyer, as a third party, pays the purchase price into an account of the trustee even though that account may be labelled as a "trust account". This is also the case where the trustee uses trust money to buy shares or where trust assets have been destroyed or damaged and the trustee is paid damages by the tortfeasor or insurance moneys by an insurance company. Academic writers have argued the case for such an extension pointing out that the doctrine of "real subrogation" which is applicable under §§ 2041, 2111 BGB to a deceased's estate should be applied by analogy to property held by a trustee. However, there is no judicial authority for this proposition yet, and the position must be viewed therefore as unsettled (for details see *supra* n. 8).

Article IV. Trusts for beneficiaries or for enforceable purposes

German law is in line with the rules laid down in Article IV. Note, however, that the beneficiary's rights listed in paragraphs 1, 2, 3 and 5 must be derived from the parties' intention and will therefore be enforced only when a basis for them can be found in an express or implied contractual agreement.

Article V. Trustees' duties and powers

The trustees' duties laid down in Article V will be recognized and enforced by German courts if they can be derived from the "trust agreement" (see *supra* n. 6).

Article VI. Remedies against trustees for breach of trust

Remedies against the trustee for specific performance, for an injunction to prohibit particular conduct, or for the payment of damages for breach are available to the settlor or beneficiary under the general law of contract. There is also a right for the settlor or beneficiary to terminate the "trust agreement" for cause (§ 626 BGB) and thus to put an end to the trustee's powers. However, there is no general jurisdiction of the German courts to remove and appoint a trustee, to advise a trustee on his rights and duties in an unexpected situation or to permit him to deviate from the terms of the "trust agreement" when changed conditions make deviation essential to achievement of its primary purposes (see *supra* n. 6 *in fine*).

Article VII. Liabilities of third parties

As to the liabilities of third parties to whom trust assets have been transferred by the trustee in breach of trust see *supra* n. 9.

Article VIII. Termination of a trust

The rules laid down in Article VIII would be enforced by a German court if, and only if, sufficient authority can be found for them in the "trust agreement". Few problems will arise if the "trust agreement" makes elaborate provision dealing with the problems listed in Article VIII. To the extent to which the parties have provided no solution in the "trust agreement" the court will normally fill the gap either by resorting to "default rules" supplied by the rules of the Civil Code or case law or by engaging in what is called "constructive interpretation" (*ergänzende Vertragsaus-*

legung[15]). However, in the field of "trust agreements", only few statutory or judge-made "default rules" are available, and it is to be hoped that the court, in attempting a "constructive interpretation" of the "trust agreement", will be guided in the future by the Principles of European Trust Law.

15 For more detailed information on "constructive interpretation" see Kötz, European Contract Law, Vol. I (translated by Tony Weir, 1997), p. 115-123.

National Report for Switzerland

A.E. von Overbeck*

A. Introduction

There is no institution called "trust" in Swiss law, and until recently no other institution which could meet the conditions of the Principles. However, a recent change of the Swiss Banking law which will be explained in part B of the present paper, permits so-called *Trust Agreements* that seem to fall within the Principles.

The question whether trusts should be introduced into Swiss law has been raised from time to time. In particular it has been discussed at the Swiss *Juristentag*, the meeting of the very influential Swiss Lawyers' Association, in 1954. Discussions of fiduciary relationships, inevitably raising also the question of trusts, took place at a Colloquy in Lausanne in 1994 and at the *Juristentag* of 1995. We will examine the results of these meetings in part C of the present paper[1].

Swiss writers and some court decisions have generally held that foreign trusts, with which practitioners have regularly to deal, are recognised. The

---

* Prof. A.E. von Overbeck is professor emeritus, University of Fribourg, and former Director of the Swiss Institute of Comparative Law.

1 C. Reymond, *Le trust et le droit suisse*, Zeitschrift für schweizerisches Recht (ZSR) 1954, p. 119a, F.T. Gubler, *Besteht in der Schweiz ein Bedürfnis nach Einführung des Instituts der angelsächsischen Treuhand (trust)?*, *ibid*, p. 215a, discussion *ibid*, p. 504a; Michel Jaccard éd., *Droit et pratique des opérations fiduciaires en Suisse*, CEDIDAC vol. 29, Lausanne 1994 (hereafter cited as: CEDIDAC 29), R. Watter, *Die Treuhand im Schweizer Recht*, ZSR 1995 II, p. 179 (hereafter cited by N°); L. Thévenoz, *La fiducie, cendrillon du droit suisse*, *ibid*, p. 253; discussion, *ibid*, p. 509. See also: P. Breitschmid, *Trust und Nachlassplanung*, in: *Rechtskollisionen, Festschrift für Anton Heini*, Zurich 1995, p. 49; P. Supino, *Rechtsgestaltung mit Trust aus Schweizer Sicht*, St. Gallen 1994; D.A. Dreyer, *Le trust en droit suisse, Etudes suisses de droit international*, vol. 21, Geneva 1981. On the practice see two contributions by A. Necker, Fiduciary Institutions in Swiss Law, and Attorneys Acting as Trustees/ Fiduciaries in Switzerland, in: The International Academy of Estate and Trust Law, Switzerland 4, 1991 and 12, 1996.

most often quoted decision is the *Harrison Trust* case of 29 January 1970[2]. However, the situation was somewhat special in that case. The trustee of a "settlement" which had all the characteristics of a trust was a Swiss bank and in an additional arrangement the Canton of Zurich was chosen as forum. The Federal Court considered that in Swiss law there was no institution corresponding exactly to the "settlement", stating in particular that the Swiss legal order did not allow for the split ownership which it considered characteristic for the trust. It asked itself which Swiss institutions had effects most similar to those of a trust and was thus able to qualify the "settlement" *lege fori* as a mixed contract governed by Swiss law according to Swiss conflict rules. In addition, the Court considered that the choice of a Swiss forum constituted a presumption for the choice of Swiss substantive law. This reasoning is not convincing and the substantive content of the "settlement" would rather have suggested an implied choice of the common law system of the settlor's domicile[3]. Having decided on the application of Swiss law, the Court then proceeded to bring the effects of the "settlement" under a number of Swiss institutions such as power of attorney (*mandat*), fiduciary transfer of ownership, gift (*donation*) and stipulation for a third person (*stipulation pour autrui*) and finally managed to a large extent to give effect to the intentions of the settlor.

Swiss law not offering any institution equivalent to the trust, practice tends to have recourse to trusts of other jurisdictions. This is mainly the case for foreign clients of Swiss banks, notaries or attorneys, while the possibilities for Swiss persons domiciled in Switzerland are limited. One should note that foreigners domiciled in Switzerland can choose in their wills their national law to govern their succession upon death instead of Swiss domiciliary law[4]. A trust valid under that chosen law is effective in Switzerland.

---

2 *Harrison g. Schweiz. Kreditanstalt*, Arrêts du Tribunal fédéral suisse, Recueil officiel (ATF) 96 II 79, Journal des Tribunaux (JT) 1971 I 329, note C. Reymond, p. 322; Supino, p. 81; Dreyer, p. 118, 125; Necker, p. 4.5.

3 Such an approach would have made the Court's task much easier. It was followed by the Appellate Court of Paris in the case *Courtois c. Ganay* of 10 January 1970, Revue critique de droit international privé 1971, p. 518, note G. Droz, p. 525; Journal du droit international, 1973, p. 207, note Y. Loussouarn, p. 214.

4 Federal act on private international law of 18 December 1987, Recueil systématique du droit fédéral (RS) 291, Article 90,2.

There are no Swiss opinions according to which a trust under a foreign law could be created in purely internal situations. But if a situation presents sufficient relations to a foreign jurisdiction, there may be a Swiss trustee of a trust governed by foreign law. However, there are some uncertainties as to the extend to which foreign law applies, especially as far as separation of assets is concerned[5].

A Swiss banker, Ms. Durr Gerber[6], compares advantages and disadvantages of trust companies in Switzerland or offshore. She concludes that, at least as long as the Hague Convention of 1 July 1985 on the Law Applicable to Trusts and on their Recognition has not been ratified, Switzerland is "a very thorny environment for trust services" and that a fully operative trust company in an offshore jurisdiction is preferable. This view is confirmed by other practitioners[7].

The ratification of the Hague Convention would of course facilitate the operations with trusts in Switzerland. On the other hand the reinforced *fiducie* which, as we shall see, has been proposed by several Swiss writers, could be recognised under the Convention[8]. At the Lausanne Colloquy Prof. Giovanoli stressed this point and its importance for the Swiss place in the world of finance[9]. Similar opinions were expressed at two Seminars organised by the Society of Trust and Estate Practitioners in Geneva and Zurich in May 1996 and at a meeting of Swiss private international law professors in Lausanne in March 1997. Banking circles, which used to be opposed to the Convention, seem to have become more favourable[10].

B. Existing law

In Swiss law various institutions can be used to fulfil some of the purposes of trusts. In fact, as Dr. P. Supino has convincingly demonstrated in his

5 H.C. Schulthess and A.C. Limburg, *Rechtsfragen der Ausübung von Trustee-Funktionen durch schweizerische Trustees, Der Schweizer Treuhänder*, 1996, p. 57.
6 2 Trust & Trustees (1996) N° 5, p. 38.
7 See also Watter N° 2.
8 Thévenoz, p. 350; Watter N° 217.
9 CEDIDAC 29, p. 216.
10 See recently, A. Fuchs, *Soll die Schweiz die Haager Trust-Konvention ratifizieren?, Publikation der Swiss Banking School*, Zurich, N° 188, 1998.

doctoral thesis, some parallelisms between Swiss institutions and the trust can be discovered, but none of the former can be assimilated to the latter[11]. For example, the representative of a community of bondholders is not owner of the assets mortgaged in favour of the bondholders[12]. We shall discuss only two institutions, the foundation and the *fiducie*, which can be used to fulfil purposes similar to an *inter vivos* trust.

1. *The foundation*

The foundation (*Fondation, Stiftung*) is governed by Articles 80 to 89bis of the Swiss Civil Code (CCS)[13]. To create a foundation, a patrimony has to be affected to a special purpose by will or by a public deed. The foundation becomes a legal person by its registration in the *registre du commerce*[14]. This formality is not necessary for ecclesiastical and family foundations. The foundation is organised according to the act creating it and, again for ecclesiastical and family foundations, placed under the supervision of the federal, cantonal or communal authority depending on the scope of its activities.

Exceptionally, foundations may have a commercial purpose, but in principle they should only pursue philanthropical aims. They are very widely used for charitable, cultural and similar purposes. Foundations for social security of employees are very numerous, specially since the introduction of a compulsory pensions scheme in 1982[15]. One can say that the foundation functions as do charitable trusts in common law countries, even if it lacks the flexibility of trusts[16].

The foundation cannot easily be used for beneficiaries in the manner in which this is done by trust law. Swiss law has its own brand of rule against perpetuities. *Fidéicommis de famille* may not be constituted (Article 335,2

---

11 Supino, p. 112, see also Thévenoz, p. 296.

12 Supino, *ibid*, p. 98; Swiss Civil Code, Article 875; Code of Obligations, Article 1157-1186.

13 See Tuor/Schnyder/Schmid, *Das schweizerische Zivilgesetzbuch*, 11th edn, Zurich 1995, p. 143; H.-M Riemer, *Berner Kommentar zum schweizerischen Privatrecht*, Bd. I 3. Abt. 3. Teilbd, Article 80-89bis ZGB, *Die Stiftungen*.

14 ATF 120 II 141.

15 Tuor/Schnyder/Schmid, p. 145.

16 Necker, p. 4.7.

CC)[17] and *substitution fidéicommisaire* is limited to one reversionary heir (Article 488 CCS)[18].

A foundation cannot be constituted for the benefit of a specified person. Family foundations may be created by dedicating a patrimony to a certain family. However, such a foundation can only provide for special purposes such as to cover the cost of education, outfitting, or support in case of need, of the family members. It cannot simply provide income to the family. The Federal Court has construed the statute narrowly[19]. It has been maintained by several writers that the scope of the family foundation should be broadened to allow trust-like arrangements. The objections against perpetuity could be met if the duration of such a foundation was limited[20].

2. *The fiducie*

The institution with the closest relations to trusts is the *fiducie*, or *acte fiduciaire* (*Treuhand*), as developed by case law[21]. It is used either as *fiducia cum creditore* for security, or as *fiducia cum amico* for purposes of administration or disposition of assets. We shall concentrate here on the latter and also leave aside special questions which may rise about immovables[22]. Rapp gives the following definition of *fiducie*[23].

> "Contrat par lequel une personne, le fiduciant, transfère un droit à une autre, le fiduciaire, qui s'oblige à en user selon les indications du fiduciant, en général à le retransférer dans certaines conditions."

---

17 Tuor/Schnyder/Schmid, p. 143.

18 A few ancient *Fidéicommis* still exist, see R. Pahud de Mortanges, *Gegenwarts-lösungen für ein historisches Rechtsinstitut: Das Familienfideikommiss*, in: *Famille et Droit*, Mélanges Bernhard Schnyder, Fribourg 1995, p. 499.

19 ATF 73 II 86, 89 II 473. In 93 II 439 it has converted a family foundation which did not meet its criteria in an ordinary foundation. In 108 II 293 it decided that maintaining a vacation chalet could not be the purpose of a family foundation.

20 A.F. Schnitzer, *Revue critique de droit international privé*, 1965, p. 479; P. Hefti, ZSR 1954, p. 551a, Thévenoz, p. 300.

21 It was first recognised in 1905 by the Federal Court, *Grüring-Dutoit c. Kappeler*, ATF 31 II lo5. See: C. Reymond et J. Revaclier, *Les opérations fiduciaires en droit suisse*, in: *Les opérations fiduciaires (pratiques, validité, régime juridique dans plusieurs pays européens et dans le commerce international)* Colloque de Luxembourg des 20 et 21 septembre 1984, Paris 1985 (hereafter cited: *Opérations fiduciaires*) published under the direction of Claude Witz.

22 On the *fiducie-sûreté* see Rapp, CEDIDAC 29, p. 32.

23 CEDIDAC 29, p. 27.

The differences with trusts are obvious. The *fiduciant* (*Treugeber*) is much less protected than the parties to a trust. None of the structures which under common law permit supervision of the trust exist (experienced courts, protectors, enforcers). One author qualifies the *fiducie* as *Cendrillon* (Thévenoz), another as *Colosse au pieds d'argile* (Giovanoli).

The Swiss fiducie derives from the rules on mandate (*mandat, Auftrag*). The *fiduciant* can give the fiduciary any instructions at any time, while normally the settlor cannot interfere with the management or disposition of the trustee. Also, in principle, a *mandat* can be revoked at any time (Code of Obligations - CO - Article 404). However, according to recent doctrine, the *mandant* may have only the power, but not the right, to revoke, if the contract provides to the contrary[24]. Some authors even contend that revocation can be altogether excluded by contract[25]. But the Federal Court, in an unpublished decision of 26 March 1997, has rejected these opinions and maintained the obligatory character of the revocation[26].

The *fiducie* is based on the *Vollrechtstheorie*, which means that the fiduciary (*fiduciaire*, the trustee) is full owner of the property[27]. He has more power than needed to fulfil his duties. On the death, incapacity or bankruptcy of the *fiduciaire* the fiduciary agreement ends (Article 405 CO), unless it continues after his death by virtue of the will of parties or because of special circumstances[28]. In that case the fiduciary assets become part of the trustee's estate but his heirs shall be bound by his obligations.

The weakest point of the *fiducie* may be the situation in case of bankruptcy of the fiduciary. The fundamental principle of Swiss bankruptcy law is that all the assets of the debtor have to be realised in favour of the creditors, thus also the fiduciary assets which are the full property of the fiduciary[29].

---

24 Watter, ZSR 1995 N° 79 seq.; Thévenoz, p. 339; F. Werro, *Le Mandat et ses effets*, Fribourg 1993, p. 87, summary p. 375 N° 1116-1123.

25 P. Gauch, Article 404 OR – *Sein Inhalt, seine Rechtfertigung und die Frage seines zwingenden Charakters*, Recht 1992, p. 17.

26 Ref. 4C443/1996/zus.

27 Thévenoz, p. 274.

28 Watter, N° 87-88.

29 See ATF 117 II 430.

However, there are some exceptions to this rule.

1) Compensation and retention are restricted in some respect[30].

2) Article 401,3 of the Code of Obligations (CO) on undisclosed agency states:

> "Le mandant peut, de même, revendiquer dans la faillite du mandataire les objets mobiliers acquis par ce dernier en son propre nom, mais pour le compte du mandant; sauf à la masse à exercer le droit de rétention qui appartiendrait au mandataire."

Should this provision be applicable in case of *fiducie*? Older authors answered in the negative[31]. The Federal Court applied Article 401,3 in a case which is considered the most favourable to *fiducie*[32]. This means that the *fiduciant* can withdraw any values received by the fiduciary on his behalf, on condition that they are separated from other assets.

However, there are uncertainties as to the precise scope of this right. In a case decided in 1976 the Federal Court has emphasised the exceptional character of the *Vallugano* solution[33]. In a more recent *obiter dictum* it raises the question whether the application of Article 401,3 should not be restricted to short-time *fiducies* the only purpose of which is to procure as soon as possible the rights acquired by the fiduciary to the *fiduciant*[34].

As Giovanoli shows, at different stages of a same operation, separation of assets may or may not be possible[35].

And it has to be stressed that Article 401,3 does not apply to assets given by the *fiduciant* to the fiduciary, but only to those received by the latter

30 Thévenoz, p. 329; Watter N° 75-76, in Banking Law see Giovanoli, CEDIDAC 29, p. 221. E.g. the *fiduciaire* cannot compensate the *fiduciant's* claim for restitution of assets with a claim of his own without any connexity to the fiduciary relationship.

31 Gubler ZSR 1954, p. 261a.

32 *Feras Anstalt e diversi contro Banca Vallugano,* ATF 99 II 393, JT 1974 I, p. 588, note C. Reymond (referring also to former cases) p. 596; see Thévenoz, p. 277.

33 ATF 102 II 103, 108, see on this case *infra* D, Article III.

34 ATF 117 II 429.

35 CEDIDAC 29, p. 198, but see *infra* the changes resulting from the new provisions on banking law.

from third persons. In the case just cited[36], the Court recognises that the interests are the same in both cases, but feels unable to further enlarge, contrary to its clear wording, the scope of Article 401,3.

3) The legislation on investment funds also provides for a right of withdrawal[37]. I shall leave this aside, as well as some special provisions of lesser importance[38].

4) By far the most important application of *fiducie* in Switzerland is in the field of banking law[39]. The main operations are the following:

(a) The bank is acting as *fiduciaire* in its own name but on behalf of the client (*fiduciant*) to invest funds in banks or companies abroad against the payment of a fee (*placements fiduciaires*). This operation requires the conclusion of a written contract between the client and the bank. It is interesting to note that the model agreement drafted by the Swiss Bankers Association (*Treuhandvertrag, Contrat fiduciaire*) is called *Trust Agreement* in English. The client bears the risk of currency and transfer of the foreign bank or company. The bank has the obligation to make the clients the beneficiaries of all income which arises from the investment. The volume of these operations, which appear below the line in the balance sheets of the banks, was in 1992 of 320 billion Swiss francs, mostly placed by foreigners in foreign institutions[40]. An elaborate system of prescriptions by the Swiss Banking Commission and of directives of the Swiss Bankers Association tend to minimise risks for clients and to prevent money laundering[41]. The contracts with clients generally provide that the *fiduciaire*

36 P. 432.

37 Thévenoz, p. 279.

38 Bankruptcy statute, RS 281.1, Article 201, Statute on insurance contracts, RS 221.229.1, Article 79 and 80.

39 On fiduciary operations of banks in Switzerland see: G. Ferrero, *Les opérations fiduciaires dans la pratique bancaire*, CEDIDAC 29, p. 89; Necker, p. 12.4; a statutory definition CEDIDAC 29, p. 121; M. Giovanoli, *Les opérations fiduciaires dans la pratique bancaire suisse*, in: *La fiducie et ses applications dans plusieurs pays européens*, Colloque du 29 novembre 1990, éd. par Claude Witz, Bulletin Jolly, 1991, N° 4bis, p. 31; Reymond/Revaclier, *Opérations fiduciaires*, p. 428, and C. Reymond, *Aspects fiduciaires de quelques opérations bancaires, principalement dans l'Euromarché, ibid*, p. 13.

40 Ferrero, CEDIDAC 29, p. 90.

41 See P.-Y. Despland, *Aspects prudentiels des opérations fiduciaires, surveillance des banques et des marchés financiers, diligence et vigilance*, CEDIDAC 29, p. 109.

is free to choose the foreign correspondent within the mentioned regulations[42].

(b) Loans and fiduciary credits made by the bank as *fiduciaire* for the benefit and the risk of the client to third parties chosen by the latter (*prêts et crédits fiduciaires*).

(c) Acting as nominees in relation to foreign corporations (in particular US corporations): The Swiss banks act as shareholders of the corporation, but on behalf of their clients[43].

(d) The fiduciary transfer for pledge purposes: It occurs for instance, when the *fiduciant* transfers to the bank (the *fiduciaire*) some shares, a mortgage title or assets in a fiduciary manner for the guarantee of a debt towards the bank, and the bank will transfer it back when the client will have paid his debts.

The most important recent development in the matter are the new provisions of the Banking statute introduced by the revised Bankruptcy statute which entered into force on 1 January 1997[44]. Their text is the following[45]:

> "Art. 16 - Sont réputées valeurs déposées selon l'article 37b de la loi:
> 1. les choses mobilières et les titres déposés par les clients;
> 2. les choses mobilières, les titres et les créances que la banque détient à titre fiduciaire pour le compte des clients déposants;
> 3. les prétentions disponibles de la banque à des livraisons à l'encontre de tiers, résultant d'opérations au comptant, d'opérations à terme échues, d'opérations de couverture ou d'emissions pour le compte des clients déposants."

> "Art. 37 b - En cas de faillite de la banque, les valeurs déposées, au sens de l'article 16, seront distraites de la masse en faillite au bénéfice du déposant, sous réserve des droits de la banque à l'encontre du déposant.

42 Examples in CEDIDAC 29, p. 99.

43 See recently: L. Olgiati, *Schweizerische Nominees im Aktienregister amerikanischer Publikumsgesellschaften*, Zurich 1997.

44 B. Kleiner and B. Lutz, *Kommentar zum Bundesgesetz über die Banken und Sparkassen*, 9. Nachlieferung, Zurich 1997; U. Bertschinger, *Zum neuen bankgesetzlichen Aussonderungsrecht, Aktuelle juristische Praxis*, 1995, p. 426; D. Zobl, *Kollisionen zwischen Sachen- und Zwangsvollstreckungsrecht*, in: *Rechtskollisionen, Festschrift für Anton Heini*, Zurich 1995, p. 543, 547; Thévenoz, p. 282; Giovanoli, CEDIDAC 29, p. 216.

45 *Feuille fédérale*, 1995 V, p. 1065.

> Si la banque en faillite est elle-même déposante auprès d'un tiers, les valeurs déposées seront présumées être celles de ses clients; elles seront dès lors distraites de la masse en faillite, conformément au premier alinéa.
> L'administration de la faillite de la banque doit remplir à l'encontre d'un tiers dépositaire les obligations relatives au dépôt et les obligations résultant d'opérations prévues à l'article 16, chiffre 3."

Article 16,1 goes without saying and confirms existing law.

Article 16,2 contains the presumption that movables, shares and bonds (*titres, Effekten*) and claims held by the bank as fiduciary are *valeurs déposées* (*Depotwerte*), deposited assets. This is the most important provision because shares and bonds are generally not kept by the banks themselves but deposited in central institutions (such as, for Switzerland, the SEGA, *Schweizerische Effekten-Giro AG*). The provision does only cover claims against third persons held by the bank as fiduciary, not debts of the bank itself resulting e.g. out of current accounts[46]. It applies to the *fiducie* for administration as well as to the *fiducie* for security.

The essential difference from the current interpretation of Article 401,3 CO is that Article 16,2 applies to all values including those remitted directly by the *fiduciant* to the fiduciary.

Article 16,3 provides for the same presumption as far as liquid claims of banks against third persons on behalf of clients are concerned. This disposition was aimed at a case where the engagement to deliver bonds, which had been firmly subscribed by a bank, was considered to be not a mandate but a sales contract[47]. Consequently, separation in case of bankruptcy by the bank was not possible. The provision might cause some problems. Sometimes it shall be difficult to find out which values due by a third person are to be allocated to which client. And what if the values do not cover the claims of all clients[48]?

Article 37b,1 provides for separation of assets in case of bankruptcy in favour of the deponent who has fulfilled all his obligations. Article 37b,2 extends this solution to values deposited in a third bank and presumes that

46 See Kleiner/Lutz N° 20 ad Article 16.
47 *Leclerc*, ATF 112 II 444, Kleiner/Lutz N°22 ad Article 16.
48 Zobl, p. 553.

such depots belong to the clients. Thus if the bank has deposited assets of clients as well as its own assets of the same type (e.g. shares of the same company) the client is first served if the third person is not able to return all the assets[49]. Article 37b,3 preserves the rights of third persons.

Article 37b introduces a special procedure which, compared to the normal bankruptcy proceedings, facilitates the separation of assets. It is applicable as well in bankruptcy as in the procedure called *concordat par abandon d'actif* where the assets are liquidated without a formal bankruptcy. In German terminology one has chosen the term *Absonderung* for this procedure, to distinguish it from the *Aussonderung* (*revendication*) in other bankruptcy proceedings. According to Article 37b the liquidators have the duty to separate the values *ex officio*, while in normal bankruptcy proceedings assets must be claimed.

C. Proposals for further development of trusts

a) The *Juristentag* 1954. The position of trusts in Swiss law and the question whether this institution should be introduced is not a new one. Thirty-four years ago, it was discussed at the meeting of the Swiss Lawyers Association (*Juristenverein*), the reporters being two practising lawyers of high standing, Dr. F.T. Gubler and (later Prof.) C. Reymond[50]. Reymond mentioned the remark of an English author, F.W. Weiser[51], according to which nowhere else than in Switzerland is there such a contrast between the large use of the *fiducie* and an absence of efforts to introduce something similar to a trust.

Both reporters concluded that it was not possible to constitute a trust according to Swiss law, and that introduction of the institution would be contrary to the spirit of Swiss law and would meet dogmatic objections, especially because of the unity of property and the *numerus clausus* of real rights. They wished to improve the system of the *fiducie*, notably as far as protection of the assets is concerned, and possibly develop other

49 Kleiner/Lutz N° 19 ad Article 37b.
50 ZSR 1954, p. 119a-476a and 504a-551a.
51 Trust on the continent of Europe, London 1936, p. 45.

institutions such as the testamentary executor and the family foundation[52]. In the discussion, Wyler, who had already published articles in favour of the trust in the thirties, defended the possibility of introducing such an institution. However, especially in view of an investigation amongst interested circles, he accepted the idea that there was no need for a trust in Switzerland[53].

The negative attitude of Swiss lawyers was criticized in 1955 by P. Lepaulle who affirmed that the lack of the concepts of legal or equitable title in Swiss law ought not to prevent the introduction of a reasonable trust[54].

A more positive attitude has also been taken by other authors, most notably by A.F. Schnitzer. He challenges the current conviction that real and obligatory rights are hermetically separated and that the principles of real rights of continental jurisdictions cannot be touched[55]. According to this writer, the theory of *numerus clausus* of real rights is only a scientific affirmation which is not laid down in any law. He shows then that trusts have been introduced in many mixed and civil law jurisdictions.

b) The Lausanne colloquy of 1994. In 1994 the *Centre du droit de l'enterprise* of the University of Lausanne (CEDIDAC) organised a colloquy on *Droit et pratique des opérations fiduciaires*[56]. A draft on *fiducie* along the lines of the new provisions of the banking statute was discussed and the hope was expressed that the courts could extend the solutions of that statute to the *fiducie* in general.

c) The *Juristentag* of 1995. In September 1995 the Swiss Lawyers Association again discussed the *fiducie* and, inevitably, the trust[57]. Both reporters spoke strongly in favour of a reinforced *fiducie* which would in fact have the main features of a trust. Thévenoz was in favour of legislative action, while Watter would rather have relied on another interpretation of existing

---

52 See Supino, p. 143.

53 ZRS 1954, p. 549a.

54 *Réflexions sur l'expansion des trusts, Revue internationale de droit comparé*, 1955, p. 318, cited by Supino, p. 144.

55 *Die Treuhand - Der Trust - und das Internationale Privatrecht*, in: *Gedächtnisschrift Ludwig Marxer*, Zurich 1963, p. 79.

56 The results are published in CEDIDAC 29.

57 ZSR 1995 II, p. 179-363 and 509-535.

law, without excluding legislation. He questioned the value of the dogmatic arguments founded on the theory of real rights[58]. And why should what was possible for banks not be extended to other fiduciary relationships[59]?

The reporters at the *Juristentag* stated that:

- Fiduciary assets should be segregated from the private patrimony of the *fiduciaire*[60];
- Contrary to Article 404 CC, the *fiduciant* must have the possibility to stipulate a certain duration and to renounce to, or restrict, his right to cancel the *fiducie*. However, a time limit must be fixed for the case of death of the *fiduciant;*
- The *fiduciant* must be able to renounce to give instructions to the *fiduciaire;*
- The *fiduciant* must be able to confer rights to beneficiaries and to name a protector[61].

The reporters were of the opinion that such a reinforced *fiducie* would render unnecessary the formal introduction of trusts[62].

It is notable that in these discussions the case where a "settlor" irrevocably transfers assets to a "trustee" in favour of "beneficiaries" has hardly been mentioned at all. Especially in banking operations, if it is true that funds are lent to a third party, they finally come back, with interest, to the *fiduciant* who is thus, to speak in terms of trust law, at the same time the settlor and the real beneficiary. However, an improved Swiss *fiducie* could well be used to achieve the same purposes as the "classical" settlor-trustee-beneficiary figure. Thévenoz describes what such a *fiducie-libéralité* could be[63].

---

58 N° 192.

59 Thévenoz, p. 283.

60 Thévenoz, p. 313; Watter N° 210-211.

61 Thévenoz, p. 347; Watter N° 30, 214.

62 Thévenoz, p. 348; Watter N° 217-218, after N° 49 he gives a table showing various functions of trusts, their possible construction under present Swiss law and the perspectives of assuming these functions by means of a *fiducie* corresponding to his interpretation and proposals for change.

63 Thévenoz, p. 300, see also Reymond/Revaclier, p. 440.

D. Commentary on the Principles article by article

Article I. Main characteristics of the trust

At present, the constitution of a trust as understood by the Principles, comprising a segregated fund, is only possible as far as the Articles 16 and 37b of the Swiss Banking statute apply. It would be possible in other cases if the point of view of the reporters to the *Juristentag* 1995 and other writers were to prevail, specially in respect to separation of assets.

Article II. Creation of the trust

No comment.

Article III. Trust fund

The new provisions on banking law provide for separation of assets as far as operations by banks are concerned.

However, they do not solve the problem of pooling of assets. In a case decided in 1976, the Federal Court refused separation, in favour of the owner of immovables, of an account in the name of a real estate agent (who became bankrupt) into which rents had been paid[64]. The main argument of the Court was that there was a manoeuvre to privilege a certain creditor. However, it also held that there could be no separation if the sums on the account could not be individualised. Giovanoli has criticised this decision and considers that the impossibility of opening an *Anderkonto* as known in Germany constitutes a serious flaw. According to Giovanoli this problem should be dealt with by legislation[65].

Outside the field of banking operations, separation of assets is only possible if Article 401,3 CO applies as described above. This applies also to foreign trusts having effect in Switzerland. It might be possible to

64 ATF 102 II 103.

65 CEDIDAC 19, p. 193, 199, 222 and a proposed provision, p. 227; see also Watter N° 117-119 and note 219.

safeguard the trust assets from the trustee's private creditors by having them held by a separate trust company[66].

One should note that the Federal Court decided in 1992 that if one of several fiduciaries dies, the property of the assets accrues to the remaining fiduciaries[67].

According to both reporters to the *Juristentag*[68] the new *fiducie* would provide for separation of the trust assets; if disposed of, they would be replaced by their counter-value[69]. The fiduciary assets would only be liable for debts contracted by the fiduciary acting as such.

Article IV. Trusts for beneficiaries or for enforceable purposes

The Swiss foundation is perfectly suited to fulfil the functions of a charitable trust. For the reasons indicated above, it is only of very limited use for beneficiaries.

If the *fiducie* was reinforced as proposed at the 1995 *Juristentag*, it could fulfil the tasks of trusts *inter vivos*.

Article V. Trustees' duties and powers

In Swiss law, the *fiduciaire* (the trustee) is considered the absolute owner of the assets.

The Rules of Article 394 and seq. CO on *mandat*, especially Article 398 CO on responsibility, seem to correspond to the rules of Article IV of the Principles[70].

66 Schulthess and Limburg, p. 60.

67 *Böckli g. Masse Mayer*, ATF 78 II 445, 452, JT 1953 I, p. 523; see also *Thorwart*, ATF 91 II 442, 448, JT 1966 I 337; M. Schwartz, *Essai d'analyse de la propriété en main commune de plusieurs fiduciaires*, Schweizerische Juristen-Zeitung, 1966, p. 319; Thévenoz, p. 276.

68 Watter N° 192; Thévenoz, p. 313.

69 *Subrogation patrimoniale*, Thévenoz, p. 317.

70 Watter N° 14-18; Thévenoz, p. 333.

One may note that under Swiss law, unless the parties have agreed otherwise, the *fiduciaire's* personal assets can be held liable for claims of third persons against the fiduciary assets[71].

Article VI. Remedies against trustees for breach of trust

There are no specific provisions of this kind in Swiss law. The sanctions of violations of his obligations by the *fiduciant* could be payment of damages or restitution of assets.

According to A.F. Schnitzer the greatest obstacle to trusts is the difficulty for Swiss courts to exercise supervision to which English courts are used[72]. Recently, however, a registrar of the Zurich *Obergericht* and lecturer, P. Breitschmid, expressed the opinion that Swiss judges could quite well fulfil such a function[73]. But what may be possible in Zurich might not be possible everywhere as Swiss organisation of courts and civil procedure are mainly a matter of law of the twenty-six Cantons.

Thévenoz deems it possible *de lege ferenda* to institute a protector having more or less extended powers over the fiduciary assets[74]. Watter recommends the creation of a private supervision[75]. According to Necker, it is not uncommon for Swiss notaries or attorneys to serve as protectors to trusts created abroad for clients[76].

Article VII. Liabilities of third parties

Under present Swiss law, if assets have been wrongfully transferred to third persons, the counter-value received by the *fiduciaire* is due to the *fiduciant*. But the rights of the *fiduciant* against third persons are limited, there is nothing comparable to the tracing rights of the beneficiaries[77]. The

71 Watter, N° 134.

72 *Trust und Stiftung*, Schweizerische Juristen-Zeitung, 1965, p. 197, 213 and 215; see also Gubler, ZSR 1994, p. 420a.

73 Breitschmid, p. 65.

74 P. 347.

75 N° 30, 214.

76 P. 12.5.

77 Thévenoz, p. 338, 274 note 77; Schulthess and Limburg, p. 59; ATF 91 III 104 obiter.

acquisition by a third person to whom a *fiduciaire* has transferred assets is upheld even if that person was in bad faith. In the latter case such a person may, however, have to pay damages[78]. If a bank, in breach of its obligation towards a client, has pledged the clients assets to a third party, the client has no right of separation in the bankruptcy of the bank, but can only claim damages against the estate in bankruptcy[79].

According to the reporters at the *Juristentag*, the *fiduciant* and possible beneficiaries ought to be allowed to trace trust assets transferred to third persons of bad faith and ought to have proprietary rights in the assets so traced[80]. Watter proposes even *de lege lata* a clause in the contract according to which assets which the *fiduciaire* tries to transfer to a third person shall fall back into the ownership of the *fiduciaire*. However, the validity of such a resolutive condition under present Swiss law is doubtful[81].

Article VIII. Termination of a trust

Termination of a *fiducie* in a way corresponding to the present Article should not raise any problems.

---

78 Watter, N° 140-143, contrary to the dominant opinion, held that a third person of bad faith does not acquire the property from the *fiduciaire*.

79 Kleiner/Lutz N° 17 ad Article 37b.

80 Thévenoz, p. 338; Watter N° 139, 211.

81 Watter, N° 149 – 150, see also N° 114 – 116 about a similar clause to save the trust assets in case of bankruptcy.

National Report for Italy

M. Lupoi and T. Arrigo*

A. Introduction

Trusts as legal relationships of *general application* exist only in England and in those countries which have inherited them from England. Nowhere has a *legislative* enactment on trusts brought about a *general* acceptance of trusts: see Liechtenstein and Japan where after more than seventy years of legislation trusts are still either almost unknown (Liechtenstein) or used only for specific purposes (Japan).

If one puts the question: "Does Italian law have rules governing relationships which are homologous to some type of trust?" one would have to decide whether analytical or structural or functional techniques are to be employed[1].

If, on the other hand, one puts the question: "Does Italian law have trusts as described in Article I of the Principles?" the reply would be "yes" and the reasons for this will be explained presently.

B. Existing law

1. *Fondo patrimoniale*

Under Articles 167 to 171 of the Italian civil code, one of the spouses, both of them or a third party, *inter vivos* or by will, may burden certain assets to satisfy the needs of the family. This is effected by a unilateral declaration

* Prof. M. Lupoi is professor of comparative legal systems, University of Genoa. T. Arrigo is research fellow at the Institute of Private Law, University of Genoa.

1 My stand on this matter has been set out elsewhere: M. Lupoi, Trusts, Milan, 1997 (an English translation of this book is about to be published by Cambridge University Press); for a somewhat different approach see D.W.M. Waters, The institution of the trust in civil and common law, Dordrecht, 1995.

of both spouses or by the declaration of one spouse followed by the acceptance of the other or by the transfer of the assets from the third party to both spouses. Unless the "settlor" has decided otherwise (in the second or third of the three instances made above), the ownership of the assets vests in both spouses, who are then proper trustees. The assets constitute a fund which is termed *fondo patrimoniale* (trust fund).

Any income of the assets in the *fondo patrimoniale* must be applied to the needs of the family.

Parties claiming against one spouse or both spouses cannot attack the assets in the *fondo patrimoniale* if the defendant contracted with them for reasons unconnected with the furtherance of the family requirements. There is therefore segregation of the trust assets.

The *fondo patrimoniale* ceases when the marriage ceases. However, if one or more of the children of the marriage are not of age, the *fondo patrimoniale* will continue until all children are of age.

It is clear that the children of the marriage enjoy no property rights over the assets in the *fondo patrimoniale* (which is the proper description of the legal position of the beneficiaries under a trust).

The *fondo patrimoniale* is homologous to an English trust devoted to the same purposes. It is interesting to note that the *fondo patrimoniale* instituted by both spouses has the same structure as a trust declared unilaterally.

2. *Undeclared testamentary trusts (secret trusts)*

Under Article 627 of the Italian civil code nobody can allege that a testamentary disposition is to enure to the benefit of a party other than its ostensible beneficiary even if the disposition is so worded as to warrant such inference. The testamentary disposition can, however, be challenged, if it aims at benefiting someone who could not receive a bequest.

Article 627 is all that remains of the fiduciary heir, of the *tacitus fideicommissus* and of the *fraus legis* (that is, when the will is in favour of a disqualified person).

3. *Unilateral segregation*

One of the peculiar features of the Hague Convention is that its notion of "trust" (as laid down in Article 2) does not correspond to the English notion of trust. The "trust assets" (as defined in the Convention) may belong to the so-called "settlor" rather than to the trustee, for nowhere in the Convention is the vesting of the trust assets in the trustee made a structural element of express trusts.

It follows that the numerous Italian legislative provisions which bring about a segregation of assets as a consequence of the "settlor" transferring control rather than ownership may well be "trusts" under the Hague Convention, while one would not consider them to be "trusts" in the English sense nor homologous to trusts from a comparative standpoint.

Pension funds, investment funds, professional management of assets: these are all instances of assets which belong to parties other than those in whose name the title stands (e.g. the pension fund managing company, and so forth). The latter would *appear* to be the owners of the assets and yet they are not. The consequence is that there is a discrepancy between title and ownership: the title-holder can deal with the assets, sell them and reinvest the proceeds, almost as an agent, but he is not in any sense the owner of the assets.

By leaving "ownership" of the assets with the party which transferred control to the professional manager, Parliament believed that the "owner" was afforded the highest possible level of protection. That has proved not to be the case, since the "owner" can only act in *reivindicatio* and that requires that he be able to identify the assets specifically and individually, a task almost always impossible to fulfil where fungible assets are concerned (such as sums of money, shares, debentures). The regular outcome of most lawsuits against professional managers has been that the "owners" lost their case.

Italian law provides special rules for "fiduciary companies" or *società fiduciarie* (Law n. 1966 of 23rd November 1939). Whatever the potential scope of the legislation on *società fiduciarie,* in practice they confine their activity to taking title to shares and behaving as an agent with limited authority. The most recent rules enacted on this matter require the *società fiduciaria* to vote at any company meeting according to the written instructions of its client. The client is actually the owner of the shares even if the name of the *società fiduciarie* appears on the share-certificate and in the register of shareholders of the company.

In all the situations mentioned in this section, the creditors of the owner can attach the assets placed under the control of the professional manager or *società fiduciaria*.

4. *Nominee accounts*

Nominee or fiduciary accounts are not recognised by Italian law. A fungible asset which is added to a person's patrimony loses its identity and can no longer be singled out.

In the most common case of a sum of money entrusted to a professional who is to deposit it with a bank until an event occurs, the professional becomes the owner of the money irrespective of whether he opens a specially-designated account or mingles that money with his own.

More generally, one cannot segregate a fungible asset except physically. For instance, if a sum of money entrusted to a professional is not deposited with a bank but is kept in a sealed envelope bearing appropriate marks, the obligation on the professional is not to repay that amount of money. Instead he must give back the very banknotes which were deposited with him. In the typical case of a professional who is asked to deposit money with his bank and perhaps purchase State bonds in order to obtain a yield for the duration of the deposit, the money becomes his; but he is bound (either to the party who entrusted the money to him or to the party to whom the money or part of it will belong upon the occurrence of a specified condition) to repay the sum of money with any accrued interest.

This is a debt which enjoys no particular form of protection. Any third party to whom the professional owes money can seize the professional's bank accounts, regardless of the origin of the funds.

5. *Special cases of segregation*

In some quite common cases, the mingling of certain assets with others belonging to the same person is prevented. These run against the widely held prejudice that in civil law countries a notion of unitary patrimony exists which admits of no exception.

- When a life annuity is granted to a beneficiary by way of gift the grantor may provide that the creditors of the beneficiary cannot attach it other than for those amounts which exceed the basic maintenance needs of the beneficiary (civil code, Article 1881).
- An heir is entitled to keep the deceased's estate (or that share of the estate which was left to him) separate from his own assets and proceed to pay the deceased's debts only through the sale of the assets which are

in the estate. Should those assets not be sufficient, he will not be liable for the difference (civil code, Articles 484 to 511).

- The creditors of the deceased are entitled to require that their debts be satisfied with the estate's assets, without confusing them within the heir's patrimony (civil code, Articles 512 to 518).
- A testamentary or *inter vivos* gift to a minor may include the appointment of a curator who will manage the asset until the minor comes of age. The powers ordinarily enjoyed by the parents of a minor are taken by the curator who is bound by the rules concerning tutors (civil code, Article 356).
- The executor under a will (civil code, Articles 700 to 712) bears a striking resemblance to a trustee or personal representative. The following rules apply to executors and trustees alike:
  - (a) If there are several executors they must always act together.
  - (b) The deceased may appoint a substitute executor in case the one named in the will cannot or will not accept the appointment.
  - (c) The executor may appoint someone else to take his place.
  - (d) The executor may be one of the beneficiaries under the will.
  - (e) The testamentary estate is vested in the executor, who enjoys full management powers ("vesting" refers here to "possession" not to title).
  - (f) He may be empowered to sell assets and to reinvest the proceeds.
  - (g) He must act as a *bonus paterfamilias.*
  - (h) He may be empowered to allocate the assets of the testamentary estate among the beneficiaries.
  - (i) He must consult with the beneficiaries before allocating the assets[2].
  - (j) Any act of the executor binds the estate.
  - (k) When there is a disagreement among the executors they may apply to the court for directions.
  - (l) The executor must provide account for the assets.
  - (m) The executors are jointly liable for their acts.
  - (n) An executor may be removed from office by the court "if he behaves in such a way as to impair the trust"[3].
  - (o) The office of the executor is by nature a gratuitous one but the testator may burden the estate with a fee payable to the executor.

2 This corresponds with the new English statutory rule in respect of trusts of land.

3 "*[P]er aver commesso azione che ne menomi la fiducia*": civil code, Article 710.

(p) Any expense incurred by the executor is charged to the estate.
(q) The executor may be granted discretionary powers (possibly wider than those of a trustee).
(r) The executor is a fiduciary.

6. *Case law developments*[4]

Unilaterally declared bare trusts are not uncommon in Italian case law. The fact situations often correspond to cases of resulting trusts under English law, namely when property is purchased by X with money provided by Y for that purpose. The reported cases almost invariably concern family arrangements relating to real estate, and X has always been held to be bound to transfer the property to Y provided that a written statement by X is shown, under which he acknowledges the provenance of the money and his obligation to transfer title to Y. Writing is, of course, unnecessary for a resulting trust under English law, so that cases of this sort would probably be seen either as express trusts declared by the trustee or as trusts of the money given by Y to X and applied by X to the purchase of the property.

Two decisions of the *Corte di cassazione* in 1988 and 1990 have opened the way to as yet unfathomable developments. In both instances the defendant had taken upon himself to manage assets belonging to the plaintiff: the uncle for his young nephews in one case, the husband for his wife in the other. In both instances title to the assets stood in the name of the defendant and there was no written agreement nor acknowledgement of any kind by the defendant. In both instances the claims by the plaintiffs were upheld.

One can easily see that a "constructive trust" type of situation might come to be recognised. The reasoning of the *Corte di cassazione*, particularly in the 1988 case, where the trust existing between spouses was stressed, suggest that fiduciary obligations might arise without any formal declaration, let alone a written document, whenever the relationship between the parties is such that the defendant cannot avail himself of the ordinary rules concerning proof of title.

4 For a discussion of the cases referred to in this section see my book, *supra* note 1, pp. 554-568.

C. Proposals for further developments of trusts

I submit that the Hague Convention allows citizens of member states to form trusts governed by a foreign law. That applies equally to citizens of states which know trusts as an institution of general application and to citizens of states which know no instance of trusts or only limited instances.

Article 6 of the Convention ("A trust shall be governed by the law chosen by the settlor") covers any trust, including one which presents no connection with the law which the settlor has chosen as the governing law. The choice made by the settlor is not conditional upon the trust being international in character[5]. Contrary to a widely-held belief, the Hague Convention has nothing to do with "international trusts", nor with trust characterised by a foreign element. The only foreign element which the Convention requires is that the law governing a trust be a foreign law (that is, foreign with respect to the forum)[6].

I am strongly against any wide-ranging legislation on trusts, be it based on the Principles or otherwise. The proper way to develop trusts in Italy is to resort to trusts which, although "Italian" in their subject matter and as to the parties involved, are governed by a foreign law. No less than 80 trusts of this sort have been formed in Italy in the last three years and favourable judicial notice has been taken of two of them[7].

A proposal currently being discussed by the Italian Parliament would make it compulsory for members of the government to transfer their assets to a trust. Although the possibility of more general legislation on trusts was discussed, the final text of the proposal refers to trusts governed by a foreign law. That is a good sign. The idea that the Hague Convention makes it possible to form domestic trusts under a foreign law is gaining acceptance.

5 See the Explanatory Report, nos. 65-66.

6 For a full treatment of this position see my essay Effects of the Hague Convention in a Civil Law Country, in P. Jackson and D.C. Wilde (edd), The Reform of Property Law, Ashgate, 1997, p. 222.

7 See P. Matthews, Note, in 11 (1997) Tolley's Trust Law International 20.

National Report for France

Ph. Rémy*

A. Introduction

General

The trust is unknown in French law[1] for two basic reasons. Firstly, the notion of "split ownership" between trustee and beneficiary is contrary to the exclusive and absolute nature of the concept of ownership under French law (Article 544 of the Civil Code); the distinction between legal title and equitable title in the same property cannot be introduced in that form into our system of *in rem* rights[2]. Secondly, French law does not generally allow assets to be set aside for a special purpose (*patrimoine d'affectation*), thus ruling out the possibility of property forming a separate fund that cannot be reached by a trustee's creditors (*arg.* Article 2092 of the Civil Code). The Civil Code does not even mention the *fiducie* (which is not included among the special contracts listed therein) and there is no institution in French law similar to the "*fiduziarische Treuhand*" of German law. Recognising the disadvantages of this situation, the Ministry of Justice has devoted considerable time and effort to drafting a bill on the *fiducie*, which was introduced before the National Assembly in 1992[3]. It was

---

* Prof. Ph. Rémy is professor of Private law, University of Poitiers.

1 Lepaulle, *Traité théorique et pratique des trusts en droit interne, en droit fiscal et en droit international privé*, (A theoretical and practical treatise on trusts in domestic law, tax law and private international law), Rousseau, 1932; Motulsky, *De l'impossibilité juridique de constituer un trust anglo-saxon sous l'empire de la loi française*, (The legal impossibility of creating a common law trust under French law), Rev. Crit. DIP 1948, 451; Oppetit, *Le trust dans le droit commercial international*, (The trust in international commercial law), Rev. Crit. DIP 1973, 1; Bredin, *L'évolution du trust dans la jurisprudence française*, (Evolution of the trust in French case law), Trav. Comité Fr. DIP, 1973-75, 137; Aubert, Rep. Dr. International, Vo. Trust; Béraudo, *Les trusts anglo-saxons et le droit français*, (Common law trusts and French law), LGDJ 1992.

2 For a discussion on this point, see section C *infra*.

3 Bill AN No. 2583, filed on 20 February 1992, creating the *fiducie*. See C *infra* on this bill.

subsequently removed from the order of business in 1995 for reasons which remain obscure, but which may have included a fear of fraud and tax evasion. The current government does not appear to consider this reform a priority.

Recognition of trusts created under foreign law

The fact that the trust is unknown in French domestic law does not prevent recognition of trusts which are properly created under the foreign law that applies according to our conflict of laws rules. However, giving effect to trusts under foreign law cannot be done without distorting them. At least until implementation of the Hague Convention of 1 July 1985, concerning the choice and recognition of the law applicable to trusts[4], the solution adopted by the courts is that a trust is considered "an essentially bilateral contract" (between the settlor and the trustee) which may give rise to rights in favour of third parties (the beneficiaries); accordingly, the trust is governed by the law chosen by the parties (even where this must be implied), which makes it possible to accord broad recognition to the validity of common law trusts[5]. But viewing the trust as a contract clearly distorts the nature of the trust.

As the validity of the trust is largely upheld by reliance on the rule that the parties' intent prevails, the business of ascertaining the effects of a trust in France can result in additional distortions. The fact that the trust is so foreign to the categories into which French domestic law is organised prevents straightforward recognition in France of the effects of the trust under applicable foreign law. Because there is no comparable category in domestic law, the trust is "adapted" for various purposes. Since the trust has widely diverse uses, how it is adapted varies, depending on the purpose sought to be achieved by the trust in each individual case: thus, the trust has been treated as an agency agreement or mandate, the appointment of an executor in a will, a *fiducie*, a gift upon condition, a gift over (*substitution fidéicommissaire*), an indirect gift, etc. A quick glance at case law reveals that this process of adaptation does not generally interfere

4 Comments: Gaillard and Trautman, Rev. Crit. Dr. Int. Pr. 1985, 1; Revillard, Rep. Not. Defrénois 1986.689; Jauffret-Spinosi, J.D.I. 1987, 23; Béraudo, No. 373 *et seq.*

5 Paris, 10 January 1970, *Epoux Courtois v. Cons. de Ganay*, D. 1972.122, note Malaurie; Rev. Crit. D.I.P. 1971.518, note Droz; J.D.I. 1973.207, note Loussouarn.

with the trustee's exercise of his powers, but that French courts will see to it that the trust does not infringe the basic principles of the law of property (assignability and liability to attachment), or the law of inheritance (especially the portion of an estate set aside by statute for certain heirs); in this way, the rights of third parties (creditors and heirs - *la réserve héréditaire*) are protected[6]. If necessary, the court will seek to determine whether the settlor's choice of foreign law was an attempt to fraudulently evade the application of French law; the case law on testamentary trusts provides a number of very clear examples of this.

The approach taken by the French courts is clearly open to challenge from a theoretical standpoint. Firstly, it is incorrect to consider that the trust "essentially constitutes a bilateral contract" between the settlor and the trustee; this is a "misleading characterisation" solely designed to permit the application of the law chosen by the parties[7]. Secondly, treating a trust as if it were the same thing as, or even similar to, a domestic law institution in order to control its effects is extremely difficult, and the results are highly unpredictable for the settlor. Implementation of the Hague Convention would represent a major advance in this area (see section no. 4 *infra* on the process of adapting the trust to the requirements of domestic law).

B. Existing law

1. *Fiducie*

Because it is not mentioned in the Civil Code, the *fiducie* has long been forgotten, and only recently resurfaced in French law with Mr. Witz's remarkable thesis[8]. Many fiduciary transactions thus appear under the guise of unnamed agreements, or achieve their objectives by circuitous

6 Béraudo, No. 350 *et seq.*

7 Lequette, *De l'ordre de réduction des libéralités réalisées au moyen d'un trust entre vifs*, (Concerning the reduction of gifts by means of an *inter vivos* trust), D. 1996, Chron. 231.

8 Witz, *La fiducie en droit privé français*, (The *fiducie* in private French law), Pref. Schmidt, Economica 1981.

routes. One finds express *fiducies* or "crypto-*fiducies*" which perform exactly the same roles as the trust in commercial, family or charitable matters.

2. *Commercial uses of the trust*

The roles played by the *inter vivos* trust in business are filled by a broad variety of mechanisms. Practices have developed in the banking and securities field of using the *fiducie* for management purposes (*fiducia cum amico*) or to provide security (*fiducia cum creditore*); some agreements, like agreements for the holding of securities, involve both types of *fiducie* at the same time.

a. Fiducia cum amico

Since the legislature has not seen fit to create a *fiducie* for management purposes, the only solution appears to be the agency agreement. But an agency agreement does not place property beyond the reach of the principal's creditors, nor does it grant any but the most limited powers to the agent. In addition, it does not prevent the principal from recovering control of the assets from the agent (even where it has been stipulated that the agent's appointment is irrevocable). Thus, the agency agreement is not suited to the active, long-term management of assets, especially when those assets include negotiable securities. Thus, in order to fill these management roles, the legislature and business practitioners have developed various procedures which contain the core "fiduciary concept" as recognised by the commentators, but in a variety of different guises.

UCITS[9]

In order to divert savings towards the stock exchange, the legislature has created a variety of different types of undertakings for collective investment in transferable securities (UCITS) *(OPCVMs)*[10]. A reform bill enacted on 23 December 1988 overhauled the entire system governing these undertakings and strengthened the oversight authority of the *Commission*

9 Undertaking for Collective Investment in Transferable Securities.
10 *Organisme de placement collectif en valeurs mobilières.*

des Opérations de Bourse (COB). We will introduce the two basic types of UCITS here, neither of which constitutes a *fiducie*.

The first type of UCITS is the open-ended investment company, or *SICAV*[11]. The *SICAV* is a French limited company (*société anonyme*) whose sole object is the management of a portfolio of securities (Article 2). The company's assets are placed in the hands of a sole custodian who is separate from the company and is picked from a list drawn up by the Minister of the Economy (Article 3). Thus, the investor is a shareholder. The return on the investment, and the price of the share, depend on the investments made by the company. The rules governing the running of the company depart from the ordinary law governing *sociétés anonymes*, especially having regard to shareholders' meetings, which are largely fictitious in nature (Article 4).

A second form of UCITS is the mutual fund (*FCP*[12]), which is a joint tenancy (and hence not a legal entity) for the holding of securities. The securities are managed by a specialised commercial company (Article 12) and are deposited with a custodian chosen from a list drawn up by the Minister of Finance (Article 13). The joint tenancy, however, is governed by rules which depart from the ordinary law rules governing joint tenancies (Article 7): the shareholders do not have the power to manage the undivided shares, and cannot cause the fund to be partitioned (Article 9). In addition, they are only liable for the debts of the joint tenancy up to the assets in the fund (Article 10). Similarly, the agency agreement with the management company represents a substantial departure from the ordinary law of agency: it is absolutely irrevocable, and includes the general power to make dispositions. The "contortions" that are required to cope with the fact that the trust is unknown in the French legal system are quite amazing.

Pension funds

The prospects of the current pay-as-you-go pension system are highly uncertain. As a result, a bill enacted on 25 March 1997 created "retirement

11 *Société d'investissement à capital variable.*
12 *Fonds commun de placement.*

savings plans" which enable employees in the private sector to build up retirement funds. These retirement savings plans, which are often called "pension funds", do not employ a trust-like approach, rather, they borrow from the insurance industry: the employee joins a group insurance policy taken out by the employer. The employer and the employee's contributions are paid into a retirement savings fund, which is a legal entity in the form of an insurance company, the sole object of which is to pay the supplementary retirement annuity. The business of individual retirement insurance is already well developed (or mixed life-death insurance). In my view, adopting the *fiducie* or trust as a vehicle for the management of retirement insurance would not be of any particular interest, from a practical standpoint.

Temporary transfers of securities

Businesses have developed agreements which provide for the "holding" of securities, and allow securities to be transferred on a temporary basis[13]. The "holder" (generally a financial institution) obtains securities from the "originator" or a third party which undertakes to assign them on a given date and for a given price, to a beneficiary - who is often the originator himself, but who can also be a third party designated in the agreement. The securities "held" are thus temporarily owned by the "holder", but do not, however, constitute a segregated fund.

An agreement of this type can be used for a wide variety of purposes. These include: 1) financing transactions, by which the banker-holder acquires ownership of the securities as security ("holding for security"); 2) a way of delaying the transfer of control to heirs who are too young or inexperienced; 3) preparing for a listing by a capital increase underwritten by a financial institution, which will then market the shares to the public; 4) transferring a bond portfolio to an *ad hoc* company that will be responsible for using the interest on the "held" securities to repay some of the originator's debts ("defeasance"); 5) "discreetly" acquiring an equity interest in a company (there are, however, "transparency" requirements designed to prevent the concealed "accumulation" of listed securities).

13 Lucas, *Les transferts temporaires de valeurs mobilières - Pour une fiducie de valeurs mobilières*, (Temporary transfers of securities - Toward a *fiducie* for securities), L.G.D.J. 1997, Pref. Lorvellec.

b. *Fiducia cum creditore*

Here, the uses of the *fiducie* (*fiducie* for security) are generally more straightforward. The development of the use of ownership to provide security was hampered in France by a number of factors. These were theoretical (the impossibility of making ownership an incident of a debt or claim, the *numerus clausus* theory of *in rem* security interests), practical (how security interests are reported and published), and economic in nature (the squandering of the debtor's credit, and the harmful effects of this type of security interest for ailing firms). Until quite recently, the transfer of title to a *fiduciaire* in order to provide security has been overlooked in favour of more "advanced" types of security interests (i.e. pledges and mortgages); however, the extent to which modern bankruptcy law has undermined those "advanced" security interests has brought about a return to transfers of title to a *fiduciaire*; ownership of property as security is a rudimentary form of security interest, but it is effective (which also explains the success of retention of title clauses in contracts of sale and leases with an option to purchase)[14]. The *fiducie* to provide security will remain suspect until a law is enacted to make it generally available, as it can be viewed as a way of circumventing the prohibition against clauses entitling the pledgee to keep the pledged chattel in the event of non-payment *(pacte commissoire)* (Article 2078 para. 2 of the Civil Code). In addition, even if they were recognised, *fiducies* to provide security would not result in segregation of the transferred property from the *fiduciaire's* other assets.

Transfer of ownership of business receivables to a fiduciaire as security

This type of *fiducie* for security purposes is clearly allowed by the Act of 2 January 1981, known as the Dailly Act (*Loi Dailly*) (as amended by the Act of 24 January 1984), which governs the assignment of business receivables as security. It provides a simplified procedure for the (undisclosed) assignment of all present or future business receivables to a credit institution. The transfer is effectuated by delivery to the transferee of a statement which lists the assigned receivables. It is enforceable against third parties as from the date of the statement, and notice need not be

14 Cabrillac and Mouly, *Les sûretés*, (Security interests), 1997, No. 527 *et seq.*

given to the debtors. The assignee lending institution may allow the assignor to collect the debts as its agent; on the other hand, it may order debtors not to pay the assignor. Finally, it may secure a waiver from the debtors of any defences which they could raise against the assignor. There is discussion in the literature of the possibility of making transfers of receivables to *fiduciaires* widely available.

"Pawning" of bills

"Pawning" of bills, or the deposit of bills as collateral security, involves an agreement by which a legal entity, generally a mutual fund or a securitised debt fund, temporarily assigns commercial paper (or negotiable debt securities, government or private paper) to a lending institution which pays for them. The assignment is coupled with a two-fold, irrevocable undertaking: the assignor undertakes to buy back the assigned securities at a given price on a given date, whilst the assignee undertakes to sell the securities back to the assignor. The difference between the selling price and the resale price is the assignee's fee. Long governed by banking practice (the "*convention de place*"), today this type of transaction is governed by the Act of 31 December 1993. There was some hesitation over how this type of agreement should be classified: after having decided that it was a loan secured by a pledge, or a sale with a right of redemption (Article 1659 *et seq.* of the Civil Code), commentators today prefer to classify it as a type of *fiducie*.

Transfer of ownership of a sum of money to a fiduciaire

The transfer of ownership of a sum of money to a *fiduciaire* is controversial. Assuming that it is permitted, the advantages of a *fiducie* for security involving a sum of money over those of a pledge of cash appear slight for, with this type of pledge, the courts will uphold an agreement authorising the pledgee to keep the pledged sum in the event of non-payment.

Transfer of ownership of other property to a fiduciaire

Because there is no law authorising the *fiducie* in general, a *fiducie* for security purposes that involves other property (personal or real) would no doubt be viewed with some suspicion by the courts. It could be considered an agreement designed to conceal a pledge in which the pledgee was entitled to retain the pledged property in the event of non-payment *(pacte commissoire)* (Article 2078 of the Civil Code). This is why, in practice, the transfer of ownership to a *fiduciaire* is often replaced with a sale with a right of redemption. Sales with a right of redemption or repurchase are allowed by the Civil Code (Article 1659 *et seq.* of the Civil Code) for up to five years (Article 1660 of the Civil Code). The lender-creditor purchases property from the borrower at a price equal to the amount of a loan, coupled with a right of repurchase in the borrower at a price that reflects repayment of the loan with interest. But this procedure may well be held fraudulent in light of the prohibition against a pledge accompanied by a right to retain the pledged property in the event of non-payment *(pacte commissoire)*.

3. *Family uses of the trust*

Under French law, the role of the trust in family law is filled by special types of *inter vivos* or testamentary gifts via an intermediary. Title in the property may vest in the intermediary, along with the responsibility to manage it and pass it on (*fideicommis* and *fiducie*), or the intermediary may merely be charged with administering the property, without actually owning it (as agent or executor)[15].

Fideicommis and fiducie for purposes of a gift

Gifts subject to an obligation to pass them on are extremely limited by the public policy rules governing inheritances. Firstly, they are limited by the laws which set aside a portion of the deceased's estate for certain heirs. Secondly, they are restricted by the prohibition against agreements concerning future estates (Article 1130 para. 2 of the Civil Code). Finally, they are limited by the serious restrictions on gifts over.

Gifts over are prohibited as a rule (Article 896 of the Civil Code): even when limited to the disposable portion of an estate, a bequest or devise of property cannot be made to a "life tenant" for his lifetime, subject to an obligation to pass it on to another person upon his death ("the remainder-

15 Grimaldi, *La fiducie; réflexions sur l'institution et sur l'avant-projet qui la consacre*, (The *fiducie*: Reflections on the institution and the *fiducie* bill), Rep. Notariat Defrénois, 1991, 897 and 962.

man"). Even under the *Ancien Régime*, an effort was made to limit *fideicommis*; the Revolution and the Civil Code prohibited them in order to promote the splitting up of family fortunes in real estate, and the free movement of goods and property. As an exception, gifts over are allowed in favour of the donor or testator's grandchildren, or the nephews and nieces of a testator who dies without issue (Article 1048 and 1049 of the Civil Code). When permitted, gifts over may only be made to the next generation ("generation-skipping" gifts over are prohibited), must be limited to the disposable portion, and must inure equally to the benefit of all of the life tenant's children (Article 1050 of the Civil Code). The gift over is thus a highly imperfect means of achieving one of the goals of the family trust; preventing the family fortune from being split up. The restrictions on gifts over are more or less circumvented by bequests or devises with an obligation to pass on the property, but without an obligation to preserve it (bequests or devises *de residuo* or *de eo quod supererit*), or by vesting the right of *usufruct* in one beneficiary, and "bare" ownership (*nue proprieté*) in another (Article 899 of the Civil Code).

The method of transferring title which most closely resembles the *fiducie* is a gift upon condition in which a donor or testator gives, bequeaths or devises all or part of his property to a person, subject to an obligation to administer it, and deliver it at the agreed time to a beneficiary. The donor or testator generally prohibits the beneficiary or donee from disposing of the property given, bequeathed or devised, or only authorises sales for valuable consideration provided that the proceeds are reinvested in specific property (real estate, negotiable securities), and requires the donee or beneficiary either to accumulate the income, or pay it out periodically to the ultimate beneficiary. The fact that the property is inalienable means that it cannot be reached by the creditors of the legatee or devisee, or those of the intermediate donee. This type of gift does not fall under the prohibition against the grant of a life estate with a remainder, because the testator or donee was not seeking to control the inheritance of his property by succeeding generations. But the inalienability clause is subject to the conditions set out in Article 900-1 of the Civil Code: the prohibition against alienation must be justified by "a serious, legitimate interest" and can only be temporary (and necessarily shorter than the intermediary's lifetime). This procedure is used, in particular, to provide for the management of the estate of a beneficiary who must be protected against himself; however, it apparently cannot be used to circumvent the rules applicable in the case of guardianship or limited guardianship of a person lacking legal capacity, be he a minor or an adult: one may only give, bequeath or devise property to the minor provided that it is administered by a third party (Article 389-3 of the Civil Code) - but the third party administrator has no temporary ownership of the property, and thus is not a *fiduciaire.*

The real obstacle to using the *fiducie* in as many and varied ways as the trust is not technical, rather, it is due to considerations of social policy: public policy rules governing inheritances, the free movement of goods, and the need to protect the property of persons lacking legal capacity.

Executors and special personal representatives

Instead of title in the property vesting in the intermediary (as donee, legatee or devisee), the intermediary may receive the property as executor or special personal representative (*mandataire post mortem*). Here we are even further removed from the trust, since the executor and the representative do not own the property that is to be passed on. These procedures are subject to fewer restrictions, but they are not as effective as a gift subject to an obligation to pass it on.

The executor's appointment only lasts one year from the testator's death (Article 1026 of the Civil Code), and he does not begin to have the necessary authority to administer the property: the appointment of an executor is a process designed to dispose of the inheritance, and not a mechanism for the administration of inherited property.

The appointment of a special personal representative is permitted (notwithstanding Article 2003 of the Civil Code). More often than not, however, he is only appointed to perform specific acts, which he began while the principal was still alive (*arg.* Article 1991 para. 2 of the Civil Code); the actual appointment of a special representative to perform acts following the principal's death must be a special appointment and cannot infringe or impair the rights of the principal's heirs. Indeed, the heirs can dismiss the representative (Article 2004 of the Civil Code), or, as owners, recover administration of the property entrusted to the representative at any time.

Trust-like aspects of life insurance

As a practical matter, the role of the trust in providing for family members is increasingly being filled by life insurance, which enjoys special tax treatment and a considerable degree of autonomy from the rules applicable to inheritance and marital property. The principal sum or annuity paid to the beneficiary are not subject to the rules governing inheritance (in principle, said sums are not reincorporated into the estate before it is divided up among the heirs, nor do they give rise to any reduction on grounds of impairment of the reserved portion of the estate). In addition, they are not subject to the rules governing marital property (in principle, a husband or wife who is a policyholder does not owe anything to the community of property which paid the premiums). In addition, the beneficiary clause can be drafted in such a way as to grant a *usufruct* of the principal sum to one beneficiary, and bare ownership to another. As is the case with pension funds, in our system, life insurance fulfils some of the roles played by the trust in common law countries.

4. *Charitable trusts*

The charitable functions of the trust are generally handled either by gifts to existing legal entities (generally associations), or by the creation of a legal entity to whom the testator or donor gives the property required to achieve the desired goal (foundation). The prohibition against gifts to persons unknown does not preclude gifts to classes of ascertainable persons, and the Code itself allows gifts to "the poor of a municipality" (Article 937 of the Civil Code).

Gifts to existing associations

The traditional suspicion with which French law views associations and property in mortmain is reflected by the following principles: 1) the only associations which are entitled to receive gifts are associations which advance or promote the public welfare and are recognised as such (Act of 1901, Article 11), associations which are merely registered, but whose sole purpose is the helping the needy, the performance of charitable works, or scientific research (Act of 1901, Article 6), or religious associations (Act of 1905, Article 19 para. 4); 2) any gift to such associations requires authorisation by the authorities (Article 910 of the Civil Code and the Decree of 13 June 1966).

Foundations

The term "foundation" either refers to the irrevocable grant of assets to an institution which advances or promotes the public welfare, by means of a gift on condition made to an existing legal entity or, more specifically, the creation by the testator or donee of a new legal entity which is given the property needed to accomplish the desired objective (Article 18 Act of 23 July 1987). The second procedure has long been hampered by the inability of unborn persons to receive gifts (Article 906 of the Civil Code), and by the suspicion with which French law views mortmain alienations and collectivities; use of this procedure requires recognition in the form of a decree by the *Conseil d'Etat* that the foundation is operating to advance or promote the public welfare. Today, foundations are governed by a patchwork of provisions (Act of 23 July 1987 on Patronage, Act of 4 July 1990 on Corporate Foundations, Act of 2 July 1996 on Heritage Foundations, tax regulations and decisions by the *Conseil d'Etat*). The *Fondation de France* is authorised to receive and redistribute gifts made in the public interest, and not for profit (Decree of 9 November 1969) and enjoys certain tax benefits: thus, it acts as a genuine intermediary for the passage of title, and in the contemporary literature it is viewed as a type of *fiduciaire.* Of course, these gifts are subject to the standard rules that govern gifts, in particular, compliance with the requirements governing that portion of an estate which the law sets aside for the heirs. It is often suggested that the system of rules governing foundations should be liberalised, but there can be no question of using the foundation as a legal entity for any purpose other than the administration and distribution of assets on a non-profit basis to promote the public welfare.

C. Further development

Effect of the Hague Convention on the adaptation of the trust to domestic law

By applying the Hague Convention, French courts will doubtless develop a better understanding of the concept of the trust. This does not, however, mean that this institution will be introduced into French domestic law.

The Convention will certainly teach French courts something about trusts: "the first purpose of the Hague Convention is to explain the trust to those countries in which it is unknown"[16]. In general, French courts will no longer have to distort the trust in order to give it effect. Firstly, pursuant to Article 6 of the Convention the trust deed will be considered a unilateral act by the settlor, and not a contract. This is a conceptual advance. Secondly, in the absence of a real definition, Article 2 and 11 of the Convention will provide a clear description of the key elements of the trust and the trust system. As a general matter, this will avoid the current distortion of the trust by the courts in order to adapt it to French requirements.

In my view, however, it is doubtful that the French interpretation of the Convention will be as accepting of the trust as has been the case in Italy, according to Mr. Lupoi. In theory, a settlor could choose to have a purely "domestic" trust (a trust located in France, with a French settlor, a French trustee and a French beneficiary) governed by the laws of a foreign country in which trusts are used. Under Article 6, significant contacts with more than one country are not a prerequisite for choosing the law that will govern the trust. In my view, however, it is likely that the safeguard provisions of Article 13 will apply in that situation. Article 13 permits non-recognition of a trust which has more significant contacts with States to which the institution of the trust is foreign[17]. Thus, I do not believe that we should anticipate that the Convention will result in the trust actually being introduced into French domestic law.

---

16 C. Jauffret-Spinosi, *La Convention de la Haye relative à la loi applicable au trust et à sa reconnaissance*, (The Hague Convention on the law applicable to the trust, and its recognition), J.D.I. 1987. 23 *et seq.*

17 Jauffret-Spinosi, Op. Cit. 40-41.

Towards a fiducie with a segregated corpus?

Recently rediscovered[18] the *fiducie* has won over notaries, bankers and securities dealers alike. Well aware of the risk that trust business will shift overseas, and of the competition from trusts in common law countries[19], they have convinced the government of the need for legislative reform. A 1992 bill aimed at adding a Title 16 bis, entitled "Concerning Fiducies", to Book III of the Civil Code. The bill, which would have added twenty articles to the Code, was withdrawn for reasons which remain obscure, but which apparently included a fear of tax evasion. A recent Senate report has given the bill new life[20] but its future remains uncertain. The *fiducie* is conceived as a *fiducie* for purposes of management (*fiducia cum amico*) and to provide security (*fiducia cum creditore*). The bill enriches the Roman law tradition underlying the *fiducie* by borrowing from the trust the notion that the trust *corpus* must be segregated from the *fiduciaire*'s assets[21]. Although this approach has been criticised[22], it probably represents the most that French law can do to adapt an institution which is similar to the trust.

Consistent with Roman law tradition, the *fiducie* is defined as a contract by which a *constituant* (settlor) transfers all or part of his property to a *fiduciaire* (trustee) who "acts with a specific aim in favour of one or more

18 Witz, *La fiducie en droit privé français*, (The *fiducie* in French law), Pref. D. Schmidt, Economica 1981; *Colloque de Luxembourg sur Les Opérations fiduciaires*, (Luxembourg colloquium on transactions involving *fiducies*), L.G.D.J. 1985. Grimaldi, *La Fiducie: réflexions sur l'avant-projet de loi qui la consacre*, (The *fiducie*: Reflections on the *fiducie* bill), Rep. Not. Defrénois, 1991. 897 and 962. Jauffret-Spinosi, *Trust et fiducie, Droit et vie des affaires*, (Trust and *fiducies*, legal and commercial aspects), *Etudes à la mémoire d'Alain Sayag*, (Papers submitted in memory of Alain Sayag), Litec 1997, 329.

19 J. de Guillenschmidt, *Présentation de l'avant-projet de loi relatif à la fiducie*, (Presentation of the bill on *fiducies*), Rev. Dr. Bancaire et Bourse 1990.105 et *La France sans la fiducie?*, (France without the *fiducie*?), Rev. Jurispr. Com. 1991.49. Scholefield, Dom *et al.* (edd), *Le trust, instrument au service de l'entreprise et du patrimoine*, (The trust, a tool in the service of business and estates), Rev. de Droit bancaire et de la Bourse, No. 56 July-August 1996.

20 *Rapport Marini sur la modernisation du droit des sociétés*, (Marini report on the modernisation of company law), 1996.

21 Larroumet, *La fiducie inspirée du trust*, (The *fiducie*, inspired by the trust), D. 1990. 119.

22 Cantin-Cumyn, *L'avant-projet de loi relatif à la fiducie, un point de vue civiliste d'outre-atlantique*, (The *fiducie* bill: a North American civil law viewpoint), D. 1992, Chron. 117.

beneficiaries" (Article 2062 of the bill) and whose powers are fixed by the agreement for a term of no more than 99 years (Article 2063 of the bill). The agreement must be in writing and include certain mandatory information and, if it is designed to effect a gratuitous transfer, it must be notarised (Article 2063 of the bill). Where the *fiducie* involves property the transfer of which must be registered (e.g. real property), the *fiducie* must include the name of the *fiduciaire* in his official capacity (Article 2070 of the bill). The transfer removes the property from the assets of the *constituant*; he no longer has control or disposition over the property, and his creditors can no longer reach it, except by exercising their *droit de suite*, or right to take possession of the collateral (if they are secured creditors), or where there has been fraud (for unsecured creditors). When the *fiducie* is being used to effect a gratuitous transfer, the portion of the *constituant's* estate set aside by law for his heirs under the rules of intestacy is protected by an action in abatement (Article 2070-3 *et seq.* to 2070-8 of the bill).

Defining the *fiducie* as a contract necessarily makes it more unlike the trust. 1) One cannot enter into a contract with oneself; the *constituant* accordingly cannot be the *fiduciaire*, whereas the settlor can be the trustee. 2) When the *fiducie* is designed to provide security, the *fiduciaire* can also be the sole *bénéficiaire* (Article 2062 para. 3 of the bill), whereas the trustee cannot at the same time be the sole beneficiary. 3) Where the *bénéficiaire* is a third party, his position is that of a third-party beneficiary of a contract conferring a right on a person not a party thereto (*une stipulation pour autrui*) (Article 1121 of the Civil Code) and he accordingly has a claim against the *fiduciaire*. The bill goes beyond the ordinary law of contracts which confer rights on third parties by allowing the *bénéficiaire* to apply to a court to have the *fiduciaire* replaced, or to have the *fiducie* dissolved (Article 2070-1 of the bill). Whether the *bénéficiaire* will have an *in rem* right over the assets transferred to the *fiduciaire* is still undecided (*see infra*). 4) The *fiduciaire* is subject to contractual obligations toward the *fiduciant* (settlor), who has standing to apply for replacement of the *fiduciaire* or termination of the *fiducie* (Article 2070-1 of the bill) and to bring an action for damages in the event that the *fiducie* is not performed, or is improperly performed; unlike in the case of an agency agreement, however, a *fiducie* cannot be revoked by the *constituant* alone. 5) Court enforcement of the performance of a *fiducie* is subject to the ordinary rules governing contracts: it requires an application by the *constituant* or the *bénéficiaire*, which cannot be aimed at amending the content of the contract, even to adapt it to changed circumstances (Article 1134 of the Civil Code). Substantial differences with the trust thus remain.

The bill, however, brings the *fiducie* closer to the trust by providing that the assets transferred to the *fiduciaire* will remain "separate from his personal property" (Article 2062 para. 1 of the bill); the *fiduciaire* must take all necessary action to avoid commingling of the transferred assets with his own property or with other assets under a *fiducie* (Article 2069 of the bill). Thus, the private creditors of the *fiduciaire* cannot reach the *corpus* of the *fiducie* except where their claims arise in connection with the management of that *corpus* (Article 2069 of the bill). Although the bill does not address the issue, it is likely that the *fiducie's* creditors will not have an action against the private property of the *fiduciaire* except in the case of commingled assets. If the *fiduciaire* dies, the corpus of the *fiducie* is not included in his estate (Article 2070-2 of the bill) and is not subject to the marital property rules applicable to him. The corpus of the *fiducie* thus constitutes a veritable "segregated corpus" in the hands of the *fiduciaire*.

It is clear that this *fiducie* bill, which provides for a separate corpus, represents a radical departure from the Roman law concept of the *fiducie*, thereby creating a new concept of ownership. Some commentators describe the *fiduciaire's* title as a type of "ownership with powers", an "ownership with duties" or an "ownership for a specific purpose", as opposed to "ownership of assets" or "economic ownership". The same assets can thus be subject to both of these different types of ownership at the same time. One could object that this would be precluded by the *numerus clausus* rule theory of rights *in rem*; although a majority of the commentators follow this principle, the issue is nevertheless a murky one in French law. The Code is not clear on this point (Article 543 of the Civil Code). A famous (but hoary) decision of the *Cour de Cassation* also formally rejected the rule of *numerus clausus* (the *Caquelard* decision, Req., 13 February 1834, S. 1834.1.205) and a substantial minority of contemporary authorities reject the rule[23].

---

23 Atlas, *Les biens*, (Property), 1991, No. 39; Malaurie and Aynès, *Les biens*, (Property), 1992, No. 355 s; Terré and Simler, *Les biens*, (Property), 1992, No. 41.

D. Commentary on the Principles article by article

A *fiducie* with a separate fund, as contemplated by the 1992 reform bill, would represent a reasonably acceptable way to introduce an institution similar to the voluntary trust into French law. Of course, this would require passage of the bill: neither contractual usage, nor judge-made law can create this type of *fiducie*. Using the reform bill as a basis, I will analyse the additional changes that the introduction of the Principles would require article by article, identifying those which I believe are appropriate.

Article I. Main characteristics of the trust

Paragraph (1)
The bill's *fiducie* with a separate fund matches the description of the trust in Article I in all but two significant respects:

a) In the French bill, the *constituant* cannot himself be the *fiduciaire;* this is because the *fiducie* is a contract. In order to satisfy Article I(1), one must: 1) allow a "*fiducie*" to be created by a unilateral act; and 2) consider that the *fiducie* fund constitutes a segregated fund in the hands of the *constituant.* This change is conceivable as a technical matter; although French law stresses the principle of indivisible ownership, it does contain a few exceptions to that rule: one is the limitation of the heir's liability for the debts of the estate to the amount of the net assets he actually receives (the *bénéfice d'inventaire* of the laws of inheritance), and more recently, the creation of the sole limited proprietorship (E.V.R.L., Act of 11 July 1985). But a "*fiducie* with oneself" would clearly be viewed with greater suspicion than the *fiducie* as contract. In light of the resistance encountered by the 1992 bill, I do not believe it would be expedient to go this far.

b) The trustee cannot be the sole beneficiary, whilst the *fiduciaire* can be the sole *bénéficiaire* (Article 2060 para. 3 of the bill). The principal cases in which the *fiducie* is used to provide security fall under this heading. It would be unacceptable to rule out this use of the *fiducie* in order to bring that institution into line with the rules governing trusts in common law countries.

Paragraph (2)
The bill does not provide for there being more than one *fiduciaire*, but there is nothing to prevent it. This could be viewed as a special case of undivided ownership (a "*fiducie* with co-ownership"). The system governing this type of ownership must be adjusted in order to make it easier to manage (and in particular, to avoid the rule of unanimity). In the event of the death of one of the *fiduciaries*, or the dissolution of a fiduciary which is a legal entity, one could rely on a provision in the bill which entitles the judge to take "all measures permitting the continuation of the contract" upon application by the *constituant* or the *bénéficiaire* (see Article 2070-10 of the bill), including by continuing the *fiducie* between the remaining *fiduciaires*, or replacing the deceased *fiduciaire*. The right to apply for continuation of the *fiducie* should also be granted to each of the remaining co-*fiduciaires*.

Paragraph (3)
The application of Article I(3) does not raise any problems as long as the *fiducie* fund is treated as a separate fund. The only requirement is that suitable formal rules and rules governing registration be developed to give notice to third parties which enter into contracts with the *fiduciaire*, as contemplated by the 1992 bill.

Article I(3) does not address the rights of the *constituant's* spouse, heirs or creditors. It is clear, however, that they will be protected by the marital property rules applicable to the *constituant*, the rules of inheritance and the rules developed to protect creditors' liens.

Paragraph (4)
How Article I(4) is applied will depend on how the *bénéficiaire's* position is conceived of.

Approach through tort and contract. As regards the *fiduciaire*, the *bénéficiaire* is in the position of a third-party beneficiary of a contractual provision *(stipulation pour autrui)*: as a result, he has a direct *in personam* right. Under the bill, this right entitles him not only to demand performance of the *fiducie* in his favour, but also to apply to have the *fiduciaire* replaced or the *fiducie* terminated in the event of material breach by the *fiduciaire*. The *bénéficiaire* would not have an action in detinue against a third party acquiring the property in bad faith, but rather an action for damages in tort. It is considered that a third party who takes part in a breach of contract is liable under Article 1382 and 1383 of the Civil Code (see Article VII *infra*).

Proprietary Approach. If we view fiduciary ownership as nothing more than a type of "ownership with powers" over assets specially earmarked for third parties, this would lead us to recognise that the *bénéficiaire* of "ownership of the asset" has an action to enforce a right *in rem* against the *fiduciaire* and third parties[24].

The registration system contemplated by the bill, especially in the area of real property, requires that the *fiduciaire* be identified in his official capacity, which makes the restrictions on the *fiduciaire*'s ownership enforceable against third parties. It does not, however, provide for identification of the *bénéficiaire*, despite the fact that this would be necessary if he were allowed an action to enforce a right *in rem* against third parties.

Article II. Creation of the trust

Subject to what has been said in relation to Article I(1) above, the application of this Article does not present any problems. It should, however, be noted that in French law, transfer of title is an immediate effect of the contract (without there being any need for a deed of conveyance or delivery of the thing). A *fiducie* is thus formed once the parties agree to do so, provided that the formal requirements applicable to contracts are met (a written document containing certain information, see Article 2063 of the bill). Neither registration nor acceptance by the *bénéficiaire* are required for a *fiducie* agreement to be formed. The *fiducie* must, however, be express (Article 2063 *in fine*); thus, the introduction of constructive trusts and implied trusts is not to be feared (moreover, they do not appear to be of any practical use in our legal system).

Article III. Trust fund

Paragraph (1)

Real subrogation (the legal fiction that one object in a group of assets takes on the legal qualities and purpose of the object it replaces) only applies by

24 Grimaldi, No. 58; contra, Jauffret-Spinosi, 340-341.

operation of law in the case of independent, separate groups of assets or estates. In order for real subrogation to apply, therefore, the *fiducie* fund must be viewed as an actual segregated fund, which seems to be the position taken in the 1992 bill. Failing this, the application of this Article would require an agreement between the *fiduciant* and the *fiduciaire* to deal with the disposal and reinvestment of trust property. Real subrogation is particularly necessary in the management of securities portfolios. The notion that the portfolio itself is a *de facto* estate is increasingly gaining acceptance today (see Article 29 of the Act of 3 January 1983, as amended by the Act of 2 July 1996 concerning pledges of financial instruments). A legislative enactment that expressly provides for real subrogation would, however, appear to be desirable. It would also be desirable to add an optional provision to deal with what happens to the proceeds of transferred assets.

Paragraph (2)

The 1992 bill contains provisions similar to Article III(2) (Article 2069 of the bill): the *fiducie* is immune to the claims of the *fiduciaire*'s creditors, with the exception of those whose claim arose in connection with the custody and management of the fund (Article 2069 of the bill). The assets placed in the *fiducie* are not included in the estate of the *fiduciaire* as an individual; in case of the dissolution of a *fiduciaire* which is a legal entity, the assets in the *fiducie* do not form part of the entity's distributable assets (Article 2070-2 of the bill).

Having regard to the rights of the *bénéficiaire* over the assets in the *fiducie*, these depend on whether they are considered rights *in rem*, or purely *in personam* rights (*supra*, I(4)). See Article IV(1) *infra* for a discussion of enforcement of powers in a trust for purposes.

Paragraph (3)

The 1992 bill provides that where there is more than one *fiducie*, the *fiduciaire* must take all appropriate measures to avoid commingling the property of the different *fiducies* (Article 2069 of the bill) or commingling the property of the *fiducie* with his own property. This segregation is one of the consequences of the doctrine of a separate fund. In the case of the management of a portfolio of securities by a *fiduciaire*, this "segregation" will be effected simply by the *fiduciaire* keeping separate accounts.

Pooling of assets raises different issues, depending on the situation. Where there is more than one *fiducie* formed in succession by the same parties and in favour of the same beneficiaries, it is of course possible to agree that the property of the different *fiducies* will be combined into a single pool. Where the beneficiaries of successive *fiducies* are different, I believe that pooling would be prohibited by Article 2069 of the bill. The same applies where there is one *fiducie* between a single *fiduciaire* and various *constituants*, containing fungible goods. In my view, pooling the property in the *fiducie* and the *fiduciaire's* personal property would also be ruled out by the bill. But the agreement could allow the *fiduciaire* to borrow from (or lend to) the *corpus* of the *fiducie*, provided that said *corpus* was separate from his personal property.

Article IV. Trusts for beneficiaries or for enforceable purposes

Paragraph (1)

The rules of Article IV(1) are similar to those of the bill (Article 2063, 3 of the bill) as regards the designation of beneficiaries. The bill specifies that the designated *bénéficiaire* cannot be changed once the *fiducie* agreement has been entered into. This rule can be understood as a transposition of the rules governing rights conferred by a contract on third parties; the third party's rights would only be irrevocable once he had accepted them. However, since the provision does not make any reference to acceptance by the *bénéficiaire*, one could also understand it to mean that the designation is irrevocable once the *constituant* and the *fiduciaire* have reached agreement.

The existence of a person with authority to enforce the trust does not present any problem since the *fiducie* is a contract that includes a right in favour of a third party: both the *constituant* as a party to the contract and the third party as the beneficiary of the right granted in the contract, have standing to seek enforcement of the *fiducie*.

Adding the trust for enforceable purposes to our law of foundations, which appears unusually rigid, would make it considerably more flexible. The appointment of an enforcer could be understood as the appointment of an agent by the *constituant*, which would require some changes to the rules governing the appointment of special personal representatives.

Paragraph (2)
According to the bill, any *fiducie* agreement that does not designate a *bénéficiaire* is null and void (Article 2063 of the bill). Designation of a *bénéficiaire* is an essential element of the agreement. However: 1) under the bill, it is enough if the agreement merely sets out the "rules for the designation" of beneficiaries; 2) there is nothing to prevent the making of alternative designations; a third party, failing which, the *constituant* himself. In addition, in the event that the agreement is unclear as to the designation of a *bénéficiaire,* the court has the power to interpret it in such manner as to effect its purposes (Article 1156 *et seq.* of the Civil Code). When the beneficiaries themselves die during the life of the *fiducie,* the property reverts to the *constituant* or to his heirs and assigns (Article 2070-11 of the bill).

Paragraph (3)
The right to information contemplated by Article IV(3) is not the right to be informed of the performance of the trustee's duties (which is covered by Article V(3)), but the right of the *bénéficiaire* to be informed having regard to the existence of a trust created for his benefit. Under the system of the *fiducie* granting a right to a third party *(avec stipulation pour autrui),* this rule is not automatic and will require a special provision.

Paragraph (4)
The *bénéficiaire's* disposition of his rights follows from the general principle that persons have the right freely to dispose of their proprietary interests.

Approach through contract. If we consider the *bénéficiaire* as nothing more than a creditor of the *fiduciaire,* then the debt owed to him can be assigned, unless otherwise provided; however, notice of a change in beneficiaries must be served on the *fiduciaire* if it is to be enforceable against him (Article 1690 of the Civil Code).

Proprietary Approach. If we consider the *bénéficiaire's* right as a right *in rem,* then it can be assigned absent a provision which precludes alienation for a limited period of time, which must be supported by a "serious and legitimate" interest. The assignment will be enforceable against the *fiduciaire* with no notice requirement. It would be a good idea to provide not only for registration of the transfer to the *fiduciaire,* but also for registration of the *bénéficiaire's* right *in rem.*

In all cases, of course, the *bénéficiaire's* marital property regime must be taken into account.

Paragraph (5)

Regardless of the nature of his right, the *bénéficiaire* has standing to seek judicial enforcement of the *fiducie* in his favour. It should be noted that, even though his right is *in personam*, the general rules governing the enforcement of obligations permit him not only to claim damages, but also to seek specific performance whenever possible (see Article VI *infra*).

Having regard to the enforcer, he will act as the *constituant's* agent, subject to the authority granted to him by the agency agreement (Article IV(1)).

Unlike the settlor of a trust, the *constituant* of a *fiducie* also has standing to seek enforcement of the *fiducie* in court: he does not "drop out of the picture".

Article V. Trustees' duties and powers

Paragraph (1)

As ownership under a *fiducie* is a type of "ownership with duties", the *fiduciaire* only has the powers granted to him by the agreement. If the agreement fails to specify the scope of those powers, it will be null and void (Article 2063 of the bill). The *fiduciaire* is considered to have the broadest powers to deal with third parties, who may be informed of the transfer by registration, where applicable (Article 2070 of the bill), unless it is shown that the third parties knew that his powers were limited (Article 2068 of the bill). This presumption concerning powers does not, however, apply to relations between the *fiduciaire* and the *constituant*.

Paragraph (2)

The basic principles governing the performance of a trust set out in Article V(2) reflect the general principle that contracts must be performed in good faith (Article 1134 para. 3 of the Civil Code) and the special rules applicable to "fiduciary" contracts such as agency agreements. The bill expressly provides that "in the performance of his duties, the *fiduciaire* shall not abuse the trust placed in him by the *constituant*" (Article 2070-1 of the bill). As for the rest, the scope of the *fiduciaire's* obligations could be fixed by reference to the agency agreement; the effort and care owed by the *fiduciaire* will likely depend upon whether he is remunerated for his services. It is also likely that, by analogy with the agency agreement, this principle will serve as a basis for a prohibition against the *fiduciaire* himself acquiring the assets of the *fiducie* without notifying the *constituant* and the *bénéficiaire* (prohibition against undisclosed self-dealing).

Paragraph (3)
The bill sets out an obligation to take appropriate measures to avoid the commingling of private property and *fiducie* property (Article 2069 para. 1 of the bill). The duty to provide information to the *bénéficiaire* and the enforcer is also found in the ordinary law of contracts (Article 1135 of the Civil Code). It should be noted that, in the *fiducie* (unlike in the trust), this obligation, like all contractual obligations, is owed first and foremost to the *constituant* himself.

Paragraph (4)
Like the trustee, the *fiduciaire* must personally perform his functions (Article 2067 of the bill): under the ordinary law of personal contracts, he is prohibited from assigning the *fiducie*. He is only authorised to "assign" the performance of certain acts under his supervision.

Paragraph (5)
The obligation to account follows naturally from the duties entrusted to the *fiduciaire*; it is also found in the agency relationship. For a discussion of compensation of damage caused by non-performance or improper performance of the *fiduciaire's* duties, see Article VI *infra*.

Article VI. Remedies against trustees for breach of trust

Under a system of *fiducie*, breach of trust is necessarily viewed as a breach of contract. This has two types of consequences:

a) The *constituant* has standing to sue in his capacity as a party to the *fiducie* contract, even when he is not a *bénéficiaire*. All of the contractual remedies for breach are available to him. Having regard to the *bénéficiaire*, he does not sue as a party to the contract, but rather, as the *bénéficiaire* of a right conferred on him by the contract. Under the ordinary law, such a third party has an action to enforce performance of the right conferred upon him, and an action in contract for damages. He does not, however, have an action to rescind the underlying agreement. The bill expands his rights by granting him the same rights as a *constituant* (Article 2070-1 of the bill).

b) The available remedies are, firstly, the oridinary remedies available in the case of non-performance, partial performance, late performance or improper performance of a contract. The *constituant* and the *bénéficiaire* may therefore 1) seek specific performance whenever possible, if necessary subject to a fine for non-performance, enforced by the court; 2) seek damages for non-performance or improper performance of the *fiduciaire*'s duties; these damages are intended to compensate the losses incurred and lost profits (Article 1149 of the Civil Code) and French courts exercise considerable discretion in assessing them; 3) seek termination of the *fiducie* contract, with or without damages (Article 1184 of the Civil Code). The restitution of profits for breach of trust in Article VI would either be included in the "lost profits" awarded as damages, or in the restitution made upon termination of the *fiducie*. Where the *fiducie* is between a professional *fiduciaire* and a non-professional, a clause disclaiming or limiting liability will be deemed null and void.

The bill adds two specific remedies to the available ordinary law remedies when the *fiduciaire* "is in serious breach of his duties, or imperils the interests entrusted to him": 1) the appointment of a temporary administrator; 2) replacement of the *fiduciaire*, which amounts to forced replacement of a contracting party and is highly unusual.

On the other hand, it is not contemplated that the judge will become the *fiduciaire's* advisor, intervening at the *fiduciaire's* request to give his blessing to a given action, or to interpret the contract. Although non-contentious proceedings represent an important aspect of the modern functions of the courts (Articles 25-29 of the Code of Civil Procedure *(Nouveau Code de Procédure Civile)*, at this point non-contentious proceedings are reserved for family law matters; a dispute is required before the judge will intervene. In my view, the French judicial structure and the training afforded to our judges are not well suited to a transformation as far-reaching as adopting the role of the judge in common law countries.

Article VII. Liabilities of third parties

The court has long held that third parties who take part in the breach of a contractual obligation owe damages to the obligor for non-performance of the contract under Article 1382 of the Civil Code. The third-party beneficiary would thus have an action in tort against the third party who participated in the breach of the *fiducie*. According to the decisional law, it suffices that the third parties are aware of the contract out of which the breached obligation arises - there is no requirement of proof of intent to harm. Article 2068 of the bill confirms this approach. Normally, the penalty for this tortious act is an award of damages. However, it could be argued that, in the case of deliberate fraud, and not mere negligence, the most appropriate penalty would be a ruling that the contract entered into in fraud of the creditor's rights was unenforceable; this ruling would constitute an award of specific performance. The choice of how this would work would be up to the court. In the event that the right of the third-party beneficiary were treated as a right *in rem* ("ownership of assets"), he would have an action in detinue against the third party, subject to the customary conditions and reservations (Article 2279 of the Civil Code, adverse possession, doctrine of ostensible authority). The action would of course assume that the property claimed could be identified as part of the *corpus* of the *fiducie*.

Article VIII. Termination of a trust

Paragraph (1)
The action provided in Article VIII(1) for third-party beneficiaries is an action for performance of the *fiducie*. Full performance of the *fiduciaire*'s duties brings the contract to an end.

Paragraph (2)
Apart from expiration, the cause of this may be a) the *fiduciaire* completes his duties ahead of schedule; b) one or more of the beneficiaries dies or withdraws (Article 2070-110, 1 of the bill); c) an action is brought to terminate the *fiducie* (Article 2070-1 of the bill). The *constituant* himself can bring such an action. The *fiducie* may also come to an end as a result of the death of the *fiduciaire* or the dissolution of the *fiduciaire* where it is a legal entity, unless the court is asked to replace the *fiduciaire* (Article 2070-10 *in fine*). As a general matter, all of the grounds for termination of the contract

(invalidity, rescission, mutual consent, etc.) will terminate the *fiducie*. In a system of *fiducies*, the contract cannot be treated simply as a rocket launcher. But the risks of this approach should not be blown out of proportion either: 1) neither the *constituant* nor the *fiduciaire* can unilaterally terminate the *fiducie*; 2) the right of the third-party beneficiary is irrevocable, at least after it has been accepted pursuant to the ordinary law of rights conferred by a contract on third parties, if not from the moment the *fiducie* contract is entered into (*arg*. Article 2064 of the bill).

Paragraph (3) and (4)
A rule specific to the *fiducie* could satisfy Article VIII(3) and (4).

National Report for Spain

A. Borrás and C. González Beilfuss*

A. Introduction

Spanish law does not know the trust concept as such. Like other civil law systems it follows the absolute theory of property which does not allow for a division between legal rights *in rem* pertaining to the trustee and equitable rights *in rem* belonging to the beneficiary. Other obstacles against a reception of the trust, which are usually mentioned are (a) the *numerus clausus* of real rights, (b) the rules against the tying up of property, (c) the rules on publicity and (d) the principle of universal responsibility of the debtor. It is, however, our view that these obstacles could be overcome if the Spanish legislator wished to introduce a trust-like institution into Spanish domestic law.

Such an intention cannot be detected at present. There is very little authoritative writing on the common law trust[1] and those authors who have dealt with it have expressed their opinion against the reception of an institution alien to Spanish legal tradition. An institution like the trust would be difficult to fit, so it is felt, into the systematics of Spanish private law. Not even the experience of several Latin American jurisdictions, which have introduced trust-like institutions into their domestic systems, serves as a counter-argument against these kind of conceptual objections. It is, moreover, generally felt that Spanish civil law can adequately deal with the practical needs which common law jurisdictions solve by using

---

* Prof. A. Borrás and Prof. C. González Beilfuss are professor of Private international law, University of Barcelona.

1 Arroyo, I., *Trust y ley civil*, RJC, 1983, pp. 95-108; Asin Cabrera, M.A., *La ley aplicable al trust en el Derecho internacional privado español*, RGD, 1990, pp. 2089-2120; Claret Marti, P., *De la fiducia y del trust*, Barcelona, 1947; Garrigues Diaz Cañabate, J., *Negocios fiduciarios en el Derecho mercantil*, Madrid, 1981; González Beilfuss, C., *El trust. La institución angloamericana y el derecho internacional privado español*, Barcelona, 1997, Minaña, E., *Los trusts. Breves consideraciones acerca de los medios de su implantación en España*, RGLyJ, 1931, pp. 597-616.

the trust. When discussing those institutions of our law most similar to the trust, such as the *fiducia cum amico* or the foundation, we will try to show that this common opinion is not sustainable and that there are, indeed, several practical advantages which Spanish law could gain if a trust-like institution were introduced into our domestic system. It is however also our opinion that the introduction of a trust-like institution should follow the lines of civil law tradition. This is why we think that the creation of a legal *fiducia*, which involved the segregation of patrimonies, would be the most adequate and feasible alternative. Even the use of common law terminology should be carefully considered since it might deter some from implementing the Principles.

In the case of Spain there are psychological objections against anything like the trust, which have been noticed by common law legal writers and practitioners. According to some, Spain is the European civil law jurisdiction with the most hostile attitude towards foreign trusts. This can be explained by two reasons. Firstly, Spanish Private international Law has hardly dealt either in theory or in practice with foreign trusts. The Hague Convention on the law applicable to trusts and on their recognition has not been ratified, because, as our Ministry of Justice informally stated, Spanish law does not know the institution. This is, of course, a terrible misconception and some authors have recently argued in favour of the ratification of a Convention that is needed by practitioners. Although hardly visible at first sight, there are more and more cases involving foreign trusts which are commonly dealt with by either assimilating the trust to the contract of mandate or deposit or by creating a legal entity wholly controlled by the trustee. These solutions are, however, either inadequate or expensive. Practitioners resort to them, and thereby conceal the existence of a foreign trust, because Spanish law does not offer a better alternative. This situation is detrimental to Spanish economic interests because it detracts foreign trustees from investing trust funds in Spain.

The second reason that might explain Spanish hostility towards the trust is the association of the institution with fraud and especially with tax evasion. Some recent and very notorious cases involving offshore trusts have even reinforced this association. There is a need for much more information about perfectly defendable uses of the trust.

B. Existing law

Spanish law has functional equivalents to the common law trust. There is however not a single institution which in itself can fulfil all of the purposes of trusts. These functional equivalents fall somehow short of the trust and it will be our aim to show to what extent the reception of a trust-like institution would ameliorate our law. This is, as we have already stated, particularly necessary in the case of Spain because there is no common opinion in favour of changing the law in order to introduce the "trust".

Since it is not the purpose of these Principles to focus on family or succession law aspects of the trust we will leave out institutions like the *fideicommissum* or the *herencia de confiança* of Catalan civil law. We will instead concentrate on *fiducia cum amico,* pension and investment funds and foundations.

1. *Fiducia cum amico*

The institution of Spanish law most similar to the trust is the *fiducia cum amico* as developed by legal writing and case law. The *fiducia* is an institution which is not contemplated in the Spanish Civil Code and there are even some authors who consider that should positive law deal with it this would imply a change in its nature.

According to Spanish law, *fiducia cum amico* involves the transfer of property from one person (called *fiduciante*) to another person (called *fiduciario*) who acquires full ownership over the transferred property but is tied up by a personal obligation to deal with the property as agreed in the so-called *pactum fiduciae.*

The main differences between the *fiducia* as known by Spanish law and the common law trust are two. Only the *fiduciario* is to be considered the property owner, whereas the *fiduciante* would have merely rights *in personam* against the *fiduciario*. This position derives from the absolute concept of property still prevailing in Spanish law. It leaves the *fiduciante* or the third person in whose benefit the property is to be administered quite unprotected, something which in Spanish legal writing is seen as an inherent flaw of the institution[2]. This is the reason why one author (De Castro)[3] argues that the transfer of assets and the ownership of the fiduciary are only fictitious, a position which has been upheld by the Spanish Supreme Court in at least two decisions on *fiducia cum creditore* (Judgements of 25th February and 8th March 1988).

The second main difference between the common law trust and the Spanish *fiducia* is that the Spanish *fiducia* does not involve the creation of a separate patrimony. The transferred property is part of the fiduciary's patrimony and is therefore not safe from the fiduciary's private creditors in the event of bankruptcy. That is why practitioners advise foreign trustees who wish to invest trust funds in Spain to create a legal person wholly controlled by the trustee.

It is our view that the above mentioned characteristics of the Spanish *fiducia* explain the little use made of this figure in Spanish legal practice. As will be shown these are precisely the reasons why the Spanish legislator opted against the institution of *fiducia cum amico* when ruling on pension and investment funds.

2. *Pension and investment funds*

For different reasons pension and investment funds are becoming increasingly popular in Spain. In order, especially, to guarantee an adequate protection of the public both the pension fund and the investment fund have been regulated by law[4].

Although these statutes deal quite extensively with pension and investment funds the legal nature of these institutions is still disputed. It seems however quite clear that they differ significantly from both the common law trust and Roman *fiducia*. The main difference lies in the fact that the entity or entities holding or administering the funds are not their legal

2 Spanish authors speak about the possibility of abuse or the lack of proportion between means and aim pursued through *fiducia* as an essential characteristic of the institution. See: Garrigues Diaz Cañabate, J., *Negocios fiduciarios...*, pp. 19-20; Jordano Barea, J.B., *El negocio fiduciario...*, pp. 27-28.

3 Castro y Bravo, F., *El negocio jurídico*, Madrid, 1967, pp. 379-442.

4 *Ley 8/1987, de 8 de junio, de regulación de Planes y Fondos de pensión; Ley 46/1984, de 26 de diciembre, reguladora de las Instituciones de inversión colectiva.*

owners. It is the participants or beneficiaries who have the legal title over the assets. The funds are therefore structured along the idea of co-ownership. Participants or beneficiaries are the owners of the pension or investment fund and the legal relationship with the entities administering or holding the assets is construed by using contractual figures such as mandate and deposit.

It has been, of course, pointed out that attributing property rights to the participants or beneficiaries is fictitious since they are deprived by contract of all the prerogatives of ownership. Participants or beneficiaries are not supposed to dispose, administer or use the assets they own. One can therefore say that their ownership is only nominal and not substantial. The Spanish legislator has nevertheless opted for the idea of ownership in order to guarantee the protection of the participants and beneficiaries. Attributing ownership over the assets to the entities holding and administering them would have meant adopting a fiduciary structure, which, as we have seen, does not imply the creation of a separate patrimony. The pension or investment funds would not have been safe from the entities' creditors.

The Spanish legislator could have created a legal *fiducia* with a separate patrimony that would essentially correspond with the trust concept used in these Principles. This would, however, have meant a break with the principle of universal responsibility of the debtor. According to one author (La Casa Garcia)[5] that would have been unjustified because the same practical effects can be reached by other means at a lesser cost. It is, however, to be noted that the Spanish legislator opted for a solution (co-ownership) which does as well imply a separation of patrimonies[6]. According to the law the fund's creditors cannot claim their credits against the participants or beneficiaries whose responsibility is therefore limited to the amount of their participation. The funds do not respond for debts of neither participants, beneficiaries nor the entities holding or administering the assets.

---

5 See La Casa Garcia, R., *Los fondos de pensiones*, Madrid, 1997, p. 121.

6 See Moreno Luque, J.M., *Notas para un estudio del contrato de participación en un fondo de inversión*, in: *La protección de los partícipes de los fondos de inversión*, Madrid, 1997, pp. 297-367, 355.

3. *Foundations*

One of the main difficulties of Spanish foundation law is the fact that Spain is a country with a non-unified legal system in relation to this matter. It is therefore not correct to speak about the Spanish foundation. For reasons of space we will, however, try to provide a general view of the matter.

Foundations are defined generally as non-profit personified organisations, which are created by affecting a patrimony to a charitable purpose. Foundations cannot be created for a private non-charitable purpose and they are not to pursue the making of profit. If their activities should produce benefits, they are not meant to be distributed but will increase the foundation's patrimony. This is, of course, a key difference with the common law trust, which is, as is emphasised in the Introduction to this work, widely used for commercial purposes. The functional equivalent for these kinds of trusts in Spanish law would not be the foundation but the corporation.

The Spanish foundation corresponds with the charitable trust. It is created in order to promote public interest. This concept seems, however, wider than the concept of charitable purposes in English law and more restrictive than the wide admittance of the trust for purposes in offshore jurisdictions. One type of foundation which is admitted is the so-called *fundación laboral*, which is usually created by employer and employees in the benefit of the latter. The protection of the employees is thus considered to be of public interest. Spanish law does, however, not accept the family foundation, that is a foundation created by affecting certain assets for the benefit of the members of a family. This kind of foundation is deemed to serve a purely private interest and is therefore expressly prohibited by the law.

C. Proposals for further developments of trusts

As we have mentioned, until now no serious proposal for introducing the trust into domestic Spanish law has been made. Some authors, mostly practitioners, have expressed their admiration towards the institution of the trust but they have not dared to propose its introduction into Spanish domestic law mostly, so we feel, because academics have always pointed out the incompatibilities between the trust and basic elements of Spanish private law. A change of focus would therefore be most welcome. If the similarities between domestic institutions and the common law trust were pointed out, perhaps the idea of introducing the trust into domestic law would cease to seem a legal chimera.

In any case, we think that a step by step approach would probably be the most commendable. The first step would be to ameliorate the treatment foreign trusts receive in our jurisdiction. The ratification of the Hague Convention on the law applicable to trusts and on their recognition would contribute, as it has in the Netherlands and Italy, to familiarise lawyers and businessmen with the institution. A better knowledge would dispel prejudices, such as the association with fraud, and awareness of the advantages of the trust would grow. The progressing internationalisation of business and especially of the financial sector would then do the rest. It is even likely that the ever-growing presence of Spanish banks in Latin America might provide a further incentive for such a development. A certain mimetic effect is also to be expected. If other European civil law jurisdictions such as France and Italy introduce a trust-like institution into their domestic systems, Spanish law would probably follow the track. It is, on the contrary, wholly unrealistic to expect the Spanish legislator to take the lead in this realm.

As we already stated before, it is our view that the easiest way to introduce something like the trust into our law would be to develop on the *fiducia cum amico*. If the concerned assets formed a separate patrimony they would be safe from both the "trustee's" and the "beneficiaries'" personal creditors. The notion of a separate patrimony is not alien to Spanish law. Apart from the classical examples of bankruptcy and succession law (*masa de la quiebra* and *herencia yacente*), the investment and the pension fund create, as we have seen, a segregation of assets. Nominally, at least, the funds belong to the participants. They are, however, safe from any claim of their personal creditors.

Spanish law views separate patrimonies as an exceptional, even as an anomalous situation. A development of the *fiducia cum amico* along the proposed lines would therefore require the intervention of the Spanish legislator. The principle of universal responsibility of the debtor is not likely to be left aside by case law without an express legal provision allowing the segregation of assets.

An aspect that would require special care is the protection of third parties. As far as the assets owned by the trustee were immovables, it would probably not be necessary to change the law. According to, at least, some, the *pactum fiduciae* can be annotated in the Property Register. If the concerned assets were, however, movables, the law would have to provide a duty to earmark, exactly as is the case with the common law trust.

D. Commentary on the Principles article by article

In this section of the report we will comment on the Principles of European Trust Law article by article. It will be our purpose to examine whether the Principles could be implemented into Spanish law and especially whether the legislator's intervention is necessary in order to do so. Since the Spanish attitude towards trusts is not favourable we generally think that legislative action is desirable even when not strictly necessary. In the current legal atmosphere we hardly think that case law would introduce a trust-like institution. A comprehensive trust statute is therefore to be recommended.

Article I. Main characteristics of the trust

Spanish law knows the notion of a contract for the benefit of a third party. There are therefore no difficulties in implementing the idea of the trustee acting for the benefit of other persons.

As has repeatedly been pointed out, the main difficulties arise for achieving a segregation of the trustee's personal patrimony and the trust funds. The separation of patrimonies is not unknown in Spanish law, but it is an exceptional, even an anomalous situation which needs special justification. Legislative intervention would therefore be necessary in this respect. A question, which would have to be examined carefully, is whether it is possible to create a trust by unilateral declaration of the settlor that in the future he will hold part of his property as trustee. Special provisions for the protection of third parties might be necessary in that respect.

There are as well no difficulties in accepting that the beneficiary has personal remedies against either the trustee or a third party to whom the trust funds have been wrongfully transferred. The admission of proprietary remedies is, on the contrary difficult to attain. As we have seen, one author (De Castro) tried to reach this result for the *fiducia*. He argued that the fiduciary is not the real owner of the assets that have been transferred to him, that ownership lies in the hands of the settlor. A wrongful transfer by the fiduciary to a third party could then be solved by application of the rules on a *non-domino* acquisition. Such a construction would, however, only be helpful for the implementation of Article I(4) if one held that the beneficiary is the owner of the assets. This in itself would imply that the trustee could not be considered the owner, a conclusion, which seems to be contrary to Article I(1).

Article II. Creation of the trust

The trust concept entails either a transfer of property from the settlor to the trustee or a segregation of part of the settlor's patrimony in the case that he is to be trustee of particular assets of his. The transfer of property from the settlor to the trustee is easy to achieve in Spanish law by either contract or donation. For the above mentioned reasons of third party protection the segregation of the trust fund from the trustee's personal patrimony should be provided for by Statute.

Article III. Trust fund

Paragraph (1)
The notion of a fund with changing assets can be easily dealt with by using the notion of real subrogation. It is an idea, which has been developed in the regulations on investment and pension funds that have been tackled with in part B. For the sake of clarity and legal certainty this question should be dealt with by Statute together with a regulation on the trustee's power of investment.

Paragraph (2)
In our opinion this idea is a consequence of the recognition of the trust fund as a separate fund. Since it is a crucial matter it seems advisable to provide for it in Statute.

Paragraph (3)
This rule should be easily recognised by Spanish law, which provides similarly in connection, for example, with the investment fund. No specific legal provision seems therefore to be necessary.

Article IV. Trusts for beneficiaries or for enforceable purposes

Paragraph (1)
Although, in the context of the stipulation in favour of a third party, the Spanish Civil Code is silent regarding the designation of ascertainable persons, case law is conclusive in admitting that the beneficiary or third party can be determined *a posteriori* provided the contract contains the necessary elements in order to do so (Supreme Court Judgment of 10 December 1956). As regards the trust for purposes we would recommend caution since its introduction would collide with the institution of the foundation. The legislator, who might prefer to further develop the law of foundations, should carefully consider this aspect.

Paragraph (2)
The result envisaged by Article IV(2) can be easily reached by applying Spanish law. In the context of the law of *fideicommissum*, Article 786 of the Civil Code provides that if the testator fails to create a valid *fideicomissum* the clause establishing it is treated as if it did not exist. The same idea could be used in order to implement this Article.

Paragraph (3)
In the context of the investment and the pension fund Spanish law deals extensively with the duty to keep the participants of the funds informed. A similar legislation of this crucial aspect seems advisable in order to implement these Principles.

Paragraph (4)
The rights of a beneficiary would be rights *in personam* under Spanish law. As such rights, that is, as claims, they are in principle disposable except if the law or the parties of the contract provided otherwise. See Article 1112 of the Spanish Civil Code.

Paragraph (5)
Spanish law would give standing to the beneficiary of a trust in order to enforce the terms of the trust. As we have suggested, the rights of the beneficiary would be assimilated to the rights of a third party in a contract for the benefit of a third party. The beneficiary or third party would therefore hold a claim against the trustee, which could be enforced with the intervention of the courts.

Article V. Trustees' duties and powers

Paragraph (1)
If the Spanish legislator opted to implement the Principles by developing the concept of *fiducia cum amico,* the trustee would be considered the absolute owner of the assets. Spanish law does not allow for a division of ownership. If one is considered the owner of the assets, he is the absolute owner and has all the powers of an absolute owner. In this respect it should, however, be noted that the Statutes on the Pension and the Investment Funds attribute ownership of the assets to the participants or beneficiaries. They also provide that by contract all the powers of ownership are vested in the entities administering the funds.

Paragraph (2)
These principles can be easily implemented in Spanish law since, in our opinion they are a mere development of the idea of *bona fide* execution of contractual obligations. For a very similar provision in the context of the contract of mandate see Article 1719 of the Spanish Civil Code.

Paragraph (3)
As has already been said these questions should be dealt with by Statute. Since trust funds constitute a separate fund the duty to earmark and to keep the assets separate is an essential duty of the trustee, which Spanish law would have no difficulty in accepting. The idea that the trustee has to keep accurate accounts and keep the beneficiaries informed is as well developed in the Statutes on the Pension and the Investment Funds. These matters are however so crucial that in our opinion precise rules should be laid down by the legislator.

Paragraph (4)
The idea that the trustee has to carry out his duty personally except if the trust instrument otherwise provides corresponds with Article 1721 of the Spanish Civil Code, which provides that the *mandatario* can only name a substitute if the *mandante* has not forbidden it. The idea of a *bona fide* execution of his duty can as well be found in the rules on mandate, see Article 1719 Civil Code.

Paragraph (5)
The rule that the trustee is personally responsible for any loss occasioned to the trust fund by his breach of trust can be easily accommodated since it is laid down in Article 1718 Civil Code for the contract of mandate. The idea that he must augment the fund by the amount of any profits made in breach of his duty does as well correspond with the provision laid down in Article 1720 Civil Code.

Article VI. Remedies against trustees for breach of trust

It is quite commonplace to state that the active role of the courts would be one of the main difficulties the introduction of a trust into a civil law system would pose. This would be precisely the situation in Spanish law. The remedies named in Article VI, namely an order restraining particular conduct or removing the trustee from his office and replacing him or ordering payment of damages, are all conceivable in Spanish law. There are no objections in admitting that the court declares that particular assets of the trustee have always been part of the trust fund and never became part of his private patrimony or are to be regarded as security for satisfying his liability.

It is, however, doubtful whether the intervention of the courts is the best solution in the context of property management. We do not feel that Spanish courts are prepared to exercise in this context the paternal role they do exercise in child protection or in the protection of incapacitated adults. The Statutes on the Pension and the Investment Funds have therefore attributed this role to administrative entities whose decisions can, of course, be questioned in a judicial proceeding. The idea of introducing private supervision (a protector or something similar) should be carefully considered by the Spanish legislator who could develop on the institution of *curatela*.

Article VII. Liabilities of third parties

One of the main consequences of vesting property over the assets in the fiduciary is that in Spanish law the fiduciary, as the absolute owner of the assets, always validly transfers them to third parties. If the transfer is in breach of trust he will be personally liable towards the beneficiary. Under certain circumstances, especially if full knowledge of the breach of trust is ascertainable, the third party might be liable in tort or delict against the beneficiary. The beneficiary has, however, no possibility of tracing the assets into the hands of the third party because he has no *in rem* rights over the trust fund.

In order to achieve this result one would have to vest property over the assets in the beneficiaries so that the transfer between the trustee and the third party can be treated as a *non-domino* acquisition. One author has, as we have already pointed out, proposed this solution and some court decisions have accepted it. Vesting property over the funds in the participants or beneficiaries is as well the solution adopted in the Statutes on the Pension and the Investment Funds.

In our opinion the use of the *fiducia cum amico* is however to be preferred. We feel that this construction is more respectful with the basic principles of Spanish property law. If our viewpoint were accepted, the Spanish legislator should carefully consider whether a tracing device is really necessary. The European Principles of Trust Law aim at facilitating the introduction of the trust for commercial uses. Personal liability of the trustee would therefore suffice in order to adequately protect the beneficiaries against breach of trust, if the legislator decided that only certain entities like, for example, banks or trust corporations can be office holders. This is the line, which has been followed in Mexico and in some other Latin American jurisdictions.

Article VIII. Termination of a trust

Paragraph (1)
This rule could be easily fitted into Spanish law because it does exist in the context of the contract of mandate (see Article 1733 Civil Code). For the sake of clarity it would, however, be preferable to lay down a special provision in Statute.

Paragraph (2)
These rules are not inconsistent with Spanish law. They should be developed by Statute.

Paragraph (3)
There are no apparent difficulties for achieving the results set forth under Article VIII(3).

Paragraph (4)
As we commented before, it is doubtful whether the purpose trust should be introduced into Spanish law. If it were to be introduced, the rule laid down in this paragraph should be developed in a statutory provision.

National Report for Denmark

R.K. Feldthusen*

A. Introduction

The Danish legal system is based on the Scandinavian legal system which is neither founded on common law nor civil law, but is unique. There is no statutory framework defining the right to property in Danish law and Danish jurisprudence does not agree on a definition of the right to property in a positive sense. The prevailing view in Denmark seems to be that the right to property can only be defined in a negative sense[1]; the right to property is thus a flexible term and much like an accordon which may be either contracted or expanded.

As evidenced by the present report, Danish law contains a number of legal institutions which offer points of similarity with the trust concept, as set out in the Principles of European Trust Law. In this context it is interesting to notice that the word trust most likely originates from either the Danish word *trøst*[2] or the Norwegian word *traust*, both of which originally having meant trust (confidence)[3]. Furthermore the word trustee most likely originates from the Old Norse word *Þraustr*.

It should be noted that Denmark permits *substitutio fideicommissaria* to one unborn generation. A *fideicommissum* may be set up by means of a will, a deed of gift, or a contract.

* R.K. Feldthusen is research fellow in the fields of tax law and estate planning and lecturer in estate planning, University of Copenhagen.

1 See W.E. von Eyben, *Formuerettigheder*, 7th edn, 1983, p. 17 *et seq.* with additional references.

2 In present-day Danish the word *trøst* means comfort, consolation.

3 Michel Grimaldi and François Barrière also point out the etymology of the word trust as originating from Danish but mistakenly uses the letter "o" as in *trost*, see Trust and Fiducie, Towards a European Civil Code, 2nd rev. and exp. edn, Arthur Hartkamp, Martijn Hesselink, Ewoud Hondius, Carla Joustra and Edgar du Perron (edd), 1998.

B. Existing law

1.a. Fiduciary ownership and fiducia cum amico

Reference to fiduciary ownership is virtually non-existent in both Danish legal scholarship and case-law. The concepts of fiduciary ownership and *fiducia cum amico* are in Danish legal scholarship predominantly associated with the Roman concepts[4].

Although a person may in numerous scenarios receive funds for a fiduciary purpose, the recipient is considered to be an ordinary owner, albeit subject to certain restraints e.g. the surviving spouse who has retained undivided possession of the community property (*uskiftet bo*)[5], the surviving spouse when he, and his spouse, have drawn up a mutual will[6], and presumably the lifetime beneficiary of a *fideicommissum*.

Pooling of assets for pension purposes (puljepension)

By virtue of the Banking Act, s. 42a, a pension saver may transfer assets to a bank, which then pools those assets with assets from other pension savers[7]. The relationship between the bank and the pension saver to a large extent resembles the trust, as set out in the Principles. The pooling of assets will therefore be dealt with briefly. It should, however, be noted, that radical changes of the Danish rules on pooling of assets for pension purposes are currently being contemplated. These changes will considerably reduce the resemblances with a trust, as defined by the Principles. In connection with these proposed changes, it may be better instead to consider implementing the trust, as defined in the Principles, as it seems ideally suited for this area of Danish law.

---

4 See *infra*, (b).

5 Cf. Inheritance Act, s. 13(4).

6 Cf. Inheritance Act, s. 48.

7 Apart from pooling assets, there are two other options open for pension savers: the depositing of money in an ordinary bank account, where the bank is the owner of the money and where the pension saver only has an *in personam* right, and the depositing in a separate deposit, where the pension saver is considered owner of the assets.

Pursuant to Regulation no. 879, October 28th 1992, s. 21, the bank is owner of the pooled assets and by virtue of s. 24(1), the bank is required to keep the pooled assets segregated from its other assets. The bank, as owner of the pooled assets, is entitled to dispose of the assets and it can thus pass on a good title to these assets. Nonetheless, the bank is under an obligation to keep accurate accounts and, moreover, to supply the account holders with information.

Because the account holders are not owners of the pooled assets they are reduced to non-preferential creditors in a bank's estate in bankruptcy. The account holders are, however, guaranteed full protection for the value of their assets by the Depositors' Guarantee Foundation in case of the bank's bankruptcy[8]. The account holders' interests in the deposited assets are, pursuant to Certain Civil Law Aspects of Pension Savings Act, s. 11, precluded from execution by creditors of the depositee.

Nominee accounts

Pursuant to the Danish Securities Act, s. 72(2) the owner of securities in a company may appoint a nominee whose name, instead of the owner's, will appear on the records of the company[9]. One of the purposes of the Danish Securities Act introducing nominees was to open up the prospect of owners being able to conceal their ownership of securities. The nominee may thus merely be a front man. A physical person as well as a legal entity may be a nominee[10].

Besides the company keeping the records, only the Danish Securities Centre will be aware of the identity of the owner. However, pursuant to Danish Securities Act, s. 60(2), the Danish Securities Centre must not disclose such information to anybody except affiliated firms, as set out in chapter 21 of the Securities Act.

As the nominee *de facto* replaces the owner of the securities to the outside world, the nominee is able freely to dispose of the securities, although this might be a breach of contract as between the nominee and the owner.

---

8 *Cf.* Depositors' Guarantee Act, s. 5(2)(2-4).

9 See also Regulation no. 925, October 17th 1996, s. 31(2).

10 See *Børsnoterede selskaber*, white paper no. 1230/1992, p. 87 *et seq.*

However, the nominee can pass on a good title over the securities to the *bona fide* purchaser[11].

Besides concealing the real ownership of the assets the nominee may - in the case of the securities being shares - receive dividends and other payments, along with shareholder information. The nominee is considered as handling the economical interests of the owner. Should the owner wish to grant the nominee administrative powers it will require a separate contract between the parties.

As a point of departure for general principle, the real owner is protected against the creditors of the nominee, as they do not derive a better right to the securities than the nominee. However, everything hinges on the state of the evidence.

Mutual funds

Investment funds (UCITS) are in Danish law subject to the Investment Funds Act. Besides investment funds, the Act introduces four kinds of so called special investment funds (NON-UCITS); namely, Placement Funds, Money-Market Funds, Funds of Funds, and Venture Capital Funds. Investment funds and special investment funds are, pursuant to Investment Funds Act, s. 3, incorporated as associations, which according to Danish law are legal entities. The assets contained in the fund are considered to be owned by the association, which in return issues certificates to each member, or alternatively some other kind of documentation, such as a statement of account. The assets of the association are held by a custodian and the association may further appoint a manager.

Mortgage trusts

The mortgage trust (or collective security trust) arises where the debtor enters into a covenant to pay the creditor and gives a parallel covenant to pay the trustee, and further transfers a security interest to the trustee in

11 It should be noted, that according to Danish law, donees are placed on equal footing with purchasers. Hence a beneficiary will be prevented from asserting a claim against a donee having neither actual nor constructive knowledge of the trust.

order to secure the parallel covenant, the trustee holding the security for the benefit of the creditors. Such trust is not used in Denmark because it would jeopardise the beneficiaries' interests in the security owned by the trustee if the trustee became bankrupt.

1.b. *Ordinary ownership*

As mentioned above[12], the Danish position on fiduciary ownership has only been afforded little attention in Danish legal scholarship. Most writers focus on the concept of fiduciary ownership (*fiducia cum creditore*) as opposed to the Danish law on mortgages. Fiduciary ownership in the shape of *fiducia cum amico* has thus been abandoned by Danish scholars[13].

A conveyance of property by C to F with a fiduciary obligation for reconveyance will undoubtedly be afforded protection by the Danish courts in the *inter partes* relation, thus allowing C to claim the property transferred from F. However, the Danish courts will most likely adopt a different position when confronted with F's creditors on the one hand, and a proprietary claim by C on the other hand. Where F has possession of the said property as well as being the judicial owner, F will most likely be considered as being the absolute owner. This is not, however, a foregone conclusion in the Danish courts, because regard will be had to any evidence that C might produce. Furthermore the basis of the conveyance, and its impact on third parties dealing with F, will be analysed for each case.

The Danish position on fiduciary ownership is probably one of the major obstacles to allowing the trust to operate in Danish law.

2. *Special arrangements*

Client accounts in law firms

Pursuant to Administration of Justice Act, s. 127, and the regulations laid down by the Danish Bar Association, all lawyers have an obligation to

12 See *supra*, 1.a.

13 See Torben Svenné Schmidt, Trusts and Trust-Like Devices, 1981, p. 113 *et seq.*

keep an account of their dealings with their clients. The client account is in the name of the lawyer and the lawyer has full powers of disposition over the account. The lawyer must manage the funds in the client account with the same regard to thoroughness, conscientiousness, and due consideration of the client's interests, as with any other undertaking by the lawyer.

The client account funds are protected against the lawyer's creditors in the event of the lawyer becoming bankrupt, because the clients have a claim for the funds which ranks above the lawyer's creditors[14].

Statutory custodians

Pursuant to the Danish Securities Act s. 6 a depositor has a proprietary claim for securities, although fungible, held by a security broker - the statutory custodian - in order to protect the depositor against the insolvency of the custodian. As a starting point the depositor's securities must be kept in a separate deposit.

However, the custodian may, instead, place the depositor's securities in a deposit where securities are pooled, provided that the custodian has informed the depositor of the legal effects hereof, and provided that the depositor has given his consent. Pursuant to Securities Act s. 6(1)(1) the custodian must take satisfactory measures to safeguard the proprietary claim of the depositor. This is done by the custodian making an inventory. Failing that, and unless the depositor is able to prove by some other means the identity of the securities, the depositor will not be able to enforce a proprietary claim if the custodian becomes bankrupt.

The tying up of funds (Båndlæggelse)

The Danish institution of "tying up" property for the benefit of one or more persons dates back to at least the year 1716. It was recognised in legal publications in the year 1816, and is now codified in chapter 11 of the Danish Inheritance Act. The public need for such an institution soon became apparent, which is illustrated by the fact that the value of the tied

14 The clients are further guaranteed full protection for their funds by the Depositors' Guarantee Foundation in case of the lawyer's bankruptcy, cf. Depositors' Guarantee Act, s. 5(2)(9).

up funds in the middle of this century already exceeded one billion DKK. Although the tying up of property is frequently used in Denmark, the institution has, in recent years, been subject to some criticism.

Tying up property is widely defined so as to include any disposition whereby a person stipulates that a fund (money, bonds, stocks, real estate, etc.) is to benefit one or more persons for a specified time. Virtually any asset can be tied up as long as there is an effective divestment of possession, which characterises and determines the tying up of funds. Under Danish law, a person cannot tie up his own property for himself. Instead, the owner must designate the person or persons to benefit from the tying up. The owner may for instance decide that A is to be the income beneficiary of the tied up funds and on A's death, the funds are to devolve on B as capital beneficiary. Except for the legal portion of inheritance reserved for heirs, the donor or testator is free to choose who is to administer the funds, e.g. a bank, lawyer, company, or a friend.

The effect of tying up property in accordance with the Inheritance Act, s. 62, which contains the mandatory rules for the legal portion of inheritance, is that the funds are protected against the beneficiaries' creditors and that the beneficiaries are prevented from disposing of their interests. The person appointed to administer the tied up funds is not considered owner of the funds as in the case of a trustee.

Partnership (Interessentskab)

According to Danish law two or more persons may decide to enter into a partnership, e.g. in order to carry on a business. It is not yet clear whether a partnership constitutes a separate legal entity[15]. This uncertainty is mainly due to the fact that the participants are jointly and severally liable to the full extent of their assets for the liabilities of the partnership. The creditors of the partnership have a preferential position in respect of the partnership fund compared to that of the participants' private creditors, the latter being precluded from bringing claims against the partnership fund. Instead, the private creditors may levy execution on the individual participant's net-share in the partnership.

15 See Erik Werlauff, *Dansk Selskabsret*, 3rd edn, 1997, p. 21.

3. *The foundation (fond)*

According to Danish law, donors and testators may convey assets to an institution which is governed or owned by itself (*selvejende institution*). This institution carries a lot of names such as *fond, stiftelse,* or *legat,* but most commonly the so-called *fond* (foundation) is used. The donor or testator may choose between conveying his assets to a foundation he sets up himself, or to an already existing foundation. The foundation is an independent legal entity and the administration of the foundation is carried out by a board of administrators. The board of administrators is bound only by the charter of the foundation. Thus, whether the donor sets up a foundation himself or makes use of an already existing foundation, the donor has irrevocably given up his control of the assets, as these now belong to the foundation. The assets must never again become the property of the settlor, his spouse, or his children under the age of majority and living at home[16].

The donor or settlor may set up a foundation for charitable purposes, furtherance of the common good, business purposes, or for the purpose of benefiting his family. However, in the latter case he must comply with the Danish rule against perpetuities, according to which only one unborn generation may benefit from the foundation[17].

C. Proposal for further developments of trust-like relationships under Danish law

The common law trust concept is predominantly unknown in Danish legal theory, and only a very limited amount of attention has been devoted to it in legal scholarship. The legal practitioner, when confronted with the trust, tends to associate the concept with unpredictable ownership of property and tax-avoidance, especially in connection with offshore trusts. This is illustrated by the fact that the only Danish statutory provision expressly dealing with trusts is concerned with settlors transferring property to trusts in low tax states, cf. the Taxation of Foundations Act, s. 3A(1)[18].

---

16 Cf. Lennart Lynge Andersen, *Fonde og Foreninger I - Fondslovene med kommentarer*, 4th rev. edn, 1996, p. 42.

17 Cf. Foundation Act, s. 7 and Business Foundation Act, s. 8.

18 See Aage Michelsen, *International Skatteret*, 2nd edn, 1996, p. 331 *et seq.*

In order to perceive the terminological problems that Danish legal scholars have in understanding the common law trust concept, it may be helpful to refer to Alf Ross' following comment:

> "But instead of talking of double ownership it would be more accurate to say that there exists no ownership at all in the typical sense: those functions which we think of as being combined in the typical owner are in these cases divided between different persons, neither of whom, therefore, holds the position of a typical owner."[19]

Besides fears of tax implications, Danish law hesitates to admit the trust concept due to the potential uncertainty which third parties might experience when being confronted with this unfamiliar concept.

In order to admit the trust concept, changes will most likely have to be made in the Danish system of registration. Pursuant to Danish law public registration of interests may take place in real estate[20], certain movables[21], ships[22], aircrafts[23], and securities[24].

A person appearing in the registry as the owner is, in relation to third parties, treated as being exactly that, unless a declaration to the contrary is also registered. Any restrictions upon the owner's right to make legally binding dispositions have to appear in the registry in order to afford protection against third parties to the persons in whose favour the restrictions have been imposed. In the case of assets that are not the subject matter of registration, other satisfactory means of protecting such persons are needed.

Furthermore, amendments will most likely have to be made in the Administration of Justice Act part 3, chapters 45-51 and the Insolvency Act, chapter 9, in order to ensure a satisfactory level of protection against the creditors of the trustee. For similar reasons, the Danish rules on divestment

19 Alf Ross, On Law and Justice, 1974, p. 181.
20 Registration Act, s. 1.
21 Registration Act, chapter II.
22 Ships Registration Act.
23 Registration of Interests in Aircrafts Act.
24 Securities Act, s. 66.

of possession and individualisation of assets, as a prerequisite of affording creditor protection, will most likely have to be revised.

In the area of tracing assets, Danish law seems to acknowledge that an owner may shift his proprietary interest in his assets to the debt due to a wrongdoer for the sale of the aforementioned assets, or alternatively to assets that replaced the aforementioned assets[25]. For instance, if X wrongfully sells assets owned by Y to Z, Y may be entitled to a proprietary claim against X for the money owed by Z. If, however, Z had already paid the purchase price to X, Y may be entitled to a proprietary claim against X for the moneys received, provided that these are kept segregated from X's other assets[26]. However, if the moneys are mixed with X's other assets or have been paid to a *bona fide* third party, Y is considered as having lost his proprietary claim[27]. Where X used the money received from Z to buy new assets, Danish scholars do not agree on Y's legal position, so that it is unclear whether or not a charge over the purchased assets is imposed on X as a security for Y's claim.[28]

As mentioned below[29], a beneficiary's interest in the trust property may, under Danish law, be considered as being proprietary, an *in rem* right. In this case the Danish position on tracing assets may prove to be of great interest, should the Danish legislator choose to implement the trust - or the Danish courts uphold a trust - as set out in the Principles.

Taking account of the current attitude towards trusts, one must expect that introducing the trust, as set out in the Principles, in Denmark, will be met by opposition. Nevertheless, as illustrated above, the Danish legal institution of tying up funds has flourished for over 280 years despite giving use to several of the misgivings Danish legal practitioners usually associate

---

25 See on tracing further *infra*, Article I(4) and IV.

26 See Knud Illum, *Dansk Tingsret*, 3rd rev. edn, 1976, p. 504 *et seq*. Even in the event of the money received having been replaced by other money, Y may be entitled to bring a proprietary claim, provided that the substitute moneys are still segregated from X's other assets.

27 Cf. Carl Torp, *Dansk Tingsret*, 2nd edn, 1916, p. 387 *et seq*. Whether and to what extent Y is able to follow fungible substitute assets, e.g. money, into the hands of *mala fides* third parties is - at best - not sufficiently clarified in Danish law.

28 See in this direction Henning Matzen, *Forelæsninger over Den Danske Tingsret*, 1882, p. 283 and of a different opinion Carl Torp, *Dansk Tingsret*, 2nd edn, 1916, p. 389.

29 See *infra*, Article VII.

with the trust concept. It will help pave the way for introducing trusts in Danish law, if the commercial world expresses a demand for the solutions offered by employing trusts. Sale-and-lease-back arrangements have been accepted in Danish law, although in some instances possibly circumventing the law of mortgages. Moreover, the commercial world is making much use of Special Purpose Vehicles, in the shape of subsidiary companies, in order to finance its debts, in a way that avoids the prohibition of floating charges in Danish law[30].

D. Commentary on the Principles article by article

Article I. Main characteristics of the trust

Paragraph (1)

A settlor in the capacity of contracting party, donor or testator, may transfer property to another person, a trustee, with instructions that the assets must form a separate fund segregated from the trustee's private patrimony. The trustee becomes owner of the transferred property subject to the terms set forth in the document setting up the trust[31].

It should be noted that a transfer of particular property from a person's right hand to a person's left hand, i.e. declaration of oneself as being trustee, is not likely to afford protection against the private creditors of the settlor/trustee, but the Danish position on a unilateral declaration of trust is not yet sufficiently clarified.

Paragraph (2)

Where there is more than one trustee, the trustees will be considered to be co-owners of the trust fund.

Co-ownership (*sameje*) in Danish law is closely related to the common law "tenancy in common" as each co-owner may sell or dispose of his share by will, and the share does not pass automatically by the right of survivorship

30 Here a trust proceeds clause between the vendor and a financial institution could instead be introduced.

31 Danish law does not seem to require that the formation of a trust is evidenced in writing, although this would be commendable.

on the death of the co-owner, but instead forms part of the co-owner's estate in administration and devolves upon his heirs and spouse. Provisions according to which at the death of the co-owner, the share shall vest in the remaining co-owners, must be evidenced in the deceased co-owner's will, so as not to conflict with the Danish prohibition against *donatio mortis causa*, cf. Inheritance Act, s. 70. In addition, the co-owner must comply with the Danish rules on legal inheritance, cf. Inheritance Act, s. 25.

However, where the co-ownership assets comprise the trust fund, a "stepping out" provision may be considered lawful under Danish law, so that the trustee's spouse and heirs will not derive any benefit from the trust fund due to the duties inherent in the trustee's office. Another possibility is to develop the rules on spouses' joint estate, where currently according to Matrimonial Obligations Act, s. 16(2) and 28(1)(1), the surviving spouse receives half of the deceased spouse's assets.

There is no objection in Danish law to there being more than one beneficiary under a trust. However, if the trustee is one of the beneficiaries this may entail problems in affording protection to the trust fund from the personal creditors of the trustee. Obviously, the trustee's creditors are entitled to advance claims relating to the trustee's rights in his capacity as beneficiary. However, the trustee being a beneficiary might jeopardise the remainder of the trust fund to the detriment of the rest of the beneficiaries, because the personal creditors of the trustee will have a better chance of asserting that the trust fund should be made available to them.

Paragraph (3)
See commentary to Article III(2) *infra*.

Paragraph (4)
If the trustee committed a breach of trust, the beneficiaries will have a personal claim against the trustee. This claim will not rank prior to claims made by the trustee's spouse, heirs, and creditors. However, the concept of tracing assets is not wholly unfamiliar to Danish law[32]. The beneficiaries might therefore be able to trace into the hands of the trustee. Furthermore, the beneficiaries might be able to advance a claim *in personam* against a

32 See *supra*, C and *infra*, Article VI.

mala fide third party. The prerequisite for such a claim will most likely be that the third party is considered liable in delict. Indeed, Danish law might even consider the beneficiaries having rights *in rem* against a *mala fide* third party. This would imply that a *mala fide* third party takes the assets transferred, subject to the rights of the beneficiaries[33].

Article II. Creation of the trust

A transfer of property to a trustee may take place by S entering into a contract with T for the benefit of B (promise *in favorem tertii*), as Danish law has no rules on privity of contract. When employing a contract to this end, the parties' contract should be construed as an irrevocable and proper third party contract (*Egentlig tredjemandsaftale med uigenkaldeligt tredjemandsløfte*). The beneficiary then acquires a right, as stipulated in the contract, which may not be revoked by S and T. In this case, B has a chose in action against S and T to ensure that they adhere to the contract[34]. However, by making use of a contract, S may be able to influence T pursuant to the contractual relation between him and T.

The legal effects of multi-party contracts would most likely be similar to those of two-party contracts. However, the Danish position is not yet sufficiently clear on this issue.

Instead of a contract, a gift or a will can be used to convey property to a recipient, the trustee, stipulating that the conveyed property is for the benefit of a number of persons. Unless the donor or testator was defrauded, forced, or the like, a trust thus created will be irrevocable.

Article III. Trust fund

Paragraph (1)
Besides the rules on client accounts in law firms, and the Danish Securities Act s. 6[35], the Danish law regarding a fluctuating mass of assets can be

---

33 Concerning the beneficiary's rights against *mala fides* third parties, see *infra*, Article VII.

34 On third party contracts see Lennart Lynge Andersen, Palle Bo Madsen, Jørgen Nørgaard, *Aftaler og Mellemmænd*, 3rd edn, 1997, p. 138 *et seq.*

35 See *supra*, 2.

illustrated by focusing on the law of mortgages and charges. Pursuant to Registration Act, s. 47(a), a person is prohibited from mortgaging everything he owns or his future acquisitions. Pursuant to Registration Act, s. 47b(1), a floating charge cannot be created. Only two exceptions exist to s. 47b(1) and the scope of these are limited[36].

Only in very few cases does Danish legal authority acknowledge a fluctuating mass of assets as being protected from the creditors of the owner, i.e. the trustee. In the case of a trust, the trustee is the owner of the trust fund and hence, the trustee will most likely not be able to ward off his creditors, even if he can prove that the present assets are only replacements for assets previously transferred to him. In the case of money and other fungibles comprising the trust fund, it is a principal rule of Danish law that if the fund does not consist of exactly the same money or fungibles as originally, then, although segregated, the fund is not protected from the creditors of the owner, i.e. the trustee. However, the Danish courts have made some significant rulings to the contrary.

The Eastern High-Court has decided that client funds in a lawyer's account were not subject to claims from the creditors of the lawyer's estate in bankruptcy, even though (1) the lawyer in question had not placed all the clients' funds in the account, (2) the lawyer had made unauthorised drawings on the account, and (3) identification of each of the clients' deposits was difficult as the lawyer's book-keeping was imperfect. The client in question was nevertheless entitled to assert a proprietary claim against the lawyer's estate in bankruptcy[37].

In relation to the law of mortgages and charges, the Supreme Court has recognised a pawnor's proprietary right to fungible shares against the pawnee's estate in bankruptcy, although the existence and identity of the original shares could not be established. The pawnor was in two cases allowed to claim shares of an equivalent number to those originally pawned by him[38].

---

36 Registration Act, s. 37 and s. 47b(2).

37 *Ugeskrift for Retsvæsen* 1949.691 Ø.

38 *Ugeskrift for Retsvæsen* 1927.21 H and 1928.216 H.

In a Supreme Court ruling, relating to the former Danish Securities Act, a bank was allowed a proprietary claim to fungible shares deposited in a larger pool of shares held by a Portuguese Bank in the name of a Danish stockbroker in bankruptcy, although the shares had been mingled together with other fungible shares[39].

A further elaboration of rules based on the principles of client accounts in law firms, partnership funds, and the court rulings *supra*, may afford a satisfactory level of protection against claims made by the trustee's creditors to trust funds, where the original assets have been replaced by substitute assets.

Paragraph (2)
Pursuant to Administration of Justice Act, s. 507, execution is levied on assets belonging to the debtor. Under the Bankruptcy Act, s. 32, the estate in bankruptcy consists of the debtor's assets and any assets which might devolve upon the debtor during the proceedings in bankruptcy. The mirror image of this provision is Bankruptcy Act, s. 82, according to which the estate in bankruptcy is compelled to release assets which either belong to third parties, or, for any other reason, cannot be included in the debtor's estate in bankruptcy.

It is presumed that Danish law might be willing to accept a trust fund being exempt from claims from a trustee's creditors, provided that a satisfactory method is devised for ensuring the identity of the fund as separate trust fund. In fact, this will most likely be a *sine qua non*. However, *de lege ferenda* it is recommended that a statutory basis is provided, ensuring that trust funds are exempt from claims of the trustee's personal creditors.

Paragraph (3)
This would also be the position in Danish law.

39 *Ugeskrift for Retsvæsen* 1997.762 H.

Article IV. Trusts for beneficiaries or for enforceable purposes

Paragraph (1)

The settlor would also need to designate ascertained or ascertainable persons according to Danish law. Considering that in trusts, as opposed to *fideicommissa*, there will always be an owner of the assets, i.e. the trustee, any objection against appointing beneficiaries, not yet in existence at the creation of the trust, does not seem justified, as long as the beneficiaries can be ascertained in due course[40].

For obvious reasons, Danish law does not have any rules on the existence of or necessity for an enforcer, in the case of a trust for purposes. However, in the case of a charitable trust, the office of an enforcer may be held by a Danish public authority, e.g. the Ministry of Justice.

As mentioned above[41], the use of foundations for charitable purposes is widespread in Denmark, and there does not appear to be any demand for introducing the trust in this area. However, trusts may offer a more flexible and a less costly alternative, which may very well be extended a hearty welcome.

Because Denmark has enacted legislation for the tying up of funds[42], it is likely that Danish law will be kindly disposed to introducing trusts for purposes. The enforcer would, in that case, not have to be a public authority, but could instead be a lawyer.

Paragraph (2)

Danish law recognises resulting interests in relation to the law of *fideicommissa*. Imagine that X sets up a *fideicommissum* on the terms that his son S is to a receive an interest for life with remainder to S' children, provided they survive S. Thus, if S does not have any children, or they do not survive S, the question remains as to who is entitled to the interest in remainder. If the *fideicommissum* is set up by means of a will, the interest in remainder is considered to be temporarily owned by X's estate in

40 Some restrictions may, as a matter of course, have to be imposed on the settlor's right to appoint beneficiaries coming into existence in a distant future.

41 See *supra*, part B(3).

42 See *supra*, 2.

administration, which will have to be reassumed when S dies. The answer to the question is therefore: in the case of S not having any surviving children at the time of his death, the interest in remainder will instead devolve upon X's heirs, or, failing that, to the Danish treasury. In the case of a *fideicommissum* set up by a gift, the donor X will be considered owner until S dies, at which point it may be determined whether S leaves any surviving children behind him. In the event of S not having any surviving children, X or his heirs will be considered entitled to the interest in remainder.

Taking into account that the principle of resulting interests is known to Danish law in relation to *fideicommissa*, it would seem that Danish law might also be prepared to accept a resulting trust.

Paragraph (3)
Pursuant to Inheritance Act, s. 13(4), the surviving spouse who has retained undivided possession of the community property (*uskiftet bo*) has an obligation, when decreed by the Probate Court, to forward information to the heirs of the deceased spouse about any dispositions carried out in relation to the assets of the undivided community property. Legislation to the same effect, providing beneficiaries and enforcers with a right to information, could accordingly be introduced in Danish law regarding trusts. The requirement of a prior court intervention might be altered to a court only intervening if the trustee does not comply with his obligation to provide information.

Paragraph (4)
This would also be the position in Danish law.

Introducing trusts in Danish law would require an analysis of the rights of beneficiaries in connection with the rules of division of spouses' joint estates and the rules of forced inheritance.

Paragraph (5)
According to Danish law, the courts do not, unless specifically provided for by virtue of legislation, offer advice or give opinions. There has to be a real conflict, and the Danish courts are (under Administration of Justice Act, s. 324) empowered to issue a fine, if a hypothetical case is dressed up as a real conflict. Legislation to this end may be necessary.

Article V. Trustees' duties and powers

Paragraphs (1) and (2)
This would also be the position in Danish law.

Paragraph (3)
In various cases Danish law already requires segregation and protection of funds to take place, combined with maintenance of accurate accounts. In introducing trusts, Danish law would most certainly adopt the same position.

Paragraph (4)
A trustee would, under Danish law, be expected to adhere to the trust deed, exercise caution in his stewardship, and avoid all conflicts of interest.

Paragraph (5)
This would also be the position in Danish law[43].

Article VI. Remedies against trustees for breach of trust

According to Danish law, a trustee may be held liable for any breaches committed by him which have resulted in a loss, and the courts can order the trustee to pay compensation.

The Bailiff's Court may (under Administration of Justice Act, s. 641) be petitioned to issue an order restraining particular conduct[44]. In order for the Danish courts to remove a person from an office, the person must pursuant to Penal Code, s. 78(2), be convicted of a criminal offence. As a point of departure, only persons occupying an office which requires a special public authorisation or approval may be removed from their office, although a growing number of Acts make exceptions to this rule.

---

43 See *infra*, commentary to Article VI.

44 Alternatively, the beneficiary may seek a declaratory judgment in the ordinary courts.

As mentioned above[45], rules of tracing are not wholly unfamiliar to Danish law. A statutory basis for tracing assets is found in Matrimonial Obligations Act, s. 28(3):

> "28(3) A matrimonial contract, pursuant to paragraph 1, includes any substitute for the assets the matrimonial contract pertains to (...)."[46]

If the spouses have agreed upon having separate estates (*særeje*), the assets from time to time replacing the original assets are, pursuant to s. 28(3), still affected by the rules on separate estates. If, for instance, one of the spouses sells one of the assets, the proceeds are considered to have replaced the asset disposed of. This regulation applies not only to assets, but also to liabilities. On the basis of the aforementioned provision and s. 15(1) of the Matrimonial Obligations Act, a spouse is effectively prevented from arbitrarily shifting his or her assets from one matrimonial regime to another, to the detriment of the other spouse[47].

The same applies in the case of a surviving spouse, who has retained undivided possession of the community property (*uskiftet bo*)[48]. *Inter vivos* the surviving spouse exercises the rights of an owner - although restricted to some extent - of the undivided community property[49]. The surviving spouse is thus entitled to sell assets, but the proceeds will be considered as having replaced the assets disposed of[50].

There is not a sufficient degree of clarity regarding the question of whether proceeds from a surviving spouse's disposal of assets affected by a mutual will, are to be considered as having replaced the assets disposed of[51].

Should rules on tracing of trust property be introduced into Danish law, it might require a statutory basis.

---

45 See *supra*, C and Article I(4).

46 Author's translation.

47 See Noe Munck and Finn Taksøe-Jensen, *Særeje*, 1996, p. 110 *et seq.* and Henrik Dam, *Ægtepagter*, 1997, p. 98 *et seq.*

48 Pursuant to Inheritance Act, chapter 3.

49 Cf. Inheritance Act, s. 15(1).

50 See Finn Taksøe-Jensen, *Arveretten*, 1986, 1st edn, 6th issue, p. 93 *et seq.*

51 In a case where the spouses had made a provision in the will concerning substitutes for assets, the Western High Court decided that the proceeds were to replace the assets disposed of, UfR 1986.806 VLD.

Article VII. Liabilities of third parties

The distinction between personal or obligational interests and proprietary interests is not clear cut in Danish law[52]. For this very reason, it is not possible to determine, with a sufficient degree of certainty in each particular case, the nature of a beneficiary's interest in a trust.

Should the beneficiary's interest be considered proprietary as being *in rem*, the beneficiary will be able to put forward a proprietary claim against the *mala fide* third party[53], and in the case of the latter being insolvent, the beneficiary's claim would rank ahead of the creditors of the *mala fide* third party[54].

Otherwise, in the case of the trust interest only being considered personal or obligational, the prerequisite for the beneficiary being able to put forward a claim against a *mala fide* third party, would most likely be that the third party is considered liable in delict. Hence the beneficiary will only be allowed to advance a claim for damages, and thus be prevented from claiming the assets wrongfully transferred and in the possession of the *mala fide* third party.

Article VIII. Termination of a trust

Paragraph (1)

Except in the case of the legal portion of inheritance, emphasis is placed on the wishes of the testator (or donor). For this reason, the beneficiaries would most likely not be entitled to terminate the trust, even though all of the beneficiaries are in existence, have been ascertained, and are of full capacity. The wishes of the donor/testator would thus protect a trust from being terminated. On the other hand, if the donor/testator has imposed conditions, the beneficiaries will be absolutely entitled once the conditions are met, and the trust will *eo ipso* be terminated. The Danish rules on

52 It is rather seen as an academic conceptualisation, cf. Knud Illum, *Dansk Tingsret*, 3rd rev. edn, 1976, p. 3.

53 See, in principle, Carl Goos, *Forelæsninger over den almindelige retslære*, 2nd part, 1900, p. 202.

54 Provided of course that the assets can be properly identified.

perpetuities will, of course, terminate any instrument which oversteps the bounds of propriety.

Paragraph (2)
Concerning the cases (a)-(c) this would be the same position in Danish law.

Paragraph (3)
It is not possible to give an account of how funds are to be distributed upon the termination of a trust. However, as mentioned above[55], Danish law recognises resulting interests in relation to the law of *fideicommissa,* and should thus be able to develop principles analogous to those of resulting trusts.

Paragraph (4)
In Danish law the rule is that a legal entity is set up to own funds for purposes. Most commonly, foundations are used when the object is charity or the furtherance of the common good. The Ministry of Justice has, to date, not yet issued any rules on the course of action when dissolving non-business foundations, but in practice, the cy-près doctrine is used. Hence the foundation's funds will be applied to another related charitable purpose. However, the foundation's assets will never result back to the settlor, his spouse, or children under the age of majority and living at home[56].

---

55 See *supra,* Article IV(2).
56 See *supra,* part B(3).

National Report for the Netherlands

S.C.J.J. Kortmann and H.L.E. Verhagen
with the assistance of N.E.D. Faber, D.W. Aertsen and Ch.A.M. Domingus*

A. Introduction

Dutch law does not recognise a legal institution directly equivalent to the common law trust. The prevailing view in the Netherlands is as follows. The common law trust leads to a splitting-up of ownership rights, or the creation of rights *in rem*, in a manner not provided for by law, and therefore infringes our closed system (*numerus clausus*) of rights *in rem*. Like most civil law jurisdictions, Dutch law recognises an absolute and indivisible notion of ownership[1]. A management-agreement between a trustee and a beneficiary can, therefore, not derogate from the full right of ownership of the trustee, even though the parties may have agreed otherwise. In such a case, the beneficiary merely acquires a personal right (*ius in personam*), which can only be enforced against the counterparty (i.e. the trustee), and not against third parties. In principle a third party having recourse to the trust assets does not have to respect such a personal right. According to Dutch law an agreement between two parties can only burden or bind third parties when this is permitted by law. Dutch law has a *numerus clausus* of proprietary rights and the creation of these proprietary rights is subject to strict formal requirements. A proprietary right comparable to the beneficiary's interest under a trust is not known in Dutch law.

The experience of South African law and Scots law has confirmed our view that it is possible to have a trust, albeit not an English trust, in a legal

---

* Prof. S.C.J.J. Kortmann and Prof. H.L.E. Verhagen are both professor of private law, University of Nijmegen. N.E.D. Faber is director of the Business and Law Research Centre and lecturer in private law, University of Nijmegen. D.W. Aertsen and Ch.A.M. Domingus are lecturers in private law, University of Nijmegen.

1 Cf. Article 5:1 BW: "Ownership is the most far-reaching right over a thing which a person can have."

system such as that of the Netherlands, where the law of property is civilian in character, and in which there is no division between common law and equity. This will be further developed in parts C and D of this report.

B. Existing law

1. *Fiducia cum amico (fiduciary ownership)*

The Dutch legal institution that comes closest to the express *inter vivos* trust is the *fiducia cum amico*. In most cases, *fiducia cum amico* involves a transfer. The assets concerned are given to somebody else for management purposes by transferring these assets to the manager (*fiduciarius*). Thus, the manager becomes owner of these assets and therefore has the power to manage and dispose of the assets. In connection with the transfer, the manager accepts the duty to manage the assets. The acquired assets are to be managed for the benefit of one or more beneficiaries. The transferor of the assets will in most cases also be the beneficiary, although this need not necessarily be the case.

The *fiducia cum amico* has wholly developed outside statutory law and under the regime of the previous Civil Code (*Burgerlijk Wetboek*) it was recognised for the first time in the *BUMA*-case (HR 14 June 1929, NJ 1929, 1424). Although the 1992 new *Burgerlijk Wetboek* codified most *Hoge Raad* (Dutch Supreme Court) case law, the new code does not contain general rules dealing with the *fiducia cum amico*. The question even arose whether the *fiducia* was valid at all. The majority of legal writers shared the view, in accordance with the opinion expressed in the Parliamentary History[2], that under the new *Burgerlijk Wetboek fiducia cum amico* should remain a valid institution. That prevailing view has been confirmed by the *Hoge Raad* in the *Sogelease*-case (HR 19 May 1995, NJ 1996, 119). The *fiducia cum amico* remains valid as long the manager acquires full and undivided ownership. The claims of the beneficiary to receive, for example, the proceeds of the managed assets can only be of a personal (obligational) nature. Such claims

2 See *Memorie van Antwoord II, Parlementaire Geschiedenis Boek 3*, pp. 318-319; *Nota II Voortgang, Parlementaire Geschiedenis Boek 3 (Inv. 3, 5 en 6)*, p. 1273.

therefore have no effect against third persons, unless the relevant claims happen to have been reinforced with proprietary rights such as pledge or mortgage, or unless the right of the beneficiary itself is a right *in rem* (e.g. *usufruct*).

Just as is the case with the trust (cf. Article I of the Principles) an essential characteristic of the *fiducia cum amico* is the fact that the beneficiary has the economic interest in the managed assets, while the manager legally owns the assets. However, there are also clear differences, particularly from the viewpoint of the beneficiary. The beneficiary is not regarded as equitable owner, such concept being unknown to Dutch law, nor as creditor of a high-priority claim. Under Dutch law the assets to be managed are wholly and exclusively owned by the manager. In the bankruptcy of the manager this very likely has the consequence that the assets concerned are part of the bankrupt estate of the manager. The beneficiary has a personal claim only against the manager and will therefore be a non-preferred creditor. Here one encounters a fundamental difference with the trust, where the trust fund forms a separate fund within the estate of the trustee; see Article I(1) of the Principles.

Dutch lawyers often use the following mechanism to reduce the bankruptcy risk in Dutch law: the assets are transferred to a legal person (for instance a foundation) which, except in respect of such assets, has no power according to its constitution and organisation to execute any transactions from which considerable debts can arise. To reduce the bankruptcy risk further, the assets to be managed are transferred to one legal entity (the trustee), while the actual management is performed by another legal person. There is, however, a considerable disadvantage attached to this mechanism compared with which the trust is much more flexible.

A second consequence of the personal nature of the *fiducia cum amico* becomes apparent when the manager exceeds his internal authority by transferring assets to a third party. Under Dutch law the beneficiary does not have a proprietary claim entitling him to recover the assets. The recovery *in rem* of traced property (cf. Article VI of the Principles) is unknown in Dutch law. It could well be argued that if the third party was aware of the "trustee's" capacity, as well as of his "breach of trust", he will be liable in delict. If the court does find the third party liable in delict, the court has the discretion to award the beneficiary the return of the specific assets (Article 6:103 BW). Naturally, the beneficiary can also sue the manager for violation of his contractual duties (Article 6:74 BW). It should be noted, however, that in both situations the claims are non-preferred personal claims, so that in the event of the third party's or manager's bankruptcy the beneficiary will only receive a small portion (or nothing) of the nominal value of his claim.

2. *The nominee account*

The only Dutch legal institution which is likely to be considered a trust in the sense of the Principles is the nominee account. A nominee account is a bank account which is, for example, maintained by an advocate or notary in his capacity as mandatary (agent) for the benefit of one or more clients. In *Hoge Raad* 3 February 1984, NJ 1984, 752 (*notary Slis-Stroom*) the *Hoge Raad* decided that the amount represented by the balance of such account is not part of the bankrupt estate of the account-holder. The *Hoge Raad* did not elaborate on the legal nature of the nominee account. The nominee account is explained by several writers as a special application of the *fiducia cum amico*[3]. The claim against the bank, originating from the bank account relationship, belongs to the account-holder. However, the claim forms a special case of a separate fund within the estate of the account-holder. If this conclusion is correct, which we think it is, the nominee account should be regarded as an institution having recognisable characteristics of the trust as described in the Principles.

3. *Certification*[4]

Certification concerns a special application of *fiducia cum amico*. Although certification can also concern receivables, we will discuss certification of shares only. The technique of certification is often applied to protect a company against a hostile take-over. In order to accomplish this, shares are transferred to a limited company or *stichting* (*stichting administratiekantoor*), which subsequently issues certificates and administers the shares for the

3 See, for example, C.Æ. Uniken Venema and S.E. Eisma, *Eigendom ten titel van beheer naar komend recht*, pp. 196 *ff.* and the contributions of N.E.D. Faber, H.L.E. Verhagen and S.C.J.J. Kortmann in: D.J. Hayton *et al.* (edd), *Vertrouwd met de Trust* (1996).

4 *Certificering*, the issue of units of value.

benefit of a group of certificate holders. The certificate holders are for instance investors who, on the stock exchange, or "over the counter", have purchased certificates. In order to protect the certificate holders, the Dutch legislator has incorporated a special provision in the *Burgerlijk Wetboek*. By virtue of Article 3:259 BW, the personal (obligational) claims of the certificate holders are in certain circumstances to be reinforced with a right of pledge created by operation of law. This security interest protects the certificate holders against non-payment of what is owed to them by the administration office. In this specific application of *fiducia cum amico* the beneficiary, the certificate holder, therefore has more than a mere personal right against the manager.

4. *Bewind*

Another legal institution which is used under Dutch law in order to create trust-like relationships is *bewind*. The *bewind* cannot be characterised as a trust in the sense of Article I of the Principles. A trust in the sense of the Principles only exists in situations where the trustee legally owns the assets to be managed, which is not so in the case of *bewind*. In the case of *bewind* the beneficiary is legal owner of the assets to be managed. There are, however, restrictions on the beneficiary's right to dispose of the assets placed under *bewind*. Either the legal owner cannot dispose of these assets at all, or he can only do so subject to the *bewind*. The *bewindvoerder*, as the administrator is usually called, acts in the case of *bewind* only as agent for the owner of the assets (the beneficiary). Because the assets to be managed are not legally owned by the *bewindvoerder*, the assets remain unaffected by the bankruptcy of the *bewindvoerder*. In this respect the *bewind* offers the beneficiary more protection than the *fiducia cum amico*.

However, despite these differences, there are also clear similarities between the trust and the *bewind*. As soon as certain assets have been placed under *bewind*, it is not the owner but rather the *bewindvoerder* who has authority to act with respect to those assets. The *bewindvoerder*, just as the trustee, is vested with the exclusive power to manage and dispose of the assets, the difference being that the *bewindvoerder* is only an agent of the owner-beneficiary. The assets placed under *bewind* constitute a separate fund within the estate of the owner-beneficiary. So far as creditors of the owner-beneficiary are concerned, a special regime applies to the assets placed under *bewind*. For debts concerning the assets placed under *bewind* and incurred by the *bewindvoerder* acting in his capacity as such, recourse can always be taken against those assets. For other debts recourse cannot be had to the *bewind* fund or, sometimes, only subject to the bewind.

For commercial and financial purposes the *bewind* is a form of asset-management which is not always practicable. The reason for this is that the *bewind* is utilisable only in a limited number of cases. The original draft for the new *Burgerlijk Wetboek* contained a set of general rules for a type of *bewind* to be created by the parties themselves (title 3.6 BW). It has since become clear that this part of the draft will not be enacted. Except for some instances, under current law the *bewind* can be used only in situations in which statute expressly allows it[5]. However, it is not clear how far the exceptions reach. Almost all of the cases of *bewind* that are recognised by statute concern family law or the law of succession. In commercial asset-management relationships the *bewind* is used only where a trustee is appointed in connection with a bond issue. The authoritative textbook, Asser-Van der Grinten, regards this institution as a special application of *bewind*[6]. Accepting this authority, it is usually assumed in the Netherlands that this specific type of *bewind* can be used effectively even though no express statutory basis exists[7].

5. *Mandate*

A statutory management device, which is intended to be a Dutch alternative for the trust, is the "privative" or exclusive mandate. On 1 September 1993 Article 7:423 BW was added to the *Burgerlijk Wetboek*, in which the so-called *privative* mandate is regulated. By virtue of this provision the principal has the possibility of authorising his mandatary or agent, in an exclusive manner, to execute acts of management and (most likely) acts of

5 See Asser-Van der Grinten I (*De vertegenwoordiging*), 7th edn (1990), nrs. 140-143 and 146. A new edition of this book is in preparation by S.C.J.J. Kortmann and will be published in 1999.

6 See Asser-Van der Grinten I (*De vertegenwoordiging*), nr. 144.

7 This view is, *inter alia*, based on Statements in Parliament, by the Secretary of State for Legal Affairs. In the Explanatory Memorandum accompanying the *Wet conflictenrecht trusts*, 1992-1993, 23 027, nr. 3, p. 5, the Secretary of State declares: "One cannot exclude the possibility that in certain cases the bewind-device will be employed, even when title 3.6 [bewind] will not be introduced. This is of special interest for the trustee in a bond issue".

disposition in respect of one or more of his assets. Where the parties have opted for "privative effect", this has the consequence that the mandatary is exclusively authorised to manage the assets. For the duration of the contract of mandate the principal does not have the authority to manage the assets himself[8]. This inability also affects third persons who are aware (or should have been aware) of the exclusive character of the mandate. It is precisely this external effect which constitutes the special character of the privative mandate. As a consequence the mandatary, just as the trustee, has the exclusive power to manage and dispose of the assets. However, the statutory regulation of the privative mandate has serious defects, so that the privative mandate has not yet proved to be a serious alternative to the trust. For example: if an agent is exclusively authorised by the principal to execute acts of management (but not acts of disposition) in connection with assets of the principal, it is not clear what happens if the principal should transfer the assets to a third party. Is the third party also bound by the contract of mandate? Article 7:423 BW affords no answer to this question.

Mention should also be made of Article 7:420 BW. Dutch law does not recognise a doctrine of undisclosed agency. Where the agent acts in his own name in dealing with a third party, a contract comes into existence only between the agent and the third party. Nevertheless, where the agent is declared bankrupt and in certain other instances, the principal can bring about a transfer to himself of the agent's rights vis-à-vis the third party. He does so by means of a declaration to the agent and third party[9]. Thus, in situations of indirect agency a situation is created which is not unlike the case where contractual rights are held on trust: the contractual rights against the third party are legally owned by the agent; in the agent's bankruptcy, however, they will pass to the principal and will thus remain unaffected by the bankruptcy.

8 On the privative mandate, see *inter alia*, Asser-Kortmann-De Leede-Thunnissen, Zwolle (1994), nrs. 169 *ff.*; A.F.J.A. Leijten, *Privatieve lastgeving en trustachtige verhoudingen*, in: *Vertrouwd met de trust*, pp. 419-434, S.E. Eisma, *Buitenwettelijk bewind en de trustfiguur bij obligatieleningen*, in: *Vertrouwd met de Trust*, pp. 387-395; W. Snijders, *Trustverdrag en Nederlands materieel recht*, in: *Grensoverschrijdend privaatrecht* (lib.am. Van Rijn van Alkemade) (1993), pp. 230-243.

9 Under Article 7:421 BW the third party has a similar power, enabling him to exercise against the principal the remedies the third party had against the agent under the contract existing between agent and third party. On Article 7:420/421 BW, see H.L.E. Verhagen, Agency in Private International Law (1995), pp. 43-50.

6. *The foundation (stichting)*

There is an important difference between the trust and the *stichting*. Unlike the trust the *stichting* is a legal person. Nevertheless, the *stichting* has a function under Dutch law similar to that of the charitable trust in common law countries.

In certain situations the *stichting* can be used as an alternative for the private trust as well. For example, the administration office in certification transactions often has the legal form of a foundation. The use of the *stichting* for commercial purposes is restricted however. Article 2:285 section 3 BW determines that a *stichting* may only distribute its assets (including its profits) to beneficaries if the distribution serves an ideal or social purpose.

7. *The mutual fund*

A wide variety of opinions exists in relation to the legal nature of the investment fund. So much is certain, that the investment fund does *not* have legal personality. A difference of opinion exists, however, as to who must be regarded as the owner of the assets comprised in the fund. Are these assets owned by the joint investors, by the custodian, or by the manager of the fund? Although an investment fund can be structured in different ways, we consider the following structure most desirable from a practical point of view. The assets comprised in the fund are owned by the custodian, while the investors only have contractual rights against the manager and the custodian. In relation to this, we submit that the fund assets remain separate from the other assets of the custodian. In our opinion this can be achieved under current law, *without* the necessity for the fund assets to be owned by a different legal entity from the one that acts as custodian. This separation of assets can in our view be accomplished by transferring the fund assets to the custodian in his capacity as such and by stipulating that the custody takes place "in the name of the fund". Under this approach, provided that a proper administration of the fund takes place, there is no necessity for appointing a different custodian (or sub-custodian) for each investment fund.

8. *Security trustee*

Under existing law it is unclear to what extent a trustee can act as a security trustee for the benefit of a group of changing creditors (e.g. bond loans, syndicated loans). In cases where the security interest (pledge or mortgage) is granted to the trustee, the security interest is vested in a different person from the creditors who provided the money covered by the security. Although in our view this is possible, it has been argued that the accessory nature of the rights of pledge and mortgage could vitiate this attempt to create a security[10]. It is also suggested that it follows from the accessory character of the rights of pledge and mortgage that these rights cannot be transferred separate from the secured debt. For this reason the replacement of the trustee might lead to difficulties. Even though it is possible to use mechanisms in order to overcome these uncertainties, for example by using a "parallel covenant" in favour of the trustee, a statutory provision for this matter would be extremely useful.

C. Proposals for further development of trust-like relationships under Dutch law

1. *The current state of affairs*

We have seen in part A that under Dutch law no equivalent to the common law trust exists. For this reason, there have been many proposals in Dutch legal writing for adapting existing rules on trust-like relationships, some even in favour of introducing a "proper" Dutch trust based on the Anglo-American model[11]. Organisations like the Dutch Bar Association, the Dutch Bankers Association and the Dutch Association of In-house Lawyers have made the same suggestion[12]. These organisations have proposed that a management agreement should have external effect, in the sense that the assets which are transferred "in trust" should form no part of the private

10 Cf. A.I.M. van Mierlo and M.V. Polak, *Verstrekking van zekerheden aan internationale syndicaten*, 2nd edn (1998), p. 636-637.

11 Particularly C.Æ. Uniken Venema has pleaded in many of his publications for introduction of the trust into Dutch domestic law.

12 *Memorie van Toelichting II* (*Wet conflictenrecht trusts*), 1992-1993, 23 027, nr. 3, p. 2.

estate of the manager. So far, the Dutch government has rejected these suggestions.

In Parliament, the Secretary of State responsible for these matters has declared that under current Dutch law there are adequate devices comparable to the trust that are available in order to reach the same results. Whether this view is correct is subject to serious doubts. Not all the legal consequences of the Anglo-American trust can be achieved in the Netherlands, or they can be achieved only through expensive or complicated legal mechanisms. For example, in the case of fiduciary ownership the parties themselves can reinforce the personal rights of the beneficiaries by creating a pledge or mortgage. In this way, at least in theory, a result is achieved by which a right *in rem* is conferred upon the beneficiary. However, particularly where the trust fund is a changing portfolio (e.g. shares and bonds), it will often be impracticable to employ the rights of pledge or mortgage. Similarly, in the case where the trust arrangement involves a large number of beneficiaries (e.g. investment funds) the creation of enduring security interests could meet with considerable difficulties. Another possibility for achieving a separation of assets is a transfer of the assets to be managed to a legal person, in circumstances ensuring (through its constitution and organisation) that this legal person cannot execute transactions from which considerable debts may arise. To reduce the bankruptcy risk further, the assets to be managed could be transferred to one legal entity (the trustee), while the actual management could be performed by another legal entity. Mechanisms like this have certain disadvantages. The incorporation of a legal person can be costly and the decision-making in such mechanisms can be highly complicated. A third possible way of protecting the interests of the beneficiary would be a transfer of the assets to be managed under a condition precedent or condition subsequent. Thus it is conceivable for the assets to be managed to be transferred to a manager under a condition subsequent which will become operative if the financial position of the manager deteriorates considerably. This mechanism is not very practicable either, since it might be too cumbersome or costly.

In comparison with other civil law systems Dutch law falls quite out of line. In Germany, for example, the "trust assets", although legally owned by the manager (*Treuhänder*), do under some circumstances form a separate fund. The conclusion has to be that the Dutch legal rules relating to management relationships are deviating strongly from corresponding rules in important jurisdictions such as the United States, Germany and England. Taking into account the ever progressing globalisation of the financial sector this is a highly undesirable situation, which adversely affects the competitive position of Dutch enterprises. Moreover, it must be noted that research has demonstrated that foreign trusts are used more and more by Dutch (legal and natural) persons to have effect in the Netherlands[13]. It is therefore not without reason that the above mentioned organisations indicated that they need a new trust-like institution. Furthermore the ratification by the Netherlands of the Hague Convention on the law applicable to trusts and on their recognition constitutes a powerful argument for amending current Dutch law on this point.

2. *How to introduce the trust into Dutch law?*

The common law trust is a hybrid legal institution, with proprietary and personal (obligational) effects. When answering the question whether the concept of the trust can be introduced into Dutch domestic law, one can therefore depart from an "obligational approach" (the trust as a notion primarily belonging to the law of obligations) or from the "proprietary approach" (the trust as a notion primarily belonging to the law of property). A third and completely different way of introducing the trust into domestic law would be the personification of the trust. Below we will briefly explain the different approaches.

a. *Obligational approach*

The underlying concept of this approach is the *fiducia cum amico*, where the assets concerned form a separate fund, not available for personal creditors of the fiduciary. The trustee has the right of ownership in respect of both his private assets and the trust assets. Nevertheless, private assets and trust assets, although both owned by the trustee, form two separate funds (patrimonies). Each patrimony forms a separate and exclusive fund. In principle a creditor of one patrimony has no right of recourse against assets which form part of the other patrimony. The beneficiary's preference is based not on a right *in rem* - his rights are of a personal nature - but on

13 The tax authorities have noted that trusts are used more and more, the Secretary of State for Legal Affairs stated in Parliament. See *Memorie van Toelichting II* (*Wet conflictenrecht trusts*), 1992-1993, 23 027, nr. 3, p. 11.

separation of patrimony. The personal creditors of the trustee merely have a claim against the assets comprised in the "private fund" of the trustee. They cannot take action against the trust fund. The beneficiary only has to share the proceeds of the assets of the trust fund with the creditors of the trust. If the proceeds of the private assets of the trustee are not sufficient to satisfy the trustee's personal creditors, they will not be able to take recourse against the trust assets for unpaid debts.

If the trustee sells an asset, the "replacement value" of the asset flows to the patrimony from which the asset originated: the trust fund can be a changing portfolio. Both patrimonies can separately be declared bankrupt. If a human trustee dies or a corporate trustee ceases to exist, the trust patrimony lives on, legally owned by a new trustee.

The relationship between the trustee and the beneficiary is obligational in character: it belongs to the law of obligations. This relationship can be created by contract or by a unilateral declaration of the settlor of the trust. For the trust to come into existence it is not necessary that the trust assets are already owned by the trustee. The "trust obligations" owed by the trustee to the beneficiary come into being with the settlor's declaration of trust. The separate fund, however, and the beneficiary's preferential position only come into existence when the trust assets are owned by the trustee. Therefore, in situations when the settlor is not the same person as the trustee, a transfer to the trustee is required in order to create a separate fund.

From this "separation of patrimony without separation of personality"[14] many of the consequences of the Dutch "trust" can be derived. Amending Dutch law in this manner has the effect that the most important alternative to the trust available in Dutch law, the *fiducia cum amico*, is brought much closer to the Anglo-American trust, the Scots trust, the South African trust and also to the German *Treuhand*. In our view, there are no insurmountable difficulties for realising this. German, Scots and South African law could serve as a precedent. In several instances current Dutch law already recognises the notion of a separate fund. For example, it is generally recognised in case law that the partnership patrimony of a commercial partnership

14 See National Report for Scotland.

(*vennootschap onder firma*) forms a fund which is separate from the personal estates of the partners[15]. An important consequence of this is that during the life of the partnership, private creditors of a partner cannot take action against the assets belonging to this separate fund. The experiences we have with the commercial partnership demonstrate that a separate fund, as referred to above, can well be fitted into a legal system, such as that of the Netherlands, recognising an absolute and indivisible concept of ownership[16].

b. *Proprietary approach*

Under this approach the trust can be fitted into the system of Dutch law as well. The trust can be characterised as a proprietary encumbrance (*goederenrechtelijk verband*) with which the assets are burdened. This means that the trustee is obliged vis-à-vis the beneficiaries to exercise for the benefit of the beneficiaries the rights accruing from the trust patrimony. From the proprietary encumbrance with which the assets are burdened obligations originate which are owed by the legal owner of these assets and his successors vis-à-vis the beneficiaries. This is a concept which is perfectly reconcilable with present Dutch law. Thus, the creation of a right of *emphytheusis* (*erfpacht*: long lease with proprietary effect) not only results in a proprietary burden on the right of ownership, but also creates obligations between the (successive) owners of the asset concerned and the person to whom the right of *emphytheusis* has been granted. The *bewind* can also be viewed as a proprietary encumbrance from which obligations originate. In the case of *bewind*, however, the beneficiary is the legal owner, while the legal position of the *bewindvoerder* is determined by the proprietary encumbrance which the *bewind* creates over the assets of the beneficiary.

c. *Personification: the stichting approach*

A completely different way of introducing the trust into domestic law would be personification of the trust. This can be achieved by introducing the trust as a qualified form of the *stichting*. Under this approach the trust

15 Cf. Asser-Maeijer 5-V, 6th edn (1995), nrs. 162, 171 and 173-181.

16 This matter is discussed more elaborately by N.E.D. Faber, S.C.J.J. Kortmann and H.L.E. Verhagen in: *Vertrouwd met de Trust*.

fund will be regarded as a legal person. So to speak the board of the *stichting* will be trustee. In the regulations of the *stichting* the settlor will appoint beneficiaries. Thereby the board will have a duty to manage the assets of the *stichting* for the benefit of the beneficiaries.

Accepting this approach, amendments to the law regarding the *stichting* (title 2.6 BW) would be necessary. Under current law the board of a *stichting* can only distribute assets of the *stichting* if such a distribution serves a charitable purpose (Article 2:285 section 3 BW). In order for the *stichting* to be available for a wide range of commercial purposes, Article 2:285 section 3 BW would have to allow dispositions of the assets to beneficiaries of the *stichting* as well. An advantage of the *stichting* approach is that the law regarding the *stichting* to some extent already deals with supervision by the court[17].

D. Commentary on the Principles article by article

Under all above mentioned approaches it would be possible to implement the trust in Dutch domestic law. For the time being it seems that the "obligational approach" has the most support among Dutch lawyers. In the last part of this national report therefore we will only discuss the consequences of the "obligational" approach. In respect of each Principle, we will set out how the rules contained therein could be implemented in Dutch law. In particular, we will indicate whether in our view an express statutory provision would be required for implementation. A general remark is that quite often this would not be strictly necessary, because of the possibilities the courts have to develop certain rules within the framework of currently existing law. However, in many cases it would be beneficial to legal certainty if express statutory provisions were to be enacted.

17 For instance, the court can replace the board of the *stichting* in the case of mismanagement.

Article I. Main characteristics of the trust

Paragraph (1)
In most cases a trust would be governed, directly or by way of analogy, by the rules on the contract of instruction or mandate (*opdracht/lastgeving*; title 7.7 BW) and/or deposit (title 7.9 BW). In other situations the general rules of book 6 of the *Burgerlijk Wetboek* (law of obligations) and those of title 3.2 BW (juridical acts) will be applicable. The rights of the beneficiaries against the trustee, to the extent that they are not already contracting parties, can normally be based on the device of stipulation for the benefit of a third party (Article 6:253-256 BW).

Traditional objections against the recognition of a separate fund are primarily based on Article 3:84 section 3, 3:276 and 3:277 BW. The rationale of Article 3:84 section 3 BW is that no splitting-up of ownership rights may take place in a manner not provided for by law. It can very well be argued that this does not prevent the recognition of a separate fund. The trustee would acquire all ownership rights. The right of ownership will form part of the trustee's estate. *Within* this estate the trust assets would form a separate fund, not available for private creditors of the trustee. However, this does not derogate from the fact that according to the law of property a full transfer of ownership has taken place. In the case of a declaration of trust, Article 3:84 section 3 BW would not even be applicable, because no transfer takes place at all. According to Article 3:276 BW a creditor can have recourse against all assets owned by the debtor, unless provided otherwise by a contract (between the creditor and the debtor) or by statute. Under a strict interpretation of Article 3:276 BW, this provision would prevent the recognition of a separate fund, since such recognition would entail that certain assets owned by the debtor are *not* available for all creditors. Similar reasoning applies to Article 3:277-282 BW, elaborating the statutory scheme of preferences. According to Article 3:277 BW all creditors have equal ranking, unless there are statutory preferences. However, in our view these provisions do not prevent the recognition of a separate trust fund. There is no need for an express statutory provision dealing with this. This is confirmed by the fact that certain forms of a separate fund have been developed by case law, which are not directly supported by a statutory basis. The most important examples are the nominee account and the separate fund of a commercial partnership (*vennootschap onder firma*).

However, it is our opinion that a statutory basis should be created for the separate trust fund because this will greatly enhance legal certainty.

Paragraph (2)

Concerning the remedies available to the parties the general rules of contract law apply, directly or by way of analogy (unilateral declaration of trust). This means that it is primarily for the settlor and the trustee to deal in the management agreement with matters such as replacement of the trustee, termination of the trust etc. Under the obligational approach the relationship between settlor, trustee and beneficiary is regarded as contractual. Therefore the rules on two-party contracts apply by way of analogy, provided that this is consistent with the character of the multi-party contract (Article 6:279 BW). The specific legal consequences of this are not completely clear. Thus it might be appropriate to include a specific statutory provision in the *Burgerlijk Wetboek* dealing with the aforementioned matters of replacement etc. in situations where a (large) number of beneficiaries is involved.

Paragraph (3)

See the comments to Article I(1).

Paragraph (4)

The solution which would be most reconcilable with the obligational approach is to accept that a beneficiary merely has personal rights against third parties to whom trust assets have been wrongly transferred. No statutory provision is necessary: the currently existing rules of law of delict, as developed in case law, can deal with this matter. The legal consequences of a tracing-like device cannot be achieved by Dutch law without an express statutory provision. See further the comment to Article VI.

Article II. Creation of the trust

For Article II no special statutory provision is required, except for those matters discussed in the comment to Article I(1). It should be noted, however, that under Dutch law a management relationship falling within the terms of Article I(1) can already come into existence before the assets are actually transferred to the trustee. The separate fund, on the other hand, will only be created when the assets are transferred to the trustee, or when a declaration of trust has taken place in respect of existing assets.

Article III. Trust fund

Paragraph (1)
The concept of a fund consisting of a changing portfolio is not unfamiliar to Dutch law. Thus, the separate fund of a commercial partnership is not confined to the assets originally transferred to the partnership patrimony by the partners. Also, in the case of *bewind* substitution is recognised, for some forms even by statute (Article 1:433 BW). Nevertheless, it is our view that for this crucial issue legal certainty should exist. It is therefore most desirable to include an express statutory provision to this effect.

Paragraph (2)
Although it could be argued that this rule is a consequence of the recognition of a separate trust fund and consistent with principles of other areas of law (e.g. agency), it is our view that this important matter should also be dealt with by statute.

Paragraph (3)
Under Dutch law this duty would, if not expressly provided for in the trust agreement, normally be implied by law. No express statutory provision is required. Where several trustees jointly own the trust assets, the general rules of the *Burgerlijk Wetboek* on co-ownership apply. These rules entail that where one of the co-owners "steps out" (e.g. dies etc.) his co-ownership interest does not automatically vest in the remaining trustee(s). A specific statutory provision to this effect would be required.

Article IV. Trusts for beneficiaries or for enforceable purposes

Paragraph (1)
Regarding the designation of ascertained or ascertainable persons as beneficiaries, this provision is consistent with our legal system and can easily be accommodated. Under Dutch law it is generally accepted that in relation to third party stipulations (Article 6:253-256 BW) the third party need only be ascertainable, not necessarily ascertained.

It is questionable, however, whether a purpose trust is desirable in our legal system. For, the foundation (the so-called *stichting*) can be used in a wide variety of cases.

Paragraph (2)
In our view, no specific statutory provision is required. The rules of interpretation available in Dutch law are sufficiently flexible to reach the result envisaged by Article IV(2).

Paragraph (3)
The *Burgerlijk Wetboek* contains provisions similar to that of this paragraph, especially in title 7.7 BW regarding the contract of instruction (*opdracht*) and mandate (*lastgeving*). See for example Article 7:403 section 1 BW about the right to information and Article 7:403 section 2 BW about the duty to account. To the extent that the trust, envisaged by these Principles, can be regarded as a contract of instruction, the aforementioned statutory provisions apply equally to the trust.

Paragraph (4)
This paragraph is consistent with current Dutch law. Under Article 3:83 section 1 BW claims are, in principle, transferable. Under Dutch law the rights of the beneficiary should be regarded as claims, rights *in personam*. Under Article 3:83 section 2 BW parties to a contract can exclude transferability of claims, which exclusion can be invoked against third parties.

Paragraph (5)
Dutch law will not pose difficulties regarding this paragraph. The terms of the trust give rise to obligations enforceable by any creditor thereof.

Article V. Trustees' duties and powers

Paragraph (1)
Since the trustee is owner of the trust fund, he has all the powers of an owner in respect of the trust fund (Article 5:1 BW). Dutch law does not distinguish between legal and beneficial ownership. Ownership always entails absolute ownership in respect of the assets of the trust fund. It is conceivable that by way of express statutory provision it could be made possible to place an absolute restriction upon the trustee's powers, either by the juridical act by which the trust is created or by the legal relationship between the trustee and the beneficiary.

Paragraph (2)

Title 7.7 BW (contract of instruction and mandate) contains similar provisions regarding reasonable care, e.g. Article 7:401 BW. More generally, the duty to take reasonable care in the relationship between the contracting parties is paramount to contract law, and is laid down in the Articles 6:2 and 6:248 section 1 BW.

Paragraph (3)

The trustee is under a duty to keep the trust assets separate from his private patrimony and from other trust assets. This duty naturally stems from the nature of the trust, and easily fits in with the Dutch legal system. The duties of the trustee are correlative to the rights of the beneficiaries and the enforcer of the trust. Article 7:403 section 1 and 2 BW contain a similar provision for the contract of instruction and mandate. Compare the comment on Article III(3) of these Principles.

Paragraph (4)

Under Dutch law the instructed party (*opdrachtnemer*) must personally perform his tasks, unless provided to the contrary, but is allowed assistance if necessary. The duty of the trustee to perform his functions honestly and loyally falls within the scope of Article 7:401 BW (in case of instruction and mandate) or at least under Article 6:2 and 6:248 section 1 BW.

Paragraph (5)

Liability of the trustee in case of breach of trust follows from Article 6:74 *ff* BW in conjunction with the Articles 6:248 section 1 and 7:400 *ff* BW (contractual liability). The trustee must make good any loss occasioned to the trust fund for which he is liable, and must make compensation out of his private patrimony. In some specific circumstances the trustee's breach of contract can also render the trustee liable in delict against the beneficiary.

Article VI. Remedies against trustees for breach of trust

Under the law of trusts common law courts have a more active role in supervising and rewarding remedies for breach as compared to that of Dutch courts in cases of e.g. *fiducia cum amico*. The regular Dutch remedy awarded in case of breach is damages, payable in money. Upon demand of the injured party the judge may decide to award damages in a form other than payment of a sum of money, if he so thinks fit (Article 6:103 BW). Under Article 6:104 BW the judge may at the request of the injured party estimate his loss at the profits made by the party in breach. Restitution of profits is therefore no separate remedy, but a way of estimating the injured party's loss. In some circumstances the judge may award a restraining order. Additionally, the judge can command the party in breach to execute certain acts, based on Article 3:296 BW. Such command can be combined with liability to pay a penal sum. Other remedies for breach, as mentioned in Article V of the Principles, do not exist in our legal system. In our view there is no need for such other remedies.

Under present law the parties to the contract are entitled to enforce the terms of that contract. There does not exist a special authority that can enforce the contract instead of, or as well as, the parties to the contract.

Replacement of a contractual party, such as a trustee, is not known in existing Dutch law. It is possible, though, for the parties to the contract to draw up a regulation on the subject in the trust deed, which in turn can be enforced by the court. Both the reasons for such replacement and the rules governing replacement procedures (e.g. requirements for a quorum and for a qualified majority of votes in the meeting of beneficiaries) can be laid down in the trust deed. Replacement of a manager might pose some problems in case of a security trust. Since no special provisions exist in relation to replacement of a contractual party, statutory provisions might be desirable for some particular uses of the trust. One could contemplate provisions making regulations similar to those currently existing for the replacement of managing directors of companies.

Article VII. Liabilities of third parties

According to consistent case law, third parties dealing with the trustee as such can in special circumstances be liable in delict (Article 6:162 BW) to the beneficiary, if the trustee committed a breach of contract because of his dealings with such third party. The mere fact that the third party had knowledge of the trust is probably insufficient for liability in delict. The beneficiary's claim against such third party is in principle a claim *in personam*. It entitles the beneficiary to damages payable in money, unless, as the injured party, he demands otherwise and the judge decides that a different form of award is suitable (Article 6:103 BW). Under current law the trustee's powers to dispose of the trust assets can only be restricted by a personal obligation. The trustee and the beneficiary cannot invoke such a personal restriction against third parties, the beneficiary not having a right *in rem*. If an *in rem* tracing-like device, up to now unknown in Dutch law, is desirable in our legal system then express statutory regulation will be needed. This regulation should establish the boundaries of the device. Already under Dutch law some instances of substitution are known, albeit for very specific situations.

Article VIII. Termination of a trust

Paragraphs (1) and (2)

The rules of termination of the trust correspond with the rules for terminating the contract of instruction and mandate, as laid down in title 7.7 BW. Possibly some additional provisions or amendments, tailored to the trust, are needed. On termination of the trust the trust fund must be dealt with as laid down in the trust deed or as flowing from the juridical act creating the trust.

Paragraph (3)

Dutch law will not pose serious difficulties regarding this paragraph.

Paragraph (4)

If the need for a purpose trust is established under Dutch law, a provision as laid down in this paragraph could easily be fitted into a statutory trust regulation.

LAW OF BUSINESS AND FINANCE

In the Series Law of Business and Finance have been published:

1. D.J. Hayton, S.C.J.J. Kortmann, H.L.E. Verhagen *(ed)*, Principles of European Trust Law, 1999.